INDEPENDENCE DOCUMENTS OF THE WORLD

INDEPENDENCE
OF

with
WAYNE E. OLSON
DAN B. ARMSTRONG, JR.

Sarah J. Campbell
Anna Atkins
Matthew F. Jodziewicz
Dana B. Blaustein
Barbara Kotlikoff
Sarah R. Armstrong

DOCUMENTS
THE WORLD

by
ALBERT P. BLAUSTEIN
JAY SIGLER
BENJAMIN R. BEEDE

1977 OCEANA PUBLICATIONS, INC./Dobbs Ferry, New York
A.W. SIJTHOFF/LEYDEN

Library of Congress Cataloging in Publication Data

Main entry under title:

Independence documents of the world.

    1. Constitutional Law — Sources. I. Blaustein,
Albert P., 1921-   II. Sigler, Jay A. III. Beede,
Benjamin R.
K3157.A2B6   342.02   77-7333
ISBN 0-379-00795-9 (v. 2)
      90 286 0527 4 (Sijthoff)

Manufactured in the United States of America

TABLE OF CONTENTS

v

EDITORS' NOTE

While most of the independence documents are
reprinted in full, there are some situations where
the editors judged it appropriate to use excerpts.
This is particularly true in regard to the states
which were granted their independence by British
Independence Acts -- for those acts all incorporated details of government and transition matters
which go far beyond the actual independence process. Excerpts have also been chosen when the
nation's independence is pronounced in a portion
of its constitution.

State of Kuwait

Kuwait is located in the northeastern corner of the Arabian Peninsula. Kuwait has been governed by members of the Al-Sabah dynasty since 1756. By virtue of an agreement between the Kuwaiti ruler and the British government signed on January 23, 1899, Kuwait came under British administration. It remained a British protectorate until 1961 as Britain administered its foreign relations. On June 19, 1961, an agreement was signed by the British Political Resident in the Persian Gulf and the Amir of Kuwait in the form of an exchange of notes. This exchange provided for Kuwaiti independence of Britain.

KUWAIT

Note from Her [Britannic] Majesty's Political Resident in the Persian Gulf to His Highness the Ruler of Kuwait:

Your Highness,

I have the honour to refer to the discussions which have recently taken place between Your Highness and my predecessor on behalf of Her Majesty's Government in the United Kingdom about the desirability of adapting the relationship of the United Kingdom of Great Britain and Northern Ireland and the State of Kuwait to take account of the fact that Your Highness' Government has the sole responsibility for the conduct of Kuwait's internal and external affairs.

The following conclusions were reached in the course of these discussions:

(a) The Agreement of the 23rd of January, 1899, shall be terminated as being inconsistent with the sovereignty and independence of Kuwait.

(b) The relations between the two countries shall continue to be governed by a spirit of close friendship.

(c) When appropriate the two Governments shall consult together on matters which concern them both.

(d) Nothing in these conclusions shall affect the readiness of Her Majesty's Government to assist the Government of Kuwait if the latter request such assistance.

If the foregoing correctly represents the conclusions reached between Your Highness and Sir George Middleton I have the honour to suggest, on the instructions of Her Majesty's Principal Secretary of State for Foreign Affairs, that the present Note together with Your Highness' reply to that effect shall be regarded as constituting an Agreement between the United Kingdom and Kuwait in this matter which shall continue in force until either party gives the other at least three years notice of their intention to terminate it, and that the Agreement of the 23rd of January, 1899, shall be regarded as terminated on this day's date.

I have the honour to be,
With the highest consideration,
Your Highness' obedient
servant,

W H LUCE

(Her Majesty's Political Resident)

Note from His Highness the Ruler of Kuwait to Her [Britannic] Majesty's Political Resident in the Persian Gulf.

(Translation)

His Excellency,

Her Britannic Majesty's Political Resident in the Persian Gulf,

Greetings,

I have the honour to refer to Your Excellency's Note of today's date which reads as follows:

(As above)

I confirm that Your Excellency's Note correctly represents the conclusions reached by myself and Sir George Middleton and I agree that Your Excellency's Note and my reply shall be regarded as constituting an Agreement between Kuwait and the United Kingdom in this matter. With best regards.

ABDULLAH AL SALIM AL SABAH

Kuwait
June 19, 1961
Provided by the Kuwaiti Foreign Ministry
Translation by the British Embassy, Kuwait

Lao People's Democratic Republic

Situated between Vietnam and Thailand, Laos
shares borders with Burma, Cambodia, and China.
Laos became a French protectorate in 1893. On
June 19, 1949, as a member of the French Union,
Laos was granted limited self-government. A
treaty of friendship between Laos and France
on October 22, 1953, granted full sovereignty and
recognized the Kingdom of Laos as an independent
state. It became the Lao People's Democratic
Republic in 1976.

TREATY OF FRIENDSHIP BETWEEN THE REPUBLIC OF FRANCE AND THE KINGDOM OF LAOS

22 October 1953

M. Vincent Auriol, President of the French Republic, President of the French Union;

and

His Majesty Sisavang Vong, King of Laos,

Noting that France has fulfilled, in their entirety, the commitments which she made to ensure to Laos the exercise of her full sovereignty and complete independence, confirmed, by the declaration of July 3, 1953;

Prompted by the mutual desire to maintain and strengthen the bonds of traditional friendship which unite their two countries and which have been confirmed and strengthened by the adherence of the Kingdom of Laos to the French Union,

Have agreed as follows:

Article 1. The French Republic recognizes and declares that the Kingdom of Laos is a fully independent and sovereign State. Consequently, it shall replace the French Republic in all rights and obligations resulting from any international treaties or special agreements entered into by the French Republic on behalf of the Kingdom of Laos or French Indo-China prior to the present agreement.

Article 2. The Kingdom of Laos freely reaffirms its adherence to the French Union, an association of independent and sovereign peoples, free and equal in rights and duties, in which all the members pool their means of guaranteeing the defence of the whole Union.

It reaffirms its decision to sit on the High Council wherein, under the Chairmanship of the President of the French Union, the co-ordination of such means and the general direction of the Union are ensured.

Article 3. France undertakes to support and uphold the sovereignty and independence of Laos before international courts.

Article 4. France and Laos undertake to participate jointly in any negotiations to modify the existing agreements between the Associated States.

Article 5. Each of the High Contracting Parties undertakes to guarantee to nations of the other in its territory the same treatment as that accorded to its own nationals.

Article 6. Should the agreements now governing their trade relations be modified, the two High Contracting Parties undertake to accord each other advantages, especially preferential tariffs.

Article 7. Special agreements shall define the terms and conditions of the association between the French Republic and the Kingdom of Laos. The treaty and the special agreements shall render void and supersede all acts of the same kind previously concluded between the two States.

Article 8. The present treaty and the special agreements shall, except in case of stipulations to the contrary, enter into force on the date of their signature. The instruments of ratification of the present treaty shall be exchanged as soon as they are approved by the French and Lao constitutional processes.

Entered into, Paris, October 22, 1953

Republic of Lebanon

Lebanon, a middle-eastern state bordered by
Israel, Syria and Turkey was ruled as part of
Turkish Empire since early in the sixteenth
century. In 1919, after the collapse of the
Ottoman Empire, France controlled the territory.
On September 1, 1920, the French High Commissioner
proclaimed the creation of Lebanon. In 1923 the
Lebanon mandate to France was approved by the
League of Nations. The defeat of France by Nazi
Germany in 1940 led to the ouster of the Vichy
French administration. In 1941, under Free French
and British forces, the independence of Lebanon
was proclaimed. By November 22, 1943, full power
over government and finances was relinquished by
French forces, as the French accepted Lebanon's
Constitutional Law of November 9, 1943. French
and British forces withdrew from Lebanon in 1946,
following discussions in the U.N. Security Council.

PROCLAMATION OF THE ESTABLISHMENT
OF THE STATE OF LEBANON

MADE IN BEYROUTH ON SEPTEMBER 1, 1920,
BY GENERAL GOURAUD, HIGH COMMISSIONER
OF THE FRENCH REPUBLIC AND COMMANDER-
IN CHIEF OF THE EASTERN ARMY

I solemnly proclaim the establishment of Lebanon and in the name of the French Republic I salute it in its grandeur and in its strength from Nahr-el-Kebir to the gates of Palestine.

People of Lebanon:

I told you several weeks ago at a serious hour: "The day that your forefathers looked forward to in vain, and which you, being more fortunate than they will see is coming closer."

Today it is here.

Before all the people assembled, people of every religion, over which Mt. Lebanon looks out -- yesterday merely adjacent to one another, henceforth united in one country strong in its past and great in its future.

At the foot of these majestic mountains which have been the strength of your country by remaining an impregnable bulwark of its faith and its freedom; by the edge of the legendary sea that could see the triremes of Phoenicia, Greece and Rome, this sea which carried your ancestors all over the world -- your ancestors subtle in mind, canny in negotiations and eloquent in speech, and who by their fortunate return bring you the consecration of a great and ancient friendship and the help of the French peace.

Before all these witnesses of your hopes, of your battles and of your victory, I share your pride as I solemnly proclaim the State of Lebanon and as I, in the name of the French Republic salute it in its grandeur and in its strength from Nahr-el-Kebir to the Gates of Palestine.

It is in Lebanon with its great mountain where the warm heart of this country beats.

With the fertile Békaa, whose unforgettable
day of Zahlé consecrated the healing union;

With Beyrouth, the principal port of the new
State, seat of its government, enjoying a wide
municipal independence, possessing its budgetary
statute and a municipality with wide-spread powers
emanating directly from the highest authority of
the State.

With Tripoli, also possessing a wide administrative and budgetary independence, stretching all
the way to its Moslem suburbs.

With Sidon and Tyre with their famous past who
will, from this union, find a new youth.

Here is the country which you have just ac-
claimed.

Before determining the boundaries of this
country, I consulted the various populations and I
can say that, faithful to the French commitments,
to the principles which inspired the League of Nations, I had as my guide nothing except the satisfaction of the wishes liberally expressed by the
various populations and a desire to serve their
legitimate interests. Every human endeavor is subject to perfectibility and if that endeavor which
starts today should some day reveal gaps and weak-
nesses, France, who has watched over its birth, who
will continue tomorrow to surround it with her soli-
citude, will not hesitate (ever-faithful to her love
and respect for liberty) to propose remedies to you.

But you are too shrewd to get involved in ster-
ile criticism, at an hour when you have been offered
the heavy, but magnificent task of giving to your
new country love, order and prosperity with the help
of France.

The life which the soul of a great country
will create; inspiration which makes nations strong
and which gives them sons worthy to serve them and
defend them; order in a security guaranteed by its
organized forces in which already the bravest of
your sons have asked to serve and which will be increased by all the volunteers which patriotic faith

411

will give them;

Order which alone permits a wise, equitable, charitable administration;

Finally, prosperity.

The time has come for this country to awaken free, having escaped from the heavy bonds which for so many centuries shackled it, able to apply to its own development the talents which your fathers and you yourselves used too often to utilize in other lands.

And France, the trustee, who could profit from the lessons of your merchants, will bring you the help of its industries, of its capital, of its transportation, of its powerful economic apparatus, and of its advisors.

Gentlemen, I would be negligent of the confidence you have given me and of which I am so proud if I didn't add that becoming a free people and wishing to become a great people mean that you must fulfill many duties.

The first and most sacred: union, which will create your greatness, just as rivalries in races and in religions caused your weakness in the past.

Lebanon is created for the benefit of all. It is against no one. Political and administrative unity permits only those religious differences which guide the conscience of each person toward beliefs and practices which he considers to be his own sacred duties.

I mention to you as proof and as a pledge of this union the enthusiasm which has brought together here the chiefs and representatives of all religions and all beliefs.

Do not forget that you must be ready to do real sacrifices for your country. A country can only be created by the self-effacement of individual interest in the face of the general interest which is governed by faith in national destiny. From every side already I have been shown proof of this spirit of sacrifice. Haven't several of you told me: "We are ready henceforth to hold our privileges cheap, for these privileges were a guarantee and one should take guarantees only when faced with our enemy. Now, here is France: we are familiar with her honest and generous traditions; we know that her advisors are making sure that the sum of money with which the public treasury has filled our coffers will be used only for our benefit.

These sums would have been used formerly to enrich our hated masters; they will only be able henceforth to assure us the dignity necessary to a State worthy of the name. Our taxes will profit from now on only the country itself. They will be the fertile sowing from which will come a harvest of wealth and this harvest will be ours."

Gentlemen: such words honor both those who uttered them and the great people to which they belong.

The first task of the counselors who will be your guides will be to see that duties are assigned according to individual talents. If the role of the counselors seems necessary today, I foresee that in the future it will depend on you and your wisdom to set the progress of Lebanon on the road toward self-government, as the political education of the people develops and as cooperation and competency form a greater and greater part in your meetings.

Behold, People of Lebanon, the sacred destiny of hope and sacrifice that this solemn occasion brings to you.

I realize that you, proud of your triumph, conscious of your future, face the future with confidence and you know that tomorrow as well as today you can count on the help of France.

Five weeks ago, the ordinary soldiers of France, the brothers of those whom you admired, envied perhaps for four years, gave wings to all your hopes by dispelling in one short morning of fighting the evil power that claimed to be serving your interests. The French soldiers are the godfathers of your

independence. And you will never forget that the
generous blood of Frenchmen flowed for you as well
as for so many others. That is why you have chosen
her flag, the symbol of liberty to be your symbol
as well, by adding your own national symbol, the
cedar.

And now, saluting the two brother flags, I
cry out with you "Long live Lebanon, Long live
France, forever united!"

Translated by Adrienne Constant de Vergie

LEBANON

CONSTITUTION OF MAY 23, 1926

Article I. Lebanon announces that Greater Lebanon is a unified and independent state whose borders have recently been officially recognized by the French Mandate Government and by the League of Nations.

Compilation of the Laws of Lebanon v. 5
Constitution Chapter, p. 1.

415

PROCLAMATION DU GRAND LIBAN

Faite à Beyrouth le 1er. Septembre 1920 par le GÉNÉRAL GOURAUD

Haut-Commissaire de la République Française
Commandant en chef l'Armée du Levant

--« Je proclame solennellement le Grand Liban,
et au nom de la République Française,
je le salue dans sa grandeur et dans sa force,
du Nahr-el-Kébir aux portes de Palestine
et jusqu'aux crêtes de l'Anti-Liban».

Le 1er septembre 1920, à Beyrouth, en présesnce des patriarches, des chefs de toutes les confessions, devant une foule enthousiaste de plusieurs milliers de personnes, le Général Gouraud, entouré de son Etat-Major, proclama officiellement la **constitution du Grand Liban.** Beyrouth était la copitale du nouvel Etat, qui s'étendait depuis la frontière Palestinienne jusqu'au Nahr-el-Kébir (au nord de Tripoli), englobant Baalbek et la Béqâ'.

La cérémonie de la proclamation du Grand Liban

Discours du Général Gouraud

Libanais :

Je vous disais, il y a quelques semaines, à une heure grave :

« Le jour que vos pères ont espéré en vain et que plus heureux vous verrez luire, approche :

Ce jour, le voici :

Devant tout le peuple assemblé, peuple de toutes les religions que domine le Mont Liban, hier voisines, désormais unies en une patrie forte de son passé et grande dans son avenir.

Au pied de ces montagnes majestueuses qui ont fait la force de votre pays, en demeurant le rempart inexpugnable de sa foi et de ses libertés.

Au bord de la mer légendaire qui vit les trirènes de la Phénicie, de la Grèce et de Rome, qui porta par le monde vos pères à l'esprit subtil, habiles au négoce et à l'éloquence et qui par un heureux retour vous apporte la consécration d'une grande et vieille amitié et le bienfait de la paix française.

Par devant tous ces témoins de vos espoirs, de vos luttes et de votre victoire, c'est en partageant votre fierté que je proclame solennellement le Grand Liban et qu'au nom de la République Française, je le salue dans sa grandeur et dans sa force, du Nahr - el-Kébir aux portes de Palestine et aux crêtes de l'Anti - Liban.

C'est le Liban avec sa montagne où bat le cœur chaud de ce pays.

Avec la fertile Bekaa, dont l'inoubliable journée de Zahlé a consacré l'union réparatrice,

Avec Beyrouth, port principal du nouvel Etat siège de son gouvernement, jouissant d'une large autonomie municipale, possédant son statut budgétaire et une municipalité à pouvoirs étendus, relevant directement de la plus haute autorité de l'Etat.

Avec Tripoli, pourvue elle aussi d'une large autonomie administrative et budgétaire, s'étendant à sa banlieue musulmane.

Avec Sidon et Tyr au passé fameux, qui de cette union à une grande patrie tireront une jeunesse nouvelle.

Voilà la Patrie que vous venez d'acclamer.

Avant d'en déterminer les limites, j'ai consulté les populations et je puis dire que, fidèle aux engagements de la France, aux principes qut inspirent la Société des Nations, je n'ai eu pour règle que de satisfaire les vœux librement exprimés des populations et de servir leurs légitimes intérêts.

Toute œuvre humaine d'ailleurs est perfectible; et si celle dont l'avenir s'ouvre aujourd'hui venait à révéler des lacunes et des faiblesses, la France qui a veillé sur sa naissance, qui continuera demain à l'entourer de sa sollicitude, n'hésiterait pas, fidèle à son amour et à son respect de la liberté, à vous proposer d'y remédier.

Mais vous êtes trop avisés pour vous laisser aller à la stérile critique, à l'heure où vous est offerte la tâche lourde et magnifique de donner à votre nouvelle patrie avec la collaboration de la France, la vie, l'ordre et la prospérité.

La vie que créera l'âme d'une grande patrie, souffle inspirateur qui fait les nations fortes et qui leur donne des fils dignes de la servir et de la défenre.

L'ordre dans la sécurité garantie par les forces organisées, dans lesquelles déjà les plus vaillants de vos fils, ont demandé à servir et qui seront grossies de tous les volontaires que leur foi patriotique leur donnera.

L'ordre, qui seul permet une administration sage, équitable, bienfaisante.

LA PROSPERITE enfin.

Voilà que ce beau pays s'éveille, libre, échappé des lourdes mains qui, pendant tant de siècles ont pesé sur lui, il va pouvoir appliquer à son développement propre les qualités que vos pères et vous mêmes alliez si souvent, trop souvent, déployer outre-mer.

Et la France tutélaire, qui pourrait recevoir des leçons de vos commerçants, vous apportera l'aide de ses industries, de ses capitaux, de ses transports, de son puissant outillage économique et de ses conseillers.

Messieurs, je manquerais à la confiance que vous m'accordez et dont je suis si fier, si je n'ajoutais pas que, devenant un peuple libre, et voulant devenir un grand peuple, vous avez des devoirs à remplir.

Le premier de tous, le plus sacré: l'union, qui fera votre grandeur, comme les rivalités de races et de religion avaient fait votre faiblesse.

Le Grand Liban est fait au profit de tous. Il n'est fait contre personne. Unité politique et administratiure, il ne ccmported 'autres divisions religieuses que celles qui orientent la conscience de chacun vers des croyances et des pratiques qu'il considère comme des devoirs sacrés qui gardent à ce titre le droit au respect de tous.

Je veux évoquer comme preuve et comme gage de cette union l'élan qui a conduit ici près de moi, dans une émouvante communion nationale, les chefs et les représentants de toutes les religions, de toutes les confessions.

N'oubliez pas non plus que vous devez être prêts pour votre nouvelle patrie à de réels sacrifices.

Une patrie ne se crée que par l'effacement de l'individualisme devant l'intérêt général commandé par la foi dans les destinées nationales.

De tous côtés déjà les témoignages affluent pour me manifester cet esprit de sacrifice. N'est-ce pas plusieurs des vôtres qui m'ont dit :

« Nous sommes prêts désormais à faire bon marché de nos privilèges, car ces privilèges étaient une garantie et on ne prend de garantie que devant des ennemis. Or voici que la France est là, nous connaissons ses traditions probes et généreuses ; nous savons que ses conseillers veilleront à ce que les sommes dont le fisc aura rempli nos caisses ne soient emloyées qu'au profit de nous-mêmes.

Ces sommes auraient pu servir jadis à enrichir un maître détesté; elles ne pourront plus que nous assurer par nos propres moyens la dignité nécessaire à un Etat digne de ce nom.

Notre impôt ne profitera plus qu'au pays lui-même. Il sera la semence féconde qui fera lever la moisson de la richesse et cette moisson sera la nôtre.

Messieurs, de telles paroles honorent et ceux qui les ont prononcées et le grand peuple auquel ils apartiennent

Le premier devoir des conseillers qui seront vos guides sera de veiller à ce que les charges soient réparties proportionnellement aux moyens de chacun.

Si le rôle des conseillers apparaît nécessaire aujourd'hui, j'entrevois dans un avenir, qu'il dépend de vous et de votre sagesse de fixer, le progrès du Grand Liban vers un gouvernement par lui-même au fur et à mesure que l'éducation politique du peuple se sera développpée et que par la voie du concours, la compétence aura pris une part de plus en plus grande dans vos conseils.

Voici, Libanais, le lot sacré d'espérance et de sacrifice que vous apporte cet instant solennel.

Je sais que fiers de votre triomphe, conscients de votre devoir, vous bravez l'avenir avec confiance et vous savez de votre côté que demain comme hier vous pouvez compter sur l'aide de la France.

Hier, il y a cinq semaines, les petits soldats de France, les frères de ceux que vous avez admirés, enviés peut-être pendant quatre ans, donnaient l'essor à tous vos espoirs en faisant s'évanouir en une matinée de combat, la puissance néfaste qui prétendait vous asservir.

Les soldats français sont les parrains de votre indépendance. Et vous n'oublierez pas que le sang génèreux de la France a coulé pour elle comme pour tant d'autres.

C'est pourquoi vous avez choisi son drapeau qui est celui de la liberté pour le symbole de la vôtre en y ajoutant votre cèdre national.

Et en saluant les deux drapeaux frères je crie avec vous: le Vive Grand Liban, Vive la France

A jamais unis !

Kingdom of Lesotho

    Lesotho, a kingdom within the borders of the Union of South Africa, became a British protectorate in 1868 at the request of Moshesh, its Paramount Chieftain. A government was formed in 1959 under a constitution granted by the British. The British dependency, once known as Basutoland, became independent on October 4, 1966, pursuant to the August 3, 1966, Lesotho Independence Act.

Lesotho Independence Act 1966

1966 CHAPTER 24

An Act to make provision for, and in connection with, the establishment of Basutoland, under the name of Lesotho, as an independent kingdom within the Commonwealth. [3rd August 1966]

BE IT ENACTED by the Queen's most Excellent Majesty, by and with the advice and consent of the Lords Spiritual and Temporal, and Commons, in this present Parliament assembled, and by the authority of the same, as follows:—

1. On 4th October 1966 (in this Act referred to as "the appointed day") the territory which immediately before that day constitutes the Colony of Basutoland shall cease to form part of Her Majesty's dominions and shall become an independent kingdom under the name of Lesotho.

Lesotho Independence Act 1966, c.24

Republic of Liberia

American philanthropic societies, in an effort
to establish freed American slaves in Africa,
helped found Liberia. The first settlement was in
1820. On July 26, 1847 the new state constituted
itself as the Free and Independent Republic of
Liberia. Control over the indigeneous tribes was
not secured until about 1860.

REPUBLIC OF LIBERIA

DECLARATION OF INDEPENDENCE.

We the representatives of the people of the Commonwealth of Liberia, in Convention assembled, invested with authority for forming a new government, relying upon the aid and protection of the Great Arbiter of human events, do hereby, in the name, and on the behalf of the people of this Commonwealth, publish and declare the said Commonwealth a FREE, SOVEREIGN, AND INDEPENDENT STATE, by the name and title of the REPUBIC OF LIBERIA.

While announcing to the nations of the world the new position which the people of this Republic have felt themselves called upon to assume, courtesy to their opinion seems to demand a brief accompanying statement of the causes which induced them, first to expatriate themselves from the land of their nativity and to form settlements on this barbarous coast, and now to organize their government by the assumption of a sovereign and independent character. Therefore we respectfully ask their attention to the following facts.

We recognise in all men, certain natural and inalienable rights: among these are life, liberty, and the right to acquire, possess, enjoy and defend property. By the practice and consent of men in all ages, some system or form of government is proven to be necessary to exercise, enjoy and secure those rights; and every people have a right to institute a government, and to choose and adopt that system or form of it, which in their opinion will most effectually accomplish these objects, and secure their happiness, which does not interfere with the just rights of others. The right therefore to institute government, and to all the powers necessary to conduct it, is, an inalienable right, and cannot be resisted without the grossest injustice.

Official Text

424

Libyan Arab Republic

Libya, a north African state adjacent to
Tunisia, Egypt, Algeria, Chad, and Niger, had
been under the domination of other states since
ancient times. The Carthaginians, the Romans,
the Vandals, the Arabs, and the Turks each
occupied the area in turn. In 1911 the Turks were
driven out by the Italians. The defeat of the
Axis powers in World War II led to the independence
of Libya after a postwar period of Franco-British
administration. Gmir Mohammed Idris El Senussi
promulgated a constitution to set up a government
for internal affairs on September 18, 1949, and
Libya received its independence under United
Nations auspices. A U.N. Resolution of December 21,
1949, made Libya independent, with January 1, 1952,
being the effective date. However the National
Constituent Assembly issued its own declaration on
December 5, 1950, and King Muhammed Idris al Sanussi
issued his own Formal declaration on December 24, 1951.

LIBYA

Resolution of the National Constituent

Assembly of Libya of 1950

In the Name of God, the Bountiful, the
Merciful

Verily those who plight their fealty to
thee do no less than plight their fealty
to God: The Hand of God is over their
hands: Then any one who violates His
oath, does so to the harm of his own
soul, and any one who fulfills what he
has covenanted with God, God will soon
grant him a great reward.

We, the representatives of the people of Libya, from Cyrenaica (Bargah), Tripolitania (Tara-
bulus), and Fezzan, have, by the will of God, gath-
ered at Tripoli as a National Constituent Assembly,

Vested with complete authority whose validity
is recognized and in due legal form,

Being resolved to form a federation among us
and establish a federated, democratic, independent,
and sovereign state whose form of government shall
be a constitutional monarchy,

Having started our action by praising the Lord
and thanking Him for what He bestowed upon us in
the liberation and independence of our land, and

In appreciation of the dedication of His Ex-
alted Highness As-Sayed Mohammad Idris Al-Mahdi As-
Sanussi, Prince of Bargah, and his long and fruitful struggle for the welfare of Libya and its people, and

In fulfilling the general desire of the people, and

Affirming the former legal fealties which were
vowed by the legitimate representatives of the

people to His Highness, and

Being concerned for the happiness of our country and its unity under a crown of a King in whom
we find the ideal example for the qualities that
such a sublime position requires,

Proclaim

His Royal Highness As-Sayed Mohammad Idris
Al-Mahdi As-Sanussi, Prince of Barqah, and vow our
fealty to him as a constitutional monarch for the
Federated Kingdom of Libya and we beg His Majesty
to accept that, therefore,

We have decided that the entire National Con-
stitutent Assembly should go to Benghazi in order
to present to His Majesty this historical decision
and to receive from His Majesty the acceptance of
that fealty.

Tripoli, Saturday, 22 Safar 1370 A.H.
[December 2, 1950]

Signatures

Translated by Frank H. Stewart and David E.P. Jack-
son

LIBYA

Declaration of Independence

In the Name of God the Merciful the compassionate
To our Noble People:

We have the pleasure to announce to the noble
Libyan nation that as a result of its struggle and
in execution of the resolution of the United Nations issued on 21st November, 1949, with the help
of God, the independence of our dear country was
realized. We supplicate to the Almighty our sin-
cerest thanks and best praise for his graces and
extend to the Libyan people our cordial congratulations on the occasion of this happy, historic
event. We declare officially that with effect from
today, Libya became an independent sovereign state
and we assume henceforth for ourselves, subservient
to the resolution of the Libyan National Assembly,
issued on 2nd December, 1950, the title of His Majesty King of the United Kingdom of Libya.

We feel also great delight for the coming into force, as from now, of the Constitution of the
country as laid down and issued by the National
Assembly on 6th Muharram, 1371, corresponding to
7th October, 1951 A.D. It is our dearest aspirations, as you know, that the country maintains a
sound constitutional life and we will exercise from
today our powers in accordance with the provisions
of this Constitution.

We make a covenant with God and our country
at this critical period in which the country is
passing through to do our best for the interest
and welfare of our noble people, so that our sublime goals are realized and our dear country occu-
pies its proper position among free nations. We
all have to safeguard what we have won at high cost
and pass this sincerely and honestly to our next
generation. We, at this blessed hour, should remember our heroes, invoke mercy and blessing on
the souls of our righteous martyrs, and salute the
holy flag which is the symbol of struggle, union
and heritage of our ancestors, hoping that the new

era commencing today be an era of prosperity and peace to the country. We beg the Almighty to assist us to this end and bestow upon us success and guidance in doing right . . .He who is the best helper.

                                    Idris

25th Rabi Al-Awwal, 1371 A.H.
24th December, 1951

Official Gazettee of the United Kingdom of Libya - Issue No. 1 dated 22nd January, 1952.

Translation by Dr. Yorguy Hakim, Legal Specialist, Near Eastern and African Law Division, Law Library, Library of Congress.

A

Whereas, in accordance with the provisions of article 23 and paragraph 3 of annex XI of the Treaty of Peace with Italy, the question of the disposal of the former Italian colonies was submitted on 15 September 1948 to the General Assembly by the Governments of France, the Union of Soviet Socialist Republics, the United Kingdom of Great Britain and Northern Ireland and the United States of America,

Whereas, by virtue of the above-mentioned provisions, the four Powers have agreed to accept the recommendation of the General Assembly and to take appropriate measures for giving effect to it,

Whereas the General Assembly, by its resolutions of 21 November 1949 and of 17 November 1950, recommended that the independence of Libya should become effective as soon as possible, and in any case not later than 1 January 1952,

Whereas paragraph 19 of annex XIV of the Treaty of Peace with Italy, which contains the economic and financial provisions relating to ceded territories, states that "The provisions of this annex shall not apply to the former Italian colonies. The economic and financial provisions to be applied therein will form part of the arrangements for the final dispoal of these territories pursuant to article 23 of the present Treaty",

Whereas it is desirable that the economic and financial provisions relating to Libya should be determined before the transfer of power in that territory takes place, in order that they may be applied as soon as possible,

The General Assembly

Approves the following articles:

Article I

1. Libya shall receive, without payment, the movable and immovable property located in Libya owned by the Italian State, either in its own name or in the name of the Italian administration of Libya.

2. The following property shall be transferred immediately:

(*a*) The public property of the State (*demanio pubblico*) and the inalienable property of the State (*patrimonio indisponibile*) in Libya, as well as the relevant archives and documents of an administrative character or technical value concerning Libya, or relating to property the transfer of which is provided for by the present resolution;

(*b*) The property in Libya of the Fascist Party and its organizations.

3. In addition, the following shall be transferred on conditions to be established by special agreement between Italy and Libya:

(*a*) The alienable property (*patrimonio disponibile*) of the State in Libya and the property in Libya belonging to the autonomous agencies (*aziende autonome*) of the State;

(*b*) The rights of the State in the capital and the property of institutions, companies and associations of a public character located in Libya.

4. Where the operations of such institutions, companies and associations extend to Italy or to countries other than Libya, Libya shall receive only those rights of the Italian State or the Italian administration which appertain to the operations in Libya. In cases where the Italian State or the Italian administration of Libya exercised only managerial control over such institutions, companies and associations, Libya shall have no claim to any rights in those institutions, companies or associations.

5. Italy shall retain the ownership of immovable property necessary for the functioning of its diplomatic and consular services and, when the conditions so require, of the schools necessary for the present Italian community whether such property is owned by the Italian State in its own name or in the name of the Italian administration of Libya. Such immovable property shall be determined by special agreements concluded between Italy and Libya.

6. Buildings used in connexion with non-Moslem public worship and their appurtenances shall be transferred by Italy to the respective religious communities.

7. Special agreements may be concluded between Italy and Libya to ensure the functioning of hospitals in Libya.

Article II

Italy and Libya shall determine by special agreements the conditions under which the obligations of Italian public or private social insurance organizations towards the inhabitants of Libya and a proportionate part of the reserves accumulated by the said organizations shall be transferred to similar organizations in Libya. That part of the reserves shall preferably be taken from the real property and fixed assets in Libya of the said organizations.

Article III

Italy shall continue to be liable for the payment of civil or military pensions earned as of the coming into force of the Treaty of Peace with Italy and owed by it at that date, including pension rights not yet matured. Arrangements shall be concluded between Italy and Libya providing for the method by which this liability shall be discharged.

Article IV

Libya shall be exempt from the payment of any portion of the Italian public debt.

Article V

Italy shall return to their owners, in the shortest possible time, any ships in its possession, or that of its nationals, which are proved to have been the property of former Italian nationals belonging to Libya or to have been registered in Libya, except in the case of ships acquired in good faith by Italy or its nationals.

Article VI

1. The property, rights and interests of Italian nationals, including Italian juridical persons, in Libya, shall, provided they have been lawfully acquired, be respected. They shall not be treated less favourably than the property, rights and interests of other foreign nationals, including foreign juridical persons.

2. Italian nationals in Libya who move, or who have since 3 September 1943 moved, to Italy shall be permitted freely to sell their movable and immovable property, realize and dispose of their assets, and, after settlement of any debts or taxes due from them in Libya, to take with them their movable property and transfer the funds they possess, unless such property and funds were unlawfully acquired. Such transfers of property shall not be subject to any import or export duty. The conditions of the transfer of this movable property to Italy will be fixed by agreement between the administering Powers or the Government of Libya upon its establishment on the one hand, and the Government of Italy on the other hand. The conditions and the time-periods of the transfer of the funds, including the proceeds of above-mentioned transactions, shall likewise be determined.

3. Companies incorporated under Italian law and having their *siège social* in Italy shall be dealt with under the provisions of paragraph 2 above. Companies incorporated under Italian law and having their *siège social* in Libya and which wish to remove their *siège social* to Italy shall likewise be dealt with under the provisions of paragraph 2 above, provided that more than 50 per cent of the capital of the company is owned by persons usually resident outside Libya and provided also that the greater part of the activity of the company is carried on outside Libya.

4. The property, rights and interests in Italy of former Italian nationals belonging to Libya and of companies previously incorporated under Italian law and having their *siège social* in Libya, shall be respected by Italy to the same extent as the property, rights and interests of foreign nationals and of foreign companies generally. Such persons and companies are authorized to effect the transfer and liquidation of their property, rights and interests under the same conditions as may be established under paragraph 2 above.

5. Debts owed by persons in Italy to persons in Libya or by persons in Libya to persons in Italy shall not be affected by the transfer of sovereignty. The Government of Italy and the administering Powers or the Government of Libya after its establishment shall facilitate the settlement of such obligations. As used in the present paragraph, the term "persons" includes juridical persons.

Article VII

Property, rights and interests in Libya which, as the result of the war, are still subject to measures of seizure, compulsory administration or sequestration, shall be restored to their owners, and, in cases submitted to the Tribunal referred to in article X of the present resolution, following decisions of that Tribunal.

Article VIII

The former Italian nationals belonging to Libya shall continue to enjoy all the rights in industrial, literary and artistic property in Italy to which they were entitled under the legislation in force at the time of the coming into force of the Treaty of Peace. Until Libya becomes a party to the relevant international convention or conventions, the rights in industrial, literary and artistic property which existed in Libya under Italian law shall remain in force for the period for which they would have remained in force under that law.

Article IX

The following special provisions shall apply to concessions:

1. Concessions granted within the territory of Libya by the Italian State or by the Italian administration of Libya, and concession contracts (*patti colonici*) existing between the *Ente per la Colonizzazione della Libia* or the *Istituto della Previdenza Sociale* and the concessionaires of land to which each contract related shall be respected, unless it is established that the concessionaire has not complied with the essential conditions of the concession.

2. Land placed at the disposal of the *Ente per la Colonizzazione della Libia* and of the colonization department of the *Istituto della Previdenza Sociale* by the Italian State or the Italian administration of Libya and which has not been the object of a concession shall be transferred immediately to Libya.

3. Land, buildings and their appurtenances referred to in sub-paragraph (*d*) of paragraph 4 below shall be transferred to Libya in accordance with the arrangements to be made under that sub-paragraph.

4. Special agreements between Italy and Libya shall provide for:

(*a*) The liquidation of the *Ente per la Colonizzazione della Libia* and of the colonization department of the *Istituo della Previdenza Sociale*, the interim status of those institutions for the purpose of enabling them to fulfil their obligations towards concessionaires whose contracts are still in operation, and, if necessary, the taking over of their functions by new organizations;

(*b*) The repayment by those institutions to financial concerns of the quotas subscribed by the latter in the establishment of the *Ente per la Colonizzazione della Libia*, and, in the case of the *Istituto della Previdenza Sociale*, the reconstitution of that part of its reserves invested by that institution in its colonization department;

(*c*) The transfer to Libya of the residual assets of the institutions to be liquidated;

(*d*) Arrangements relating to land placed at the disposal of these institutions and to the buildings on and appurtenances to that land, in which, after their abandonment by the concessionaires, no further investment could be made by the institutions;

(*e*) Payments in amortization of the debts of concessionaires owed to those institutions.

5. In consideration of the renunciation by the Italian Government of its claims against those institutions, the latter shall cancel the debts of the concessionaires and the mortgages securing those debts.

Article X

1. A United Nations Tribunal shall be set up, composed of three persons selected by the Secretary-General for their legal qualifications from the nationals of three different States not directly interested. The Tribunal, whose decisions shall be based on law, shall have the following two functions:

(*a*) It shall give to the administering Powers, the Libyan Government after its establishment, and the Italian Government, on request by any of those authorities, such instructions as may be required for the purpose of giving effect to the present resolution;

(*b*) It shall decide all disputes arising between the said authorities concerning the interpretation and application of the present resolution. The Tribunal shall be seized of any such dispute on the unilateral request of one of those authorities.

2. The administering Powers, the Libyan Government after its establishment and the Italian Government shall supply the Tribunal as soon as possible with all the information and assistance it may need for the performance of its functions.

3. The seat of the Tribunal shall be in Libya. The Tribunal shall determine its own procedure. It shall afford to the interested parties an opportunity to present their views, and shall be entitled to request information and evidence which it may require from any authority or person whom it considers to be in a position to furnish it. In the absence of unanimity, the Tribunal shall take decisions by a majority vote. Its decisions shall be final and binding.

B

The General Assembly

Authorizes the Secretary-General, in acordance with established practice,

1. To arrange for the payment of an appropriate remuneration for the members of the United Nations Tribunal set up under article X above and to reimburse their travel and subsistence expenses:

2. To assign to the United Nations Tribunal such staff and provide such facilities as the Secretary-General may consider necessary to carry out the terms of the present resolution, utilizing the existing United Nations staff of the Libyan Mission in so far as possible.

Following is the text of the explanations of certain points in the foregoing resolution appended to the report of the *Ad Hoc* Political Committee (A/1726):

Article I, paragraph 2(a):

It is understood that the Italian Government will facilitate the return to Libya of any archives or documents of an administrative character or technical value, property of the Italian State, which are in Italy and which the Libyan Government would have the right to request of it under this paragraph.

The words documents of "technical value" apply, *inter alia*, to documents concerning archaeological research projects which are being carried out or are to be carried out in Libya.

Article I, paragraph 3:

Italy abandons her right to property transferred under this paragraph, as a contribution to the rehabilitation of Libya.

Article I, paragraph 3(b):

The rights mentioned in this sub-paragraph include share holdings and similar rights owned by the Italian State either in its own name or in the name of the Italian administration of Libya.

Article I, paragraph 6:

The expression "buildings used in connexion with non-Moslem public worship" includes all objects used in connexion with public worship in those buildings.

It is understood that mosques and objects used in connexion with Moslem public worship will be transferred directly to the Libyan State.

It is also understood that the maintenance of cemeteries shall be the subject of special agreements.

Article IV:

Italy renounces all her claims to any payment whatsoever from Libya in respect of debts, in view of the economic conditions of that country.

Articles V; VI, paragraph 4; VIII:

The phrase "former Italian nationals belonging to Libya" means, in particular, the indigenous population of Libya.

Article VII:

It is understood that this article does not affect the requisitions made by the authorities for the needs of the administration.

Article VIII:

It is understood that the second paragraph applies to aliens only, and not to the Libyans themselves.

Article IX, paragraph 4(c):

It is understood that if the final balance sheet of the institutions shows a debit balance, no part of such liability will be transferred to the Libyan Government.

Article X, paragraph 1:

The Tribunal "whose decisions shall be based on law" shall apply the rules of law, and shall not decide *ex aequo et bono*. It will thus apply the General Assembly resolution in the light of the principles of international law and of the rules for the interpretation of international texts.

Article X:

The Sub-Committee discussed the period during which the Tribunal should remain in existence. Although it is difficult to foresee precisely the time it will take that body to accomplish its task, the Sub-Committee believes that it might take at least two or three years. In this connexion, much will depend on the time it will take to conclude the several special Italo-Libyan Agreements provided for in the resolution.

The Sub-Committee further believes that the General Assembly should in any case examine either at its seventh, or at its eighth session at the latest, and in the light of the progress then made by the Tribunal, the question of whether its functions should be continued. By then, Italy and Libya might desire either to maintain the Tribunal jointly, assuming the corresponding financial obligations, or prefer to replace it by a different procedure.

Article X, paragraph 3 (last sentence):

In specifying that the decisions of the Tribunal should be binding, the Sub-Committee does not intend to infer that this does not apply to the instructions given by the Tribunal.

c. TECHNICAL ASSISTANCE FOR LIBYA

(1) *Consideration by the Economic and Social Council*

The General Assembly, in resolution 289 A (IV),[105] had empowered the United Nations Commissioner in Libya to offer suggestions to the Economic and Social Council and to the

---

[105] For text, see *Y.U.N., 1948-49*, p. 275-76.

Principality of Liechtenstein

Liechtenstein is a small principality on the upper Rhine River between Switzerland and Austria. After the turmoil of the Thirty Years' War, Holy Roman Emperor Charles VI, in order to bring stability to the region, sold the counties of Schellenburg and Vaduz to Anton Florian, the ruler of the House of Liechtenstein in 1719. The Palatinate Diploma of January 23, 1719 raised Liechtenstein to the status of an imperial principality, thus establishing it as a new and independent state.

LIECHTENSTEIN

Palatinate Diploma of 1719

We, Carl the Sixth, by God's will elected
(Holy) Roman Emperor, confess and announce to all
that we consequently recognize our uncle and prince
the beloved, faithful Anton Florian, the ruler of
the House of Liechtenstein, of Niclasburg, Duke in
Silesia, of Troppau, and Jagerndorff as our imperial privy councellor, colonel controller and
Knight of the Golden Fleece, in most merciful consideration of him as well as in the memory of our
glorious ancestors of the (Holy) Roman Empire in
recollection of his extraordinary and great merit.
Our imperial spirit is prompted to this because of
the faithfulness of our subject who bought the
imperial earldom and principality of Vaduz and
Schellenberg with all its lands held now or those
acquired in the future which are immediately incorporated in this new principality, a direct imperial principality. On today's date the castle
and the mark, "Vaduz" are changed and endowed
with the name "Liecntenstein" and because the beloved Prince Anton Florian of Liechtenstein
approached us and asked that in the name of the
Roman Emperor Ferdinand The Second who gloriously
remembered Prince Gundagger of Liechtenstein and
all the first born of the princely Liechtenstein
House on November 14, 1633 in his function as
Comites Palatini, the imperial county palatines
and court counts, that Prince Anton Florian have
bestowed upon him the privileges, mercy, freedom,
advantages and all the just and lawful duties
appertaining to the above new principality of
Liechtenstein as the present and future owner. We
mercifully confirm this transfer as the ruling
(Holy) Roman Emperor.

Translated by Ellen Meier and Alois Bohmer.
From: Jacob von Falke, Geschichte des Fürstlichen
Hauses Liechtenstein (Wien: Wilhelm Braumüller,
1868-1882, 3 vols.), Vol. 3, pp.77-78.

Grand Duchy of Luxembourg

Although founded in 963 Luxembourg did not gain
sovereignty until 1815. The Treaty of Vienna of
1815 made Luxembourg a part of the German Confederation, but it was administered briefly by Belgian
authorities from 1830 until 1839. In 1866 Luxembourg left the collapsing German Confederation.
The Treaty of London of May 1, 1867 proclaimed
the neutrality of the demilitarized Grand Duchy,
while guaranteeing its integrity as an independent
state.

TREATY between Great Britain, Austria, Belgium, France, Italy, the Netherlands, Prussia, and Russia, relative to the Grand Duchy of Luxemburg and the Duchy of Limburg. Signed at London, 11th May, 1867.

Translation as laid before Parliament.

In the Name of the Most Holy and Indivisible Trinity.

HIS Majesty the King of the Netherlands, Grand Duke of Luxemburg, taking into consideration the change produced in the situation of the Grand Duchy in consequence of the dissolution of the ties by which it was attached to the late Germanic Confederation (**Nos. 26, 388**), has invited Their Majesties the Queen of the United Kingdom of Great Britain and Ireland, the Emperor of Austria, the King of the Belgians, the Emperor of the French, the King of Prussia, and the Emperor of All the Russias, to assemble their Representatives in Conference at London, in order to come to an understanding, with the Plenipotentiaries of His Majesty the King Grand Duke, as to the new arrangements to be made in the general interest of Peace.

And Their said Majesties, after having accepted that invitation, have resolved, by common consent, to respond to the desire manifested by His Majesty the King of Italy to take part in a deliberation destined to offer a new pledge of security for the maintenance of the general tranquillity.

In consequence, Their Majesties, in concert with His Majesty the King of Italy, wishing to conclude a Treaty with a view to that object, have named as their Plenipotentiaries, that is to say :—

Her Majesty the Queen of the United Kingdom of Great Britain and Ireland, the Right Honourable Edward Stanley, commonly called Lord Stanley, a Member of Her Britannic Majesty's Most Honourable Privy Council, a Member of Parliament, her Principal Secretary of State for Foreign Affairs ;

His Majesty the Emperor of Austria, King of Hungary and Bohemia, the Sieur Rudolph Count Apponyi, Chamberlain and Privy Councillor of His Imperial Royal and Apostolic Majesty, his Ambassador Extraordinary to Her Britannic Majesty, &c. ;

His Majesty the King of the Belgians, the Sieur Sylvain Van de Weyer, Minister of State, his Envoy Extraordinary and Minister

Plenipotentiary to Her Britannic Majesty, &c.;

His Majesty the Emperor of the French, the Sieur Godfrey Bernard Henry Alphonse, Prince de la Tour d'Auvergne Lauraguais, his Ambassador Extraordinary and Plenipotentiary to Her Britannic Majesty, &c.;

His Majesty the King of Italy, the Sieur Emmanuel Taparelli de Lagnasco, Marquis d'Azeglio, his Envoy Extraordinary and Minister Plenipotentiary to Her Britannic Majesty, &c.;

His Majesty the King of the Netherlands, Grand Duke of Luxemburg, the Sieur Adolphus Baron Bentinck, his Chamberlain and Minister of State, his Envoy Extraordinary and Minister Plenipotentiary to Her Britannic Majesty, &c.; the Baron Victor de Tornaco, Minister of State, President of the Government of the Grand Duchy, his Honorary Chamberlain, &c.; and the Sieur Emanuel Servais, Vice-President of the Council of State and of the Superior Court of Justice, formerly Member of the Government, &c.;

His Majesty the King of Prussia, the Sieur Albert Count de Bernstorff-Stintenburg, his Minister of State and Chamberlain, his Ambassador Extraordinary and Plenipotentiary to Her Britannic Majesty, &c.;

And His Majesty the Emperor of All the Russias, the Sieur Philip Baron de Brunnow, his Actual Privy Councillor, Ambassador Extraordinary and Plenipotentiary to Her Britannic Majesty, &c.;

Who, after having exchanged their Full Powers, found in good and due form, have agreed upon the following Articles:—

Maintenance of Rights of the House of Orange-Nassau.

ART. I. His Majesty the King of the Netherlands, Grand Duke of Luxemburg, maintains the ties which attach the said Grand Duchy to the House of Orange-Nassau, in virtue of the Treaties which placed that State under the Sovereignty of the King Grand Duke, his descendants and successors (**Nos. 183, 187**).

The Rights which the Agnates of the House of Nassau possess with regard to the Succession of the Grand Duchy, in virtue of the same Treaties, are maintained.

The High Contracting Parties accept the present Declaration, and place it upon record.

Grand Duchy to form a Perpetual Neutral State under Guarantee of Contracting Parties.

ART. II. The Grand Duchy of Luxemburg, within the Limits determined by the Act annexed to the Treaties of the 19th April, 1839 (**Nos. 183, 184, 185**), under the Guarantee of the Courts of Great Britain, Austria, France, Prussia, and Russia, shall henceforth form a perpetually Neutral State.

It shall be bound to observe the same Neutrality towards all other States.

The High Contracting Parties engage to respect the principle of Neutrality stipulated by the present Article.

That principle is and remains placed under the sanction of the collective Guarantee of the Powers signing Parties to the present Treaty, with the exception of Belgium, which is itself a Neutral State.

Luxemburg to cease to be a Fortified City. Troops to be maintained by the King Grand Duke.

ART. III. The Grand Duchy of Luxemburg being Neutralised, according to the terms of the preceding Article, the maintenance or establishment of Fortresses upon its Territory becomes without necessity as well as without object.

In consequence, it is agreed by common consent that the City of Luxemburg, considered in time past, in a military point of view, as a Federal Fortress, shall cease to be a fortified city.

His Majesty the King Grand Duke reserves to himself to maintain in that city the number of troops necessary to provide in it for the maintenance of good order.

Evacuation of Fortress of Luxemburg by Prussian Troops.

ART. IV. In conformity with the stipulations contained in Articles II and III, His Majesty the King of Prussia declares that his troops actually in garrison in the Fortress of Luxemburg shall receive orders to proceed to the Evacuation of that place immediately after the exchange of the Ratifications of the present Treaty. The withdrawal of the artillery, munitions, and every object which forms part of the equipment of the said Fortress shall commence simultaneously. During that operation there shall remain in it no more than the number of troops necessary to provide for the safety of the material of war, and to effect the dispatch thereof, which shall be completed within the shortest time possible.

Demolition of Fortress of Luxemburg by the Netherlands.

ART. V. His Majesty the King Grand Duke, in virtue of the rights of Sovereignty which he exercises over the City and Fortress of Luxemburg, engages, on his part, to take the necessary measures for converting the said Fortress into an open city by means of a demolition which His Majesty shall deem sufficient to fulfil the intentions of the High Contracting Parties expressed in Article III of the present Treaty. The works requisite for that purpose shall be commenced immediately after the withdrawal of the garrison. They shall be carried out with all the attention required for the interests of the inhabitants of the city.

Fortifications not to be restored.

His Majesty the King Grand Duke promises, moreover, that the Fortifications of the city of Luxemburg shall not be restored in future, and that no Military Establishment shall be there maintained or created.

Duchy of Limburg to form an integral part of the Kingdom of the Netherlands.

ART. VI. The Powers signing Parties to the present Treaty recognise that the Dissolution of the Germanic Confederation (**No. 388**) having equally produced the Dissolution of the ties which united the Duchy of Limburg, collectively with the Grand Duchy of Luxemburg, to the said Confederation, it results therefrom that the relations, of which mention is made in Articles III, IV, and V of the Treaty of the 19th April, 1839 (**No. 183**), between the Grand Duchy and certain Territories belonging to the Duchy of Limburg, have ceased to exist, the said Territories continuing to form an integral part of the Kingdom of the Netherlands.

*Ratifications.**

ART. VII. The present Treaty shall be ratified, and the Ratifications shall be exchanged at London within the space of 4 weeks, or sooner if possible.

In witness whereof the respective Plenipotentiaries have signed the same, and have affixed thereto the Seals of their Arms.

Done at London, the 11th day of May, in the year of Our Lord, 1867.

   (L.S.) STANLEY.
   (L.S.) APPONYI.
   (L.S.) VAN DE WEYER.
   (L.S.) LA TOUR D'AUVERGNE.
   (L.S.) D'AZEGLIO.
   (L.S.) BENTINCK.
   (L.S.) TORNACO.
   (L.S.) E. SERVAIS.
   (L.S.) BERNSTORFF.
   (L.S.) BRUNNOW.

* Ratifications exchanged at London, 31st May, 1867.

Edward Hertslet, The Map of Europe by Treaty, Vol. III, pp. 1801-5 (1875).

Democratic Republic of Madagascar

Madagascar consists of the large island of Madagascar
and certain smaller islands situated in the Indian
ocean. Madagascar became a French protectorate in
1885 and was declared a French colony in 1896. The
Malagasy Republic as Madagascar was once named
declared itself independent of French rule in its
Constitution of October 14, 1958. France recognized
its independent status by an agreement of April 2, 1960.

MADAGASCAR

SPECIAL AGREEMENT

Providing for the Transfer to the Malagasy

Republic of the Jurisdictions of the Community

Instituted by Article 78 of the Constitution of

October 4, 1958

    The Government of the French Republic, on the
one hand and The Government of the Malagasy Republic, on the other hand, have agreed to the following:

    Article 1. The Malagasy Republic shall accede,
in full agreement and friendship with the French
Republic, to international sovereignty and to independence through the transfer of the jurisdictions of the Community.

    Article 2. All the jurisdictions instituted
by Article 78 of the Constitution of October 4,
1958 shall be transferred to the Malagasy Republic,
insofar as it is concerned.

    Article 3. Each of the contracting parties
shall notify the other of the completion of the
procedures required by its Constitution for putting
the present agreement into force. This agreement
shall take effect on the date of the last of these
notifications.

    Done at Paris, April 2, 1960.

        For the Government of the French Republic:

            Michel Debré.

    For the Government of the Malagasy Republic:

            Philibert Tsiranana.

Translated by Matthew Jodziewicz

Republic of Malawi

British explorers penetrated into central
Africa in the 1850's and 60's. In 1884 Cecil
Rhodes received a charter to develop the region,
but because of conflicts with the Arabs Britain
annexed the territory in 1891, making it a
protectorate in 1892. It was first called British
Central Africa and later Nyasaland. Nyasaland
became self-governing on February 1, 1963, after
years of resistance to British rule. Independence
was gained on July 6, 1964, pursuant to the
Malawi Independence Act of June 10, 1964.

Malawi Independence Act 1964

1964 CHAPTER 46

An Act to make provision for and in connection with the attainment by Nyasaland of fully responsible status within the Commonwealth.   [10th June 1964]

BE IT ENACTED by the Queen's most Excellent Majesty, by and with the advice and consent of the Lords Spiritual and Temporal, and Commons, in this present Parliament assembled, and by the authority of the same, as follows:—

1.—(1) On and after 6th July 1964 (in this Act referred to as " the appointed day ") the territories which immediately before the appointed day are comprised in the Nyasaland protectorate shall together form part of Her Majesty's dominions under the name of Malawi; and on and after that day Her Majesty's Government in the United Kingdom shall have no responsibility for the government of those territories.

(2) No Act of the Parliament of the United Kingdom passed on or after the appointed day shall extend or be deemed to extend to Malawi as part of its law; and on and after that day the provisions of Schedule 1 to this Act shall have effect with respect to legislative powers in Malawi.

(3) Subsection (1) of this section shall not affect the operation in Malawi of any enactment or any other instrument having the effect of law passed or made before the appointed day, or be taken to extend any such enactment or instrument to Malawi as part of its law.

Malaysia

Malaysia is comprised of portions of the former Malay states which had been British administered in the late 19th and early 20th century, Sabah and Sarawak. Sabah (formerly North Vorreo) was a British protectorate from 1881 until 1942, when it was occupied by the Japanese, as was nearby Sarawak. After the Japanese defeat a Union of Malaya was formed among the Malay states on April 1, 1946. On September 16, 1963, a larger federation of Malaya, Singapore, Sabah and Sarawak was formed, independent of Britain. Although Singapore withdrew in 1965, Malaysia dates its independence from the proclamation of August 31, 1957.

An Act to make provision for and in connection with the establishment of the Federation of Malaya as an independent sovereign country within the Commonwealth. [31st July, 1957]

BE it enacted by the Queen's most Excellent Majesty, by and with the advice and consent of the Lords Spiritual and Temporal, and Commons, in this present Parliament assembled, and by the authority of the same, as follows:—

1.—(1) Subject to the provisions of this section, the approval of Parliament is hereby given to the conclusion between Her Majesty and the Rulers of the Malay States of such agreement as appears to Her Majesty to be expedient for the establishment of the Federation of Malaya as an independent sovereign country within the Commonwealth.

(2) Any such agreement as aforesaid may make provision—

(a) for the formation of the Malay States and of the Settlements of Penang and Malacca into a new independent Federation of States under a Federal Constitution specified in the agreement, and for the application to those Settlements, as States of the new Federation, of State Constitutions so specified;

(b) for the termination of Her Majesty's sovereignty and jurisdiction in respect of the said Settlements, and of all other Her power and jurisdiction in and in respect of the Malay States or the Federation as a whole, and the revocation or modification of all or any of the provisions of the Federation of Malaya Agreement, 1948, and of any other agreements in force between Her Majesty and the Rulers of the Malay States.

(3) Any such agreement shall be conditional upon the approval of the new Federal Constitution by enactments of the existing Federal Legislature and of each of the Malay States; and upon such approval being given Her Majesty by Order in Council may direct that the said Federal and State Constitutions shall have the force of law within the said Settlements, and, so far as She has jurisdiction in that behalf, elsewhere within the Federation, and may make such other provision as appears to Her to be necessary for giving effect to the agreement.

(4) Any Order in Council under this section shall be laid before Parliament after being made.

(5) In this Act " the appointed day " means such day as may be specified by Order in Council under this section as the day from which the said Federal Constitution has the force of law as aforesaid.

2.—(1) On and after the appointed day, all existing law to which this section applies shall, until otherwise provided by the authority having power to amend or repeal that law, continue to apply in relation to the Federation or any part thereof, and to persons and things in any way belonging thereto or connected therewith, in all respects as if no such agreement as is referred to in subsection (1) of section one of this Act had been concluded:

Provided that—

(a) the enactments referred to in the First Schedule to this Act shall have effect as from the appointed day subject to the amendments made by that Schedule (being amendments for applying in relation to the Federation certain statutory provisions applicable to Commonwealth countries having fully responsible status within Her Majesty's dominions);

(b) Her Majesty may by Order in Council make such further adaptations in any Act of the Parliament of the United Kingdom passed before the appointed day, or in any instrument having effect under any such Act, as appear to Her necessary or expedient in consequence of the agreement referred to in subsection (1) of section one of this Act;

(c) in relation to the Colonial Development and Welfare Acts, 1940 to 1955, this subsection shall have effect only so far as may be necessary for the making of payments on or after the appointed day in pursuance of schemes in force immediately before that day and in respect of periods falling before that day;

(d) nothing in this section shall be construed as continuing in force any enactment or rule of law limiting or restricting the legislative powers of the Federation or any part thereof.

(2) An Order in Council made under this section shall be subject to annulment in pursuance of a resolution of either House of Parliament.

(3) An Order in Council made under this section may be varied or revoked by a subsequent Order in Council so made and may, though made after the appointed day, be made so as to have effect from that day.

(4) In this section " existing law " means any Act of Parliament or other enactment or instrument whatsoever, and any rule of law, which is in force on the appointed day or, having been passed or made before the appointed day, comes into force after that day; and the existing law to which this section applies is law which operates as law of, or of any part of, the United Kingdom, Southern Rhodesia, or any colony, protectorate or United Kingdom trust territory except that this section—

(a) does not apply to any law passed by the Federal Legislature of Rhodesia and Nyasaland;

(b) applies to other law of, or of any part of, Southern Rhodesia so far only as concerns law which can be amended neither by a law passed by the Legislature thereof nor by a law passed by the said Federal Legislature; and

(c) applies to other law of, or of any part of, Northern Rhodesia or Nyasaland so far only as concerns law which cannot be amended by a law passed by the said Federal Legislature.

(5) References in subsection (4) of this section to a colony, a protectorate and a United Kingdom trust territory shall be construed as if they were references contained in the British Nationality Act, 1948.

MALAYSIA

PROCLAMATION OF INDEPENDENCE

AUGUST 31, 1957

In the name of God, the Compassionate, the merciful, Praise be to God, the Lord of the Universe and may the blessings and peace of God be upon his messengers.

And whereas the time has now arrived when the people of the Persekutuan Tanah Melayu will assume the status of a free independent and sovereign nation among the nations of the world;

And whereas by an agreement styled the Federation of Malaya Agreement, 1957, between Her Majesty the Queen and Their Highnesses the Rulers of the Malay States it was agreed that the Malay States of Johore, Pahang, Negri Sembilan, Selangor, Kedah, Perlis, Kelantan, Trengganu and Perak and the former Settlements of Malacca and Penang should as from the 31st day of August, 1957, be formed into a new Federation of States by the name of Persekutuan Tanah Melayu;

And whereas it was further agreed between the parties to the said agreement that the Settlements of Malacca and Penang aforesaid should as from the said date cease to form part of Her Majesty's dominions and that Her Majesty should cease to exercise any sovereignty over them;

And whereas it was further agreed by the parties aforesaid that the Federation of Malaya Agreement, 1948, and all other agreements subsisting between Her Majesty the Queen and Their Highnesses the Rulers or any one of them immediately before the said date should be revoked as from that date and that all powers and jurisdiction of Her Majesty or of the Parliament of the United Kingdom in or in respect of the Settlements aforesaid or the Malay States or the Federation as a whole should come to an end;

And whereas effect has been given in the Federation of Malaya Agreement, 1957, by Her Majesty the Queen, Their Highnesses the Rulers, the Parliament of the United Kingdom and the Legislatures of the Federation and of the Malay States;

And whereas a constitution for the Government of the Persekutuan Tanah Melayu has been established as the supreme law thereof;

And whereas by the Federal Constitution aforesaid provision is made to safeguard the rights and prerogatives of Their Highnesses the Rulers and the fundamental rights and liberties of the people and to provide for the peaceful and orderly advancement of the Persekutuan Tanah Melayu as a constitutional monarchy based on Parliamentary democracy;

And whereas the Federal Constitution aforesaid having been approved by an Ordinance of the Federal Legislatures, by the Enactments of the Malay States and by resolutions of the Legislatures of Malacca and Penang has come into force on the 31st day of August, 1957, aforesaid:

Now in the name of God the Compassionate, the Merciful I, Tengku Abdul Rahman Putra ibni Al-Marhum Sultan Abdul Hamid Halimshah, Prime Minister of the Persekutuan Tanah Melayu, with the concurrence and approval of Their Highnesses the Rulers of the Malay States do hereby proclaim and declare on behalf of the people of the Persekutuan Tanah Melayu that as from the thirty first day of August, nineteen hundred and fifty-seven, the Persekutuan Tanah Melayu comprising the States of Johore, Pahang, Negri Sembilan, Selangor, Kedah, Perlis, Kelantan, Trengganu, Perak, Malacca and Penang is and with God's blessing shall be for ever a sovereign democratic and independent State founded upon the principle of liberty and justice and ever seeking the welfare and happiness of its people and the maintenance of a just peace among all nations.

This proclamation was read by Tunku Abdul Rahman at the celebrations held at the Stadium Merdeka, Kuala Lumpur, on August 31, 1957, at which H.R.H. the Duke of Gloucester, acting on

behalf of Her Majesty the Queen, formally handed
over to the Prime Minister the constitutional
documents signifying the independence of the
Federation of Malaya.

Republic of Maldives

These islands in the Indian Ocean were long
under the control of Ceylon. They came under
British domination in 1887 and were a dependency
of the Colony of Ceylon until 1948. An independence
agreement with Britain was signed on July 26, 1965.

No. 7980. AGREEMENT BETWEEN HER MAJESTY'S GOV-
ERNMENT IN THE UNITED KINGDOM OF GREAT
BRITAIN AND NORTHERN IRELAND AND THE GOV-
ERNMENT OF THE MALDIVE ISLANDS. SIGNED AT
COLOMBO, ON 26 JULY 1965

Her Majesty's Government in the United Kingdom of Great Britain and Northern
Ireland and the Government of the Maldive Islands ;

Desiring to consolidate the friendship and close association between their two
countries and desiring for this purpose to revise the Agreement concluded between
them on 14th February 1960, agree as follows :

Article 1

The provisions of the aforesaid Agreement of 1960 shall cease to have effect and
they shall be replaced by the provisions of this present Agreement.

Article 2

The United Kingdom Government confirm their recognition of the State of the
Maldive Islands as a composite sovereign and fully independent State possessing
all rights to have direct relations politically and otherwise with all countries and
international organisations.

Article 3

The Maldivian Government confirm the grant made by them to the United
Kingdom Government by the Agreement of 14th February 1960, [2] of the unrestricted
and exclusive use of the whole area of the island of Gan in Addu Atoll and a demar-
cated area of 110 acres on the island of Hithadoo (Maamendu) of the same atoll,
until the 15th day of December 1986 as a free gift. The said areas are hereafter
referred to as "the Agreed Areas".

The Maldivian Government undertake that during the period until 15th December
1986 they will not permit the entry into or use of the territory, territorial waters
or air space of the Maldive Islands for any purpose by any of the armed forces of any
other State or the establishment by any other State of rights or facilities of a military
character, unless the United Kingdom Government has consented thereto. This
undertaking shall not apply to courtesy visits by aircraft and by vessels of war in
accordance with normal international practice.

The United Kingdom Government may establish, operate and maintain an
Airfield on Gan Island, and a Radio Station on Hithadoo Island, and shall have
unrestricted access by sea and air to the Agreed Areas, and the unrestricted use of
the lagoon of Addu Atoll and the territorial waters adjacent to the Agreed Areas
for Her Majesty's ships as may be required. The United Kingdom Government

may further utilise the lagoon of Addu Atoll and the territorial waters adjacent to the Agreed Areas for recreational purposes for the British Forces and for the maintenance of such facilities as are specified and agreed in this Agreement and Annexure.

Until the 15th day of December, 1986, the United Kingdom Government may maintain within the Agreed Areas such Armed Forces as they may think fit for the exercise and use of the rights and facilities accorded to them under this Agreement. Nothing herein or hereafter contained in this Agreement shall impair the Sovereign Status of the Agreed Areas as part of the State of the Maldive Islands.

Article 4

The United Kingdom Government undertake to utilise the facilities granted to them by the Maldivian Government in the Agreed Areas only for Commonwealth defence.

Article 5

The Annexure which contains provisions relating to the implementation and interpretation of this Agreement shall form part of this Agreement.

Article 6

This Agreement shall come into force on the Twenty-sixth day of July 1965, from which date all previous agreements and understandings shall cease to be effective.

IN WITNESS WHEREOF the undersigned, being duly authorised by their respective Governments, have signed this Agreement.

DONE in duplicate at Colombo this Twenty-sixth day of July 1965 in the English language.

For Her Majesty's Government in the United Kingdom
of Great Britain and Northern Ireland :

Michael WALKER

For the Government of the Maldive Islands :

Ibrahim NASIR

Republic of Mali

Mali is a west African state bounded by
Mauritania, Senegal, Ivory Coast, Niger and Algeria.
France took control of the region at the end of the
last century. The French Sudan, as it was later
called, first became a colony in 1904. Once Mali
was the center of great African empires, but its
independence from French rule came finally on
September 22, 1960. Senegal seceded from a federation with Mali shortly thereafter and Mali adopted
its current name on September 22, 1960.

PROCLAIMING THE INDEPENDENT REPUBLIC OF MALI

LAW NO. 60-35/AL/RS

September 22, 1960

The Legislative Assembly of the Sudanese Republic;

Considering the Constitution of January 23, 1959, modified by Law No. 6023/AL/RS of July 26, 1960, of the Sudanese Republic;

Considering Law No. 60-1/AL/RS of June 7, 1960, ratifying the agreement on the transfer of jurisdiction to the Sudanese Republic;

Considering the needs of the State,

Has deliberated and adopted the following law:

Article 1. The Sudanese Republic, beginning September 22, 1960, at 11:25, shall take the name of: "REPUBLIC OF MALI," INDEPENDENT AND SOVEREIGN STATE.

The Independent and Sovereign State of the Republic of Mali shall be free of all commitments and political ties.

Article 2. This law shall be promulgated according to emergency procedure.

/signed/   /signed/
SESSION SECRETARY   PRESIDENT OF THE
AMADOU Thioye   LEGISLATIVE ASSEMBLY
                            MAHAMANE ALASSANE HAIDARA

Translated by Sarah J. Campbell

Article 5. This law shall be promulgated according to emergency procedure.

/signed/   /signed/
SESSION SECRETARY   PRESIDENT OF THE
AMADOU Thioye   LEGISLATIVE ASSEMBLY
                            MAHAMANE ALASSANE HAIDARA

Translated by Sarah J. Campbell

ESTABLISHING THE LEGISLATIVE ASSEMBLY OF

THE SUDANESE REPUBLIC

AS THE NATIONAL ASSEMBLY

OF THE REPUBLIC OF MALI

LAW NO. 60-36/AL/RS

September 22, 1960

The Legislative Assembly of the Sudanese Republic;

Considering the Constitution of January 23, 1959, modified by Law No. 60-23/AL/RS of July 26, 1960, of the Sudanese Republic;

Considering Law No. 60-1/AL/RS of June 7, 1960, ratifying the agreement on the transfer of jurisdiction to the Sudanese Republic,

Considering Law No. 60-35/AL/RS of September 22, 1960, proclaiming the "Republic of Mali,"

Considering the needs of the State,

Has deliberated and adopted the following law:

Article 1. The Legislative Assembly of the Sudanese Republic shall be established as the National Assembly of the Republic of Mali.

Article 2. Members of the Legislative Assembly shall take on the title of Deputies to the National Assembly of the Republic of Mali.

Article 3. The seat of the Legislative Assembly shall remain the seat of the National Assembly.

Article 4. The present Government of the Sudanese Republic shall become the Provisional Government of the Republic of Mali.

Republic of Malta

Malta, a mid-Mediterranean island, was once
the base of the Knights of St. John, who received
the islands from Charles V in 1830. Napoleon
conquered the islands in 1798, but was forced out
by superior British forces in 1799. British rule
continued until a measure of self-government was
extended on September 5, 1947. After severe
internal disorders self-government was restored.
On August 20, 1962, the Maltese Prime Minister
formally requested independence. A referendum
was held in May, 1964, to decide on the form of
an Independence Constitution. A Malta Independence
Bill was passed by the British House of Commons
and by the Malta Legislature Assembly. Malta
became independent on September 21, 1964.

Malta Independence Act 1964

1964 CHAPTER 86

An Act to make provision for, and in connection with, the attainment by Malta of fully responsible status within the Commonwealth. [31st July 1964]

B E IT ENACTED by the Queen's most Excellent Majesty, by and with the advice and consent of the Lords Spiritual and Temporal, and Commons, in this present Parliament assembled, and by the authority of the same, as follows :—

1.—(1) On and after such day as Her Majesty may by Order in Council appoint (in this Act referred to as "the appointed day") Her Majesty's Government in the United Kingdom shall have no responsibility for the government of Malta.

(2) No Act of the Parliament of the United Kingdom passed on or after the appointed day shall extend, or be deemed to extend, to Malta as part of its law; and on and after that day the provisions of Schedule 1 to this Act shall have effect with respect to the legislative powers of Malta.

Malta Independence Act 1964, c.86

Islamic Republic of Mauritania

Mauritania is located in northwestern Africa, and is bounded by Algeria, Mali, Senegal, and the former Spanish Sahara. It became a French protectorate in 1900 and was made part of the Colony of French West Africa in 1920. Mauritania became an autonomous republic within the French Community in 1958, and won full independence on November 28, 1960, following an agreement with the French government.

MAURITANIA

November 28, 1958

DELIBERATION NO. 284 -- Deliberation No. 284
of November 28, 1958, of the Territorial Assembly
of Mauritania, proclaiming the Islamic Republic of
Mauritania, and deciding to establish itself as a
deliberating constituent Assembly until the installation of new institutions, and commissioning
the Government of Mauritania to assembly a consultative constitutional Committee and to have the constitution ratified by means of a referendum.

Considering the option taken this day to act
in conformity with the Statute of a Member State of
the [French] Community,

THE TERRITORIAL ASSEMBLY OF MAURITANIA proclaims the Islamic Republic of Mauritania, and decides:

1) to establish itself as a deliberating constituent Assembly until the installation of new
institutions.

2) to commission the Government of Mauritania
to assemble a consultative constitutional Committee
composed of not more than thirty members, of which
half would be elected by the Assembly from within
its ranks and the other half would be designated
by the Government.

3) to have the constitution ratified by means
of a referendum.

Journal Officiel de la Republique Islamique de
Mauritanis, June 3, 1959. Deliberation no. 284.

Translated by Sarah J. Campbell

MAURITANIA

PRIVATE AGREEMENT

TRANSFERRING THE POWERS OF THE COMMUNAUTÉ

The Government of the French Republic, on the one hand,

The Government of the Islamic Republic of Mauritania, on the other hand,

In view of Article 66 (paragraph 3) of the Constitution of October 4, 1958, completed by the constitutional law of June 4, 1960,

Agree on what follows:

Article 1. The Islamic Republic of Mauritania accedes in full accord and friendship with the French Republic to international sovereignty and independence by the transfer of the powers of the Communauté.

Article 2. All powers instituted by Article 78 of the Constitution of October 4, 1958, are, where applicable, transferred to the Islamic Republic of Mauritania as soon as the contracting parties have fulfilled the procedure provided for in Article 37 of said Constitution.

Paris, October 19, 1960,

Prime Minister of the French Republic,

MICHEL DEBRÉ

Prime Minister of the Islamic Republic of Mauritania,

MOKHTAR OUID DADDAH

Journal Official de la Republique Francaise, November 24, 1960, p. 1045.

Translated by Sarah J. Campbell

DÉLIBÉRATION N° 284. — *Délibération n° 284 du 28 novembre 1958 de l'Assemblée territoriale de Mauritanie proclamant la République Islamique de Mauritanie décidant de s'ériger en Assemblée constituante délibérante jusqu'à la mise en place des nouvelles institutions chargeant le Gouvernement de la Mauritanie de réunir un Comité consultatif constitutionnel et de faire ratifier la constitution par voie de référendum.*

L'ASSEMBLÉE TERRITORIALE DE LA MAURITANIE

Considérant l'option faite ce jour pour le Statut d'Etat membre de la Communauté,

L'Assemblée territoriale de Mauritanie, proclame la République Islamique de Mauritanie.

ET DÉCIDE :

1° De s'ériger en Assemblée constituante délibérante jusqu'à la mise en place des nouvelles institutions.

2° Et charge le Gouvernement de la Mauritanie de réunir un Comité consultatif constitutionnel composé au maximum de 30 membres dont la moitié serait élue par l'Assemblée en son sein et l'autre moitié désignée par le Gouvernement.

3° De faire ratifier la constitution par voie de Référendum.

Nouakchott, le 28 novembre 1958.

Le Président de l'Assemblée territoriale,
SIDI EL MOKTAR.

◆◆◆

Actes de l'Assemblée constituante délibérante

N° 402. — ARRÊTÉ *rendant exécutoire la délibération n° 283 du 28 novembre 1958 de l'Assemblée territoriale de la Mauritanie.*

LE CHEF DU TERRITOIRE DE LA MAURITANIE.

Vu la Constitution.

Vu l'ordonnance n° 58-902 du 6 octobre 1958 fixant certaines conditions d'application de l'article 76 de la Constitution et le régime provisoire des pouvoirs publics dans les territoires d'Outre-Mer ;

Vu le décret n° 57-458 du 4 avril 1957 fixant les attributions des Chefs de territoire, des Conseils de Gouvernement et des Assemblées territoriales dans les territoires de l'Afrique occidentale française et de l'Afrique équatoriale française ;

Vu la délibération n° 283 du 28 novembre 1958 de l'Assemblée territoriale de la Mauritanie,

ARRETE :

Article premier. — Est rendue exécutoire la délibération n° 283 du 28 novembre 1958 de l'Assemblée territoriale de la Mauritanie portant option pour le statut d'Etat Membre de la Communauté.

Art. 2. — Le présent arrêté sera publié selon la procédure d'urgence.

Nouakchott, le 28 novembre 1958.

Pour le Chef du Territoire absent :
Le Secrétaire général, suppléant signé,
BERNARD.

━━━━━━━◆◆◆━━━━━━━

Décret n° 59-001 du 12 mars 1959 ·

Article. premier. — La Fête nationale de la République islamique de Mauritanie est fixée au 28 novembre, jour anniversaire de la proclamation de la République.

Art. 2. — Le jour de la Fête nationale de la République islamique de Mauritanie est chômé et payé dans tous les services publics et toutes les entreprises privées.

━━━━━━━◆◆◆━━━━━━━

Mauritius

The island state of Mauritius lies in the Indian Ocean near Madagascar. A British naval expedition took control of the island in 1810, following a century of French rule. A drive for independence grew after World War II but Britain was slow to depart because of fear of ethnic rivalries. Full internal autonomy was granted in 1964. Rioting against British rule broke out in the 1960's and after the 1967 elections Britain was ready to consider independence. A British parliamentary petition for independence was accepted early in 1968 and on March 12, 1968, independence was celebrated in Mauritius.

Mauritius Independence Act 1968

1968 CHAPTER 8

An Act to make provision for, and in connection with, the attainment by Mauritius of fully responsible status within the Commonwealth.   [29th February 1968]

B E IT ENACTED by the Queen's most Excellent Majesty, by and with the advice and consent of the Lords Spiritual and Temporal, and Commons, in this present Parliament assembled, and by the authority of the same, as follows:—

1.—(1) On and after 12th March 1968 (in this Act referred to as " the appointed day ") Her Majesty's Government in the United Kingdom shall have no responsibility for the government of Mauritius.

(2) No Act of the Parliament of the United Kingdom passed on or after the appointed day shall extend, or be deemed to extend, to Mauritius as part of its law ; and on and after that day the provisions of Schedule 1 to this Act shall have effect with respect to the legislative powers of Mauritius.

Mauritius Independence Act 1968, c.8

United Mexican States

The United Mexican States are bounded to the
north by the United States and to the south and
southeast by Guatemala and British Honduras. After
the Spanish conquest by Hernan Cortes in the early
1500's a colony was established. With the Napoleonic
invasions of Spain in 1810, political disintegration
began. Refusing to recognize the reign of Joseph
Bonaparte a group of conspirators led by Miguel
Hidalgo y Costilla declared their independence
in the "Grito de Delores" on September 16, 1810.
The movement soon collapsed. A successful drive
for independence came after the Spanish Revolution
of 1820 where the king was forced to abide by a
liberal constitution. Mexican conservatives and
insurgents joined together in declaring their
independence on February 24, 1821. Although
Spanish officials at the Convention of Cordoba
on August 24, 1821, recognized the independence
of Mexico, the Spanish government did not.
Nevertheless, Spain made no serious effort to
reconquer Mexico.

UNITED MEXICAN STATES
Treaty of Peace between the Armies of Spain and
Mexico. Signed at Cordova,
24th August, 1821.

Treaty concluded in the City of Cordova, on
the 24th of August, 1821, between the Senors Don
Juan O'Donoju, Lieutenant-General of the Armies
of Spain, and Don Augustin de Iturbide, First
Chief of the Imperial Mexican Army of the Three
Guarantees.

The Independence of New upon Old Spain being
declared, and it having an Army capable of
supporting this Declaration, the Provinces of the
Kingdom being subdued by it, the Capital, where
the Legitimate Authority had been deposited, being
besieged, and when there only remained for the
European Government the Fortresses of Vera Cruz
and Acapulco, dismantled and without the means of
resisting a siege, well directed, and which should
last some time; Lieutenant General Don Juan
O'Donoju arrived at the former Port, with the
character and authority of Captain-General and
Superior political Chief of this Kingdom, appointed
by His Catholick Majesty, and, being desirous of
avoiding the evils which afflict the People in
vicissitudes of this sort, and wishing to concili-
ate the interests of both Spains, invited the
first Chief of the Imperial Army, Don Augustin
de Iturbide, to an interview, in which they might
discuss the great business of the Independence,
by loosening, without breaking, the chains which
united the 2 Continents. The interview took
place in the City of Cordova, on the 24th of
August, 1821 and the first with the authority of
his Spanish Character, and the latter with that
of the Mexican Empire, after having conferred at
length on what was most proper for both Nations,
considering the present situation and the last
occurrences, agreed upon the following Articles,
which they signed in Duplicate, to give them all
the force of which Documents of this sort are
capable, each keeping an original in his possession
for greater security and validity.

Art. I. This America shall be recognized as
a sovereign and independent Nation, and shall in

future be called the Mexican Empire.

II.   The Government of the Empire shall be a Constitutional Limited Monarchy.

III.   There shall be named to reign in the Mexican Empire, (after taking the oath which the IVth Article of the Plan of Iguala points out) in the first place the Senor Don Ferinand VII.   Catholick King of Spain; upon his renunciation or non-admission, his Brother, the Most Serene Senor Infant Don Carlor; upon his renunciation or nonadmission, the Most Serene Senor Infant Don Francisco de Paula; upon his renunciation or non-admission, he whom the Cortes of the Empire shall designate.

IV.   The Emperor shall fix his Court in Mexico, which shall be the Capital of the Empire.

V.   Two Commissioners shall be appointed by His Excellency General O'Donoju, who shall go to the Court of Spain, to place in the Royal hands of Senor Don Ferinand VII. a Copy of this Treaty, with the following exposition, which shall accompany the delivery of it to His Majesty: first, that whilst the Cortes of the Empire offer him the Crown, with all the formalities and guarantees, which a business of so much importance demands; they intreat His Majesty, that, should he not be pleased to accept it, conformably to the IIId Article, he will deign to notify to their Serene Highnesses the Infants, mentioned in same Article, in the order in which they are named; interposing his benign influence, so that one of those Personages designated from his august House may come to this Empire, inasmuch as the prosperity of both Nations is concerned in it; and expressing the satisfaction which the Mexicans will receive, in adding this to the other bonds of friendship with which Spainards can and desire to be united.

VI.   There shall be immediately appointed, according to the spirit of the Plan of Iguala, a Junta, composed of the first Men of the Empire, distinguished for their virtues, stations, fortunes, authority and judgment and designated by the general opinion, the number of whom may be

sufficiently considerable, that the union of
lights may ensure the success of their determinations, which may emanate from the authority and
powers which the following Articles grant them.

VII. The Junta, of which the following
Article treats, shall be named the Provisional
Junta of Government.

VIII. Lieutenant-General Don Juan O'Donoju
shall be one of the Provisional Junta of the
Government, in consideration of the convenience
of a Person of his rank taking an active and
immediate part in the Government, and from its
being indispensable to omit some of the Persons
who were designated in the said Plan, in conformity with the exact spirit of it.

IX. The Provisional Junta of Government shall
have a President, appointed by itself, who shall
be elected from amongst its own Members, or otherwise, by an absolute plurality of their votes: if
the Election should not take effect at the first
voting, they shall proceed to a second scrutiny,
beginning with the two who may have the most votes.

X. The first step of the Provisional Junta
of Government shall be, to publish its installation,
and the motives for which it is assembled, with
the explanations which it may consider proper, to
illustrate to the People their interests, and to
explain the mode of proceeding in the election of
Deputies to the Cortes, of which mention will be
made hereafter.

XI. The provisional Junta of Government shall
appoint, after the election of its President, a
Regency composed of 3 Persons, either of its own
Members or otherwise, in which shall be vested
the Executive Power, and who shall govern in the
name of the Monarch, until He receive the Sceptre
of the Empire.

XII. The Provisional Junta being installed,
shall govern provisionally according to the existing Laws, in every thing not opposed to the Plan of
Iguala, and until the Cortes shall have framed
the Constitution of the State.

XIII. The Regency, immediately after being appointed, shall proceed to the convocation of the Cortes, agreeably to the Regulations of the Provisional Junta of Government, and in conformity with the spirit of the XXIVth Article of the said Plan.

XIV. The Executive Power is vested in the Regency, and the Legislative Power in the Cortes; but, as they have been for sometime united, in order that both may not again fall under the same Authority, the Provisional Junta shall exercise the Legislative Power; first, in such cases as occur, and which cannot wait the meeting of the Cortes, when they shall proceed in accordance with the Regency; and, secondly, in acting as an Auxiliary and Consultive Body to the Regency, in its determinations.

XV. Every Person who belongs to a Society (the system of Government being changed, or the Country passing into the power of another Prince), remains in the state of natural liberty to transport himself with his fortune, to what Place he pleases, without there being any right to deprive him of this liberty, unless he shall have contracted some debt with the Society to which he belongs, or have forfeited his liberty by crime, or in some other way known to Publicists: this rule applies to Europeans, as well as to Americans now resident in the Peninsula, admitted into New Spain; who shall, consequently, be free to remain, or to adopt another Country; and demand their Passports, which cannot be refused to them, for removing from the Realm in the time prescribed, and carrying with them their families and effects; but satisfying, on the departure of the latter, the duties of exportation now established, or which may hereafter be established by competent authority.

XVI. The foregoing alternative shall not be granted in favor of Publick Officers or Military Men, who are notoriously disaffected towards the Independence of Mexico; who shall of necessity quit this Empire within the term which the Regency may prescribe, carrying with them their property, and paying the duties mentioned in the preceeding Article.

XVII. The occupation of the Capital by the Troops of the Peninsula, being an obstacle to the realizing of this Treaty, it becomes indispensable to overcome the same; but, as the first Chief of the Imperial Army, uniting his sentiments to those of the Mexican Nation, is desirous not to take it by force, for which there are abundant resources (notwithstanding the valour and constancy of the said Peninsular Troops), independency of the want of means and ability to support themselves against the system adopted by the whole Nation-- Don Juan O'Donoju offers to use his authority, that the said Troops may complete their departure without the effusion of blood, and by an honourable Capitulation.

Done in the City of Cordova, the 24th August, 1821.

JUAN O'DONOJU.   AUGUSTIN DE ITURBIDE.

9 British and Foreign State Papers 431-432 (1821-1822).

Principality of Monaco

Located on the Mediterranean east of Nice,
France, Monaco was given to the Genoese family of
Garibaldi in the 10th century by the Roman Emperor
Otto I. On February 20, 1512, with the "Lettres
Patents of Louis XII, " France recognized Monaco
as an independent state. A 1793 national conven-
tion dispossessed the ruling family and annexed
Monaco to France. In 1814 the family was restored.
On February 2, 1861, Monaco became an independent
sovereignty as a French Protectorate. A 1918
treaty with France guaranteed independence.

Letters Patent of Louis XII recognizing the independence of Monaco "which depends only upon God and the sword," and confirming the harbor rates.

1511-12, February 20 - Blois.

Louis, by the grace of God, King of France, Count of Provence, Forcalquier and adjacent lands, to all those who will see these presents, greeting; we announce that we have received the humble supplication of our beloved, faithful Lucien de Grimault, Lord of Mourgues, stating that his said place and domain of Mourgues is held from God and the sword, without the said suppliant nor his predecessors to whom it has belonged from such ancient times that there is no memory of the beginning nor of the contrary ever having recognized a sovereign, king, or prince, except for God; however, the said suppliant and all his predecessors have always been in and under the protection of us and of our predecessors, Kings of France, Counts of Provence, friends of our friends, and enemies of our enemies; and how much the said suppliant has the firm resolution, desire, wish and intention of persevering in his loyalty to us, risking body and property in our service in following his devotion and that of his predecessors to us and to ours; nevertheless, because of, and under the color of, a complaint that some of our subjects of Languedoc and Provence have allegedly made against him, previously, from the sixth day of March, 1508, he deferred to our beloved and faithful chancellor and answered to him concerning the said complaints although this de Mourgues has neither firsts nor levy upon them nor expects such in the future, except the right of toll which he and his predecessors, Lords of Mourgues, have been accustomed to take and to levy on all ships passing before his said Mourgues, which are its ancient preeminences, for so long that there is no memory of the beginning nor of the contrary, fearing that on the occasion of the said sought-after submission that the rights, prerogatives and preeminences that in the said place he has held from God and the sword and from no other, as has been said, would be prejudiced and that his domain would have been put in servitude, humbly requesting of us that, given the forementioned things, the desire that he has to continue his loyalty toward us and to be and remain our good and loyal servant and of our successors, friend of our friends and enemy of our enemies, and that he is and will always be ready to offer for our service, to support and defend our rights, the honors of his person and property, we are pleased that each one know that we want, therefore, to provide and impart our grace, provision and proper remedy; therefore, these things considered, remembering the loyalty and services that the said suppliant and his predecessors, Lords of Mourgues, have always had and done toward us and ours, equally the said suppliant as he has demonstrated through facts in his said domain and otherwise, we want for this reason to suffer and permit that, upon the occasion of the said submission or otherwise, he have or incur no reduction of his said rights, honors, authorities, jurisdiction and preeminences, but rather to keep, support and defend him in them. For these causes and other considerations moving us, and on the condition that the said suppliant and his successors, lords of the said Mourgues, will be, remain and continue forever our servants and our successors', Kings of France and Counts of Provence, friends of our friends and enemies of our enemies, we have declared and will declare, from our certain knowledge and full power and authority, by these presents, that we do not want nor expect that because of any submissions made by the said Grimault, Lord of Mourgues, that he be in any way diminished or impeded in his rights, jurisdictions, superiorities, prerogatives and preeminences in his said place and domain of Mourgues, and the appurtenances and dependencies of it, before the said submission having been made by him, we want it to be null and void, provided, however, that the said lord of Mourgues will be satisfied and will send us within four months his letters in good and sufficient form, stating that he and his successors, lords of Mourgues, will be and remain our good and loyal servants, friends of our friends and enemies of our enemies, and that in the event that he or his wish to levy or require any tribute, salt tax, toll, or other new tax, above and beyond what he and his predecessors, lords of Mourgues, have had the custom from ancient times of requiring, taking

and collecting from our said subjects and their
property and merchandise passing by his said place
of Mourgues, that in this event he be willing and
consent to be and remain under the judgment and
cognizance of our said chancellor, without, however, prejudicing in any way his rights, preeminences, jurisdictions, authorities and prerogatives
concerning his said place of Mourgues, its appurtenances and dependencies, but that his said rights,
jurisdictions, authorities, superiorities and preeminences of his said place and domain and its appurtenances and dependencies he be and remain what
he and his predecessors have been before this, and
what the said Grimault was before the said submissions. And he, with his said place, lands, domains and other property, we have taken and put in
and under our protection, security and special
safeguard in this place and its appurtenances, we
promise to keep and maintain him as a good king
and prince ought to maintain his servant against
all comers, generally by these said presents, by
which we ask our beloved and faithful councillors,
the members of our council, the members of our
courts of parliament, governors, baillifs, senes-
chals, judges and all others, justiciaries, officers and subjects to support, keep and observe our
said present declarations, will and intention,
neither doing, nor suffering to be done, anything
which will prejudice them, or if such is done,
rectifying and revoking it forthwith and without
delay; for thus it pleases us.

In witness whereof, we have caused our seal
to be put on these presents.

Given at Blois, the twentieth day of February,
the year of grace one thousand five hundred eleven
and of our reign the fourteenth.

By the King, Count of Provence, you and others,
here present.

Robertet.

Translated by Sarah J. Campbell

Mongolian People's Republic

The Mongolian People's Republic is bounded on
the north by the Soviet Union and on the west,
south, and east by China. Formerly known as Outer
Mongolia, the Republic was from the 17th century
a province of China. Supported by Russia, nationalistic Mongolians pushed for an autonomous State.
The Treaty of Kyakhta in 1915 recognized this
status. Despite some Chinese success in 1919 in
abolishing the autonomous status, a 1921 treaty
with the Soviet Union recognized Outer Mongolia
as an independent state. On November 26, 1924, a
constitution of the Mongolian People's Republic
was promulgated which adopted that name and
declared Mongolia an independent republic.

CONSTITUTION OF THE MONGOLIAN PEOPLE'S REPUBLIC

Adopted by the First Great Huruldan

November 26, 1924

In conformity with the interests of the broad masses who manifested their will during the revolution of the eleventh year (1921), by which revolution the foreign oppressors were driven out by the revolutionary people, and also in consideration of the death of the hitherto head of state Bogda Khan Damba Hutuktu on the seventeenth day of the fourth month (May 24), the government, elected by the revolutionary people, decided:

1.   To entrust the seal of Bogda Khan to the custody of the government.

2.   To adopt in the country a republican constitution, without president as head of state, which will vest the highest authority in the People's Great Huruldan and in the government elected by it (Great Huruldan).

3.   To commemorate each year the era of the Mongolian People's Republic together with the day of the establishment of the Mongolian State on the sixth day of the sixth month.

4.   To rename the period of government of Olana Ergugdeksen from this date (10 July 1924) of this fourteenth year to such and such successive year of the Mongolian State.

The Great Huruldan of the whole nation, at this its first convention, confirms the above fundamental decrees of the government and the following Fundamental Law (Constitution) of the Mongolian People's Republic.

The above-mentioned Fundamental Law shall be made public by the central and local authorities and posted in all public places.

The Great Huruldan commits to the government the teaching of the fundamental regulations of this constitution in schools and to the military forces.

PROCLAMATION OF RIGHTS OF THE
MONGOLIAN WORKING CLASSES

1. Mongolia is declared an independent
Republic, in which all power belongs to the
working classes. The people exercise their
supreme power through the Great Huruldan of the
entire nation and through the government elected
thereby.

Assembly.

Triska, Fan F., ed., Constitutions of the Communist
Party States, Stanford, The Hoover Institution, 1968.

Translated by: Iwan Jakowiewitsch Korestovetz and
Erich Hauer.

Kingdom of Morocco

Located in northwest Africa, Morocco is
bounded on the north by the Mediterranean, on the
east by Algeria, and on the west by the Sahara.
After being conquered in the seventh century by
the Arabs, Morocco was ruled by a series of Arab
and Berber dynasties. European influence increased from the eighteenth century. In 1912,
Morocco lost its independence and was divided into
French and Spanish protectorates and the international zone of Tangier. After World War II a
nationalistic sentiment began to grow. A declaration published on November 6, 1955, stated the
desire of the Sultan of Morocco to turn Morocco
into a democratic state and constitutional
monarchy. On March 2, 1956, France recognized the
independence of Morocco.

DECLARATION OF CELLE SAINT CLOUD
OF NOVEMBER 6, 1955

Published on November 6, the Declaration of
Celle Saint Cloud constitutes, in effect, a joint
statement of the Ministry of Foreign Affairs of the
French Republic and the Sultan of Morocco.

"His Majesty the Sultan of Morocco Sidi Mohammed Ben Youssef and President Antoine Pinay,
Minister of Foreign Affairs, have met on November 6,
1955, at Chateau Celle St. Cloud.

President Pinay has outlined the general principles of the policy of the French government en-
dorsed by the statement of the Council of Ministers
of November 5, 1955.

His Majesty the Sultan of Morocco has stated
his agreement with those principles. For the duration of his absence from Rabat, he has, with the
consent of the French government, charged the Council of Trône, created on October 17, 1955, and re-
lieves of its duties on November 3, 1955, with the
continued administration of the daily affairs of
the Empire.

His Majesty the Sultan of Morocco has stated
his desire to have an administration which will
reflect the various Moroccan points of view. The
mission of the administration will be primarily to
carry out institutional reforms which will make
Morocco a democratic State and a constitutional
monarchy. The mission will also be to conduct negotiations with France with the aim of gaining for
Morocco the status of an independent State, united
with France by permanent, defined, and freely entered bonds of interdependence.

His Majesty the Sultan of Morocco and President Pinay are in accord in stating that France
and Morocco, together and without the intervention
of others, must build their futures firmly committed to each other's sovereignty and the mutual
guarantee of each other's laws and treaties."

Translated by Matthew Jodziewicz

MOROCCO

COMMON DECLARATION OF MARCH 2, 1956

The Government of the Republic of France and His Majesty Mohammed V, Sultan of Morocco, affirm their intent to give full effect to the Declaration of Celle St. Cloud, of November 6, 1955.

They state that as a result of the progress of Morocco, the treaty of Fez on March 30, 1912, no longer reflects, henceforth, the needs of modern life and is no longer appropriate for the conduct of Franco-Moroccan relations. As a consequence, the Government of the Republic of France solemnly recognizes the independence of Morocco, which requires a diplomatic corps and an army, appropriate to its right to respect for its government, and for the protection of its boundaries, guaranteed by international treaty.

The Government of the Republic of France and His Majesty Mohammed V, Sultan of Morocco declare that the negotiations which have just opened in Paris between Morocco and France, sovereign and equal States, have for their object the reaching of new accords which will define the interdependence of these two countries, their areas of common interest, and which will establish their cooperation on a basis of liberty and equality, particularly in matters of defense, foreign relations, economics and cultural affairs and which will guarantee the rights and liberties of the French living in Morocco and Moroccans living in France, based on the sovereignty of the two States.

The Government of the Republic of France and His Majesty Mohammed V, Sultan of Morocco agree that while waiting for the effective date of these accords, the relationship of France and Morocco will be governed by procedures of protocol attached to this Declaration.

Translated by Matthew Jodziewicz

People's Republic of Mozambique

Located on the southeast coast of Africa,
Mozambique was settled by the Portuguese in the
early 1500's. It remained a colony of Portugal
until 1953 when it was made an overseas province.
A nationalist movement, begun in 1964, resulted in
a transitional government in September, 1974, and
complete independence on June 25, 1975.

THE PEOPLE'S REPUBLIC OF MOZAMBIQUE

Meeting at Lusaka from 5 to 7 September 1974 and aiming at the establishment of an agreement leading to the independence of Mozambique, the Portuguese State and the Mozambique Liberation Front delegation agreed on the following points.

1. Having recognized the Mozambique people's right to independence, the Portuguese State accepts, by agreement with FRELIMO, the progressive transfer of the powers it holds over the territory, under the terms following below.

2. The complete independence of Mozambique shall be solemnly proclaimed on 25 June 1975, the anniversary of the foundation of FRELIMO.

3. The following governmental structures are created with a view to ensuring the aforesaid transfer of powers. They will be operative during the transitional period, which begins on the signing of the present agreement. They are:

(a) a High Commissioner, appointed by the President of the Portuguese Republic;

(b) a Transitional Government, appointed by agreement between the Mozambique Liberation Front and the Portuguese State;

(c) a Joint Military Commission, appointed by agreement between the Mozambique Liberation Front and the Portuguese State.

4. The duties of the High Commissioner, as representative of Portuguese sovereignty are:

(a) to represent the President of the Portuguese Republic and the Portuguese Government;

(b) to ensure Mozambique's territorial integrity;

(c) to promulgate the legislative decrees approved by the Transitional Government and to ratify the acts which involve the direct responsibility of the Portuguese State;

(d) to ensure the implementation of agreements reached between the Portuguese State and the Mozambique Liberation Front and the respect for mutual guarantee, namely those subscribed to in the Universal Declaration of Human Rights;

(e) to boost the process of decolonization.

5. The Transitional Government's task will be to promote the progressive transfer of powers at all levels and to prepare Mozambique's independence. Namely its duties are:

(a) the exercise of legislative and executive functions relating to the Territory of Mozambique. Legislative functions will be carried out through legislative decrees;

(b) the general administration of the Territory up to the proclamation of independence and the restructuring of the cadres concerned;

(c) the defence and safeguard of public order and the safety of persons and property;

(d) the implementation of agreements signed by the Mozambique Liberation Front and the Portuguese State;

(e) the financial and economic administration of the Territory, namely the establishment of structures and mechanisms of control which may contribute towards the development of an independent Mozambique economy;

(f) the guarantee of the principle of non-discrimination on the grounds of race, ethnicity, religion or sex;

(g) the restructuring of the Territory's judiciary organization.

6. The composition of the Transitional Government shall be as follows:

(a) a Prime Minister, appointed by the Mozambique Liberation Front and whose task is to co-ordinate Government action and represent the Government;

(b) nine Ministers holding the following portfolios: Internal Administration; Justice; Economic Co-ordination; Information; Education and Culture; Transport and Communications; Health and Social Affairs; Labour; Public Works and Housing;

(c) Secretaries and Under-Secretaries to be created and appointed at the Prime Minister's proposal, by the Transitional Government's decision, and submitted for the High Commissioner's ratification;

(d) the Transitional Government shall define the distribution of its competence through the respective Ministers, Secretaries and Under-Secretaries.

7. Given the transitional character of this stage of governmental action, Ministers shall be appointed by the Mozambique Liberation Front and by the High Commis-

sioner in the proportion of two thirds and one third, respectively.

8. The Joint Military Commission will consist of equal numbers of representatives from the Armed Forces of the Portuguese State and from the Mozambique Liberation Front. Its main task will be to control the implementation of the cease-fire agreement.

9. The Mozambique Liberation Front and the Portuguese State hereby agree to a cease-fire on the terms specified in the adjoining protocol.

10. In the case of serious disruption of public order requiring intervention by the Armed Forces, the command and co-ordination will be entrusted to the High Commissioner, assisted by the Prime Minister on whom the Armed Forces of the Mozambique Liberation Front directly depend.

11. The Transitional Government shall set up a police corps charged with ensuring the maintenance of order and the safety of persons. Until such a corps becomes operative, the police forces presently existing will be commanded by the High Commissioner, in accordance with the general orientation defined by the Transitional Government.

12. The Portuguese State and the Mozambique Liberation Front undertake to act jointly in the defence of the territorial integrity of Mozambique against aggression.

13. The Mozambique Liberation Front and the Portuguese State solemnly state their aim to establish and develop links of friendship and constructive co-operation between their respective peoples, namely in the cultural, technical, economic and financial fields, upon a basis of independence, equality, community of interests and respect for the personality of each people. For this and during the transitional period, specialized joint commissions will be created and, thereafter, the relevant agreements will be signed.

14. The Mozambique Liberation Front declares its readiness to accept responsibility for financial obligations undertaken by the Portuguese State in the name of Mozambique, provided that those obligations were undertaken in the effective interests of this Territory.

15. The Portuguese State and the Mozambique Liberation Front undertake to act jointly in order to eliminate all vestiges of colonialism and to create true racial harmony. In this context, the Mozambique Liberation Front reaffirms

its policy of non-discrimination, according to which the quality of Mozambican is not defined by skin colour, but by voluntary identification with the aspirations of the Mozambican Nation. On the other hand, special agreements will define the status of Portuguese citizens resident in Mozambique and of Mozambican citizens resident in Portugal, on a reciprocal basis.

16. In order to secure for the Transitional Government the means to pursue an independent financial policy, a central bank will be created in Mozambique, which will also have the functions of an issuing bank. For this purpose the Portuguese State undertakes to transfer to that bank all assets and liabilities of the Mozambique department of the Banco Nacional Ultramarino (National Overseas Bank). A Joint Commission will begin work immediately to study conditions for such a transfer.

17. The Transitional Government shall try to obtain, through international organizations, or bilaterally, the aid required for the development of Mozambique, namely for the solution of its most pressing problems.

18. The independent Mozambican State will exercise fully complete sovereignty in domestic and external affairs, establishing political institutions and freely choosing the political and social system which it considers best suited to the interests of its people.

19. The Portuguese Government and the Mozambique Liberation Front congratulate themselves for the conclusion of the present agreement which, with the end of war and the re-establishment of peace, leading to the independence of Mozambique, opens a new page in the history of relations between the two countries and peoples. The Mozambique Liberation Front which, during the course of its struggle, has always distinguished the deposed colonialist régime from the Portuguese people, and the Portuguese State, will increase its efforts to build the basis for fruitful fraternal and harmonious co-operation between Portugal and Mozambique.

United Nations translation

Republic of Nauru

Nauru is an island in the southwestern
Pacific Ocean south of the Marshall Islands.
Under German control from 1888, Nauru was taken
over by the Australian Expeditionary Force in
1914. After World War I it was under the joint
administration of Britain, Australia, and New
Zealand. In 1947 Nauru became a U.N. Trust
Territory. In 1966 the U.N. General Assembly
recommended independence for Nauru, to be obtained no later than January 31, 1968. Australia
announced that Nauru would be independent November
7, 1967, and the Nauru Independence Act was finally passed on November 10, 1967.

REPUBLIC OF NAURU

NAURU INDEPENDENCE ACT 1967

Be it enacted by the Queen's Most Excellent Majesty, the Senate, and the House of Representatives of the Commonwealth of Australia, as follows:--

1.   This Act may be cited as the Nauru Independence Act 1967.

2.--(1.) Sections 1, 2 and 3 of this Act shall come into operation on the day on which this Act receives the Royal Assent.

(2.) Section 4 of this Act shall come into operation on a date to be fixed by Proclamation, in this Act referred to as "Nauru Independence Day."

3.   The power of the Legislative Council for the Territory of Nauru conferred by section 26 of the Nauru Act 1965 to make Ordinances for the peace, order and good government of that Territory extends to the making of an Ordinance establishing a convention for the purpose of establishing a constitution for Nauru.

4.--(1.) On the expiration of the day preceding Nauru Independence Day--

(a) the Nauru Act 1965 is repealed; and
(b) all Acts that extend to Nauru as a Territory of the Commonwealth cease so to extend.

(2.) On and after Nauru Independence Day, Australia shall not exercise any powers of legislation, administration or jurisdiction in and over Nauru.

Commonwealth of Australia, Act No. 103 of 1967.

Kingdom of Nepal

Situated on the northeastern frontier of India, Nepal is also bounded by Tibet to the north, and Sikkim to the east. Originally a group of small principalities, Nepal was united by Prithui Narayan Shah beginning in 1769. A conflict with Britain in 1814 to 1816 resulted in a loss of some territory and establishment of British influence. With Indian independence in 1947, a revolutionary movement began in Nepal. A new constitution was adopted in 1959, which declares the sovereignty of Nepal and of its ruling royal house.

KINGDOM OF NEPAL

THE CONSTITUTION OF NEPAL

PREAMBLE

Whereas it is desirable in the best interest and for all-round progress of the kingdom of Nepal and of the Nepalese people to conduct the government of the country in consonance with the popular will;

And Whereas We are firmly convinced that such arrangement is possible only through Panchayat system rooted in the life of the people in general, and in keeping with the national genius and traditions, and as originating from the very base with the active co-operation of the whole people, and embodying the principles of decentralization;

And Whereas the happiness and prosperity of Our beloved subjects have been always Our only objective for the accomplishment of which We are solemnly resolved;

And Whereas it is desirable for the said purpose to enact and promulgate a Constitution for the Kingdom of Nepal;

Now Therefore, I, King Mahendra Bir Bikram Shah Deva, in exercise of the sovereign powers and prerogatives inherent in Us according to the constitutional law, custom and usage of Our country and which devolved on Us from Our August and Revered Forefathers, do hereby enact and promulgate this Constitution.

Official Translation

Kingdom of the Netherlands

The Netherlands were ruled by Spain since the early 15th century. Religious persecution led to open rebellion in 1568. In 1579 the northern provinces of the Kingdom joined in a defense organization, the Union of Utrecht. On July 26, 1581, they declared themselves independent from Spain in the Proclamation of Deposition. The Treaty of Westphalia at the conclusion of the eighty years war in 1648 recognized independence. The Union was abolished in 1795 when the Netherlands came under French domination. In 1814 with the defeat of Napoleon Belgium and the Netherlands were united by the Treaty of Paris. This union lasted until 1830 when the Kingdom of Belgium was formed.

NETHERLANDS

PROCLAMATION OF DEPOSITION (1581)

The States General of the United Netherlands.
To all and singular who shall see these presents
or hear them read, Greeting!

Whereas it is known to all persons that a
Sovereign of the Realm has been appointed by God
to rule over his subjects, to safeguard them and
to protect them from all injustice, vexation and
violence, like a good shepherd watching over his
flock;

And that his subjects have not been created
by God for their Sovereign's pleasure, to do whatever he commands them to do, whether it be godly
or ungodly, right or wrong, and to serve him like
slaves, but that the Sovereign is there for his
people, but for whom he would not be Sovereign at
all, to govern them with justice and reason, and
to defend them and to love them like a father his
children and a shepherd his flock, who will risk
his person and his life to save the latter.

But if he does not do so, and instead of protecting his subjects, tries to oppress and vex them,
to deprive them of their ancient liberties, privileges and usages, and to order them about and use
them like slaves, he cannot be regarded as a Sovereign, but as a Tyrant, and may therefore in all
justice and reason be no longer recognized by his
subjects as their Sovereign, and by the delibera-
tions of the States General in particular, and
should be deposed, so that another may be elected
in his stead without any abuse of power to ensure
the people's protection:

The more so since his subjects have, with humble representations, not been able to persuade their
Sovereign aforesaid to mend his ways, or been able
to make him turn away from his tyrannous intent and,
therefore, see no other way of safeguarding and
protecting the freedom which is their own, their
wives', their children's and their descendants'
unalienable right (to protect which the law of

500

Nature renders it their duty to risk their proper-
ties and lives), as happened on various occasions
for the same causes in various Countries and at
various times, of which many examples are known:

That which, in particular, ought to take place
and come about in the aforesaid Countries, which
have always been governed, and should continue to
be governed in conformity with the pledges made by
their Sovereigns on their accession, in accordance
with their privileges, customs and ancient usages:
having also most of the Countries aforesaid accepted their Sovereigns on such conditions and under
such contracts and agreements, is that the abuse
thereof will involve the Sovereign's being lawfully
deprived of the Country's governance.

Now it so happens that the King of Spain has,
after the decease of the Emperor Charles V of glorious memory, from whom he has inherited all the
Low Countries, ...listened and given cre-
dence to the Council of Spain,

which Council of Spain, or some of its principal members, have on several occasions advised
the aforesaid King that it would be meet, both for
his own reputation and for the Majesty of his power,
to reconquer the aforesaid Countries, to bring them
under his undisputed and absolute sway (which means
to tyrannize them as pleases him), instead of governing them under such conditions and with such
restrictions as he should have pledged himself to
observe in taking over the government of these
Countries.

Acting upon which, the King has since, by all
the means at his disposal, endeavoured to deprive
the aforesaid Countries of their ancient liberties
and to bring them, in slavery, under Spanish domination: having ....

(there follows a detailed account of the unlawful deeds of violence committed by or in the
name of the King, and of their disastrous effects)
....

All of which has given us more than lawful
cause to depose the King of Spain, and to request

501

another powerful and benevolent Sovereign[+] to help
to protect and defend the aforesaid Countries the
more so since those Countries have been left in
disorder and trouble, neglected by their King for
more than twenty years, and been treated not as
subjects but as enemies, their own Sovereign seeking to subjugate them by force of arms ....

(All attempts to make the King change his mind
through petitions or peaceful negotiation having
failed).

so we, fully despairing of any means of rec-
onciliation, and having also been deprived of all
other remedies and succour,

obeying the law of Nature for the protection
and safeguarding of our subjects' and other residents' rights; jealous of the privileges, ancient
usages and liberties customary in this Country, of
the lives and honour of our wives, children and
descendants, that they might not be subjected to
Spanish slavery,

rightly deposing the King of Spain, having
been forced to employ such means, which we have
found to be appropriate, for the safeguarding and
preservation of our aforesaid rights, privileges
and liberties.

Whereas we, having considered the foregoing
and having, compelled by dire necessity as set out
before, by common accord, deliberation and agreement, declared and declare by these presents the
King of Spain to be deprived, ipso jure, of His
Rule of the aforesaid Countries and of his title
and hereditary rights thereto: and having reserved
henceforth not to seek his opinion in any matter
concerning the person of the Sovereign, his Highness, the Jurisdiction and Domains of the aforesaid
Countries, nor to use his name any more as Over-
lord, nor to allow it to be so used by others,

Declaring also, accordingly, all Officers,

[+] i.e. Anjou

Justices, Members of the Gentry, Vassals and all
other residents of the aforesaid Countries, of
whatever condition or quality, to be henceforth
absolved from the oath which they may in any way
have taken with respect to the King of Spain, having
been the Sovereign of the aforesaid Countries, or
from their being beholden to him in any other manner.

(there follow regulations concerning the super-
session of the name, title and seal of Philip II
in official documents, and concerning the new oath
to be taken on the States General by the officers
of the State).

Done at our Convention at The Hague, this
twenty-sixth day of July MDLXXXI.

Official Translation

DE Staten Generael der Geunieerde Nederlanden, Allen den genen die dese tegenwoordige sullen sien ofte hooren lesen, Saluyt. Alsoo een yegelick kennelick is, dat een Prince van den Lande van Gode ghestelt is Hooft over syne Ondersaten, om de selve te bewaren ende beschermen van alle ongelijck, overlast ende geweldt, ghelijck een Herder tot bewarenisse van sijn Schapen: Ende dat d'Ondersaten niet en zijn van Gode geschapen tot behoef vanden Prince, om hem in alles wat hy beveelt, weder het goddelick oft ongoddelick, recht ofte onrecht is, onderdanich te wesen, ende als slaven te dienen: maer den Prince om d'Ondersaten wille, sonder de welcke hy egheen Prince en is, om de selve met recht ende redene te regeeren, voor te staen, ende lief te hebben als een Vader sijne Kinderen, ende een Herder sijne Schapen, die syn lijf ende leven settet om de selve te bewaren. Ende soo wanneer hy sulcx niet en doet, maer in stede van syne Ondersaten te beschermen, de selve soeckt te verdrucken, t'overlasten, heure oude vryheyt, Privilegien ende oude herkomen te benemen, ende heur te gebieden ende gebruycken als Slaven, moet gehouden worden niet als Prince, maer als een Tyran, ende voor sulcks nae recht ende reden mach ten minste van syne Ondersaten, besonder by deliberatie vande Staten vanden Lande, voor egeen Prince meer bekent, maer verlaten, ende een ander in sijn stede, tot beschermenisse van henlieden, voor over-hooft, sonder misbruycken, gekosen werden, Te meer soo wanneer d'Ondersaten met ootmoedige verthooninge niet en hebben heuren voorsz Prince konnen vermorwen, noch van sijn tyrannigh opset gekeeren, ende alsoo egeen ander middel en hebben om heure eygene, heure Huysvrouwen, Kinderen, ende Nakomelingen aengheboren vryheyt (daer sy nae de Wet der Natueren goet ende bloedt schuldigh zijn voor op te setten) te bewaren ende beschermen, gelijck tot diversche reysen uyt gelijcke oorsaken in diversche

Landen, ende tot diversche tyden gheschiet, ende d'exempelen genoegh bekent zijn: 't Welck principalick in dese voorsz Landen behoort plaetse te hebben, en stant te grijpen, die van allen tyden zijn geregeert geweest, ende hebben oock moeten geregeert worden, naevolgende den Eedt by heure Princen t'heuren aenkomen gedaen, na uytwijsen heurer Privilegien, Costuymen, ende oude herkomen: hebbende oock meest alle de voorsz Landen haren Prince ontfangen op Conditien, Contracten, ende Accoorden, de welcke brekende, oock naer recht den Prince vande heerschappye vanden Landen is vervallen. Nu is 't alsoo, dat den Coningh van Spaengien, naer het overlyden van hooger memorie Keyser Caerle de vijfde, van wien hy alle dese Nederlanden ontfangen hadde, vergetende de diensten die soo sijn Heer Vader, als Hy, van dese Landen ende Ondersaten der selver, hadden ontfangen, deur de welcke besonder de Coningh van Spaengien soo losselicke Victorien tegens syne Vyanden verkregen hadde, dat synen naem ende macht alle de Werelt deur, daer deur vernaemt ende ontsien werdt: vergetende oock de vermaninge die de voorsz Keyserlicke Majesteyt hem t'anderen tyden ter contrarien hadde ghedaen, heeft dien van den Rade van Spaegnien nessens hem wesende die deur dien sy in dese Landen en vermochten egeen bevel te hebben te gouverneren, oft de principale Staten te bedienen (gelijck sy in de Coninghrijcken van Napels, Sicilien, tot Milanen, in Indien, ende ander plaetsen onder des Coninghs gewelt wesende, deden, kennende den meestendeel van hen den rijckdom ende macht der selver, hadden eenen nijdt tegens dese voorsz Landen, ende de vryheydt der selver, in hen herte genomen) gehoor ende geloof ghegeven, welcken Raedt van Spaegnien, oft eenige van de principale van dien, den voorsz Coningh tot diversche reysen voor oogen ghehouden hebben, dat voor sijn reputatie ende Majesteyt beter was, dese voorsz Landen van nieuws te conquesteren, om daer over vryelick ende absolutelick te mogen bevelen ('t welck is tyranniseren na sijn beliefte) dan onder alsulcken conditien ende restrictien (als hy hadde in het overnemen van de heerschappye van de selve Landen moeten sweeren) die

B 3   te re-

.mael met fyne Brieven gheveynfdelick hadde toe-gefeyt: Ja dat hy felfs van meyninge was te komen in Perfoone, om in al tot genoege van eenen yege-licken ordre te ftellen : hebbende oock ten tyden van het vertreck van den Hertoge van Alve na defe Landen een Vloote van Schepen in Spaegnien,om hem te voeren, en een in Zeelandt om hem tegens te komen, tot groote exceffive koften van den Lan-de doen toe-reeden, om fyne voorfz Onderfaten te abuferen, ende te beter in 't net te brengen: Heeft niet te min de voorfz Hertoge van Alva terftont na fijn komfte, wefende een Vreemdelingh, ende niet van den bloede van den voorfz Coningh, verklaert gehadt Commiffie van den Coningh te hebben van opperfte Capiteyn , ende korts naer van Gou-verneur generael van den Lande, tegens de Privile-gien ende oude herkomen des felfs. Ende openba-rende genoegh fijn voornemen , heeft terftondt de principale Steden ende Sloten met Volck befet, Cafteelen ende Stercken in de principaelfte en machtighfte Steden,om die te houden in fubjectie, opgerecht : de principaelfte Heeren, onder 't dexel van heuren Raedt van doen te hebben, ende te wil-len imployeren in den dienft van den Lande , uyt laft van den Coningh vriendelijck ontboden : die hem gehoor gegeven hebben, doen vangen, tegens de Privilegien uyt Brabant, daerfe gevangen waren, gevoert, voor hem felven (niet wefende haren com-petenten Rechter)doen betichten: ten leften, fon-der hen volkomelick te hooren, ter doodt veroor-deelt , ende openbaerlick ende fchandelick doen dooden, d'Andere, beter kenniffe van de geveynft-heyt der Spanjaerden hebbende, hen uyt den Lan-de houdende, verklaert verbeurt te hebben lijf ende goet, voor fulcks hun goet aenveert ende geconfif-queert,om dat de voorfz arme Ingefetene hun niet en fouden , ten ware met hare Sterckten, oft Prin-cen die hare vryheyt fouden mogen voorftaen,kon-nen oft mogen tegens 't Spaenfch geweldt behel-pen : Behalvens noch ontallicke andre Edelmans ende trefflijcke Borgers, die hy, foo om den hals ge-bracht, als verjaegt heeft,om hare goederen te con-fifqueren. De refte van de goede Ingefetene (bo-ven den overlaft die fy in haer Wijfs, Kinderen en-de goederen leden, door gemeyne Spaenfche Sol-daten t'heuren Huyfe in guarnifoen leggende, tra-vaillerende met foo vele diverfche fchattinge , foo menfts haer dwingende tot geldinge tot bouwinge van de nieuwe Cafteelen ende Fortificatien van de Steden , tot hare eygene verdruckinge, als met op-lecngen van hondertfte, twintighfte, ende thiende penningen, tot betalinge van de Krijghs-lieden,foo by hem mede gebracht, als die hy hier te Lande op-lichtede, om te imployeren tegens hare mede-Landtfaten , ende de gene die des Landts vryheyt met perickel van haer Lijf avontuerden voor te ftaen, op dat de voorfz Onderfaten verarmt wefen-de, geen middel ter Werelct en foude over blyven om fijn voornemen te beletten , ende de Inftructie, hem in Spangien gegeven, van het Landt te tracte-ren als van nieuws geconquefteert, te beter te vol-brengen. Tot welcken eynde hy oock begoft heeft in de principale plaetfen d'ordre van Juftitie, na de maniere van Spangien (directelick tegens de Privi-legien van den Lande) te veranderen, nieuwe Ra-den te ftellen , ende ten laetften wefende buyten

alle vreefe , foo hem dochte , eenen thienden pen-ninck forteelijck willen oprechten,op de koopman-fchappen ende handt-wercken,tot gantfche bederf-feniffe van den Lande , alfoofe gheelijck op de voorfz Koopmanfchap ende Handt-wercken is ftaende, niet tegenftaende menichfuldige Remon-ftrantien by elck Landt in 't particulier , ende oock by allegader in het generael hem ter contrarien ge-daen : 't welck hy oock met gewelt foude volbracht hebben, ten ware geweeft dat deur toedoen van mynen Heere den Prince van Orangien , ende di-verfche Edelmans , en andere goede Ingeborene, by den voorfz Hertogh van Alve uyt den Lande gebannen, fyne Vorftelijcke Gen. volgende, ende meeft in haren dienft wefende , ende andere goede Ingefetene ende wel-geaffectioneerde tot de vry-heydt van het voorfz Vaderlandt , Hollandt ende Zeelandt korts daer naer niet meeft en hadde hem af-gevallen , ende hun begeven onder de befcher-minge van den voorfz Heere Prince, tegens de welcke twee Landen,den voorfz Hertoge van Alve, gedurende fijn gouvernement,ende daer naer den grooten Commandeur (die naer den voorfz Her-togh van Alve,niet om te verbeteren,maer om den felven voet van tyrannye by bedeckter middelen te vervolgen, den voorfz Coningh van Spaengien hier te Lande ghefchickt hadde) hebben d'andere Landen , die fy met hare guarnifoenen ende opge-rechte Cafteelen hielden in de Spaenfche fubjectie, bedwongen om heure Perfoonen ende alle hare macht te ghebruycken om die te helpen t'onder te brengen, dies niet meer de felve Landen, die fy tot hare affiftentie, als voren, imployeerden, verfchoo-nende,dan ofte heur felfs Vyanden waren geweeft: latende de Spangiaerden,onder het deckfel van ge-muytineert te zijn , ten aenfien van den grooten Commandeur in de Stadt van Antwerpen gewel-dighlijck komen, daer fes weecken langh , tot lafte van de Borgeren, na hare difcretie teeren,ende daer en boven tot betalinge van hare ge-eyfchte foldie, de felve Borgeren bedwingende binnen middeler-tijdt (om van het gheweldt van de Spaengiaerden ontflagen te wefen) vier hondert duyfent guldens op te brengen,hebbende daer naer de voorfz Spaen-fche Soldaten , meerder floutigheyt ende geweldt gebruyckende, hen vervoordert de Wapenen open-baerlijck tegens het Landt aen te nemen, meynen-de eerft de Stadt van Bruffel in te nemen , ende in ftede van d'ordinaire refidentie van den Prince van den Lande, daer wefende, aldaer haren roof-neft te houden, 't welck haer niet geluckende, hebben de Stadt van Aelft overweldight, daer naer de Stadt van Maeftricht, ende de voorfz Stadt van Antwer-pen geweldighlijck overvallen, gefaccageert, gepil-leert, gemoort, gebrandt, ende foo getracteert, dat de tyrannige ende cruelfte Vyanden van den Lan-de, niet meer ofte erger en fouden konnen gedoen, tot on-uytfpreeckelijcke fchade niet alleenlijck van de arme Ingefetene , maer oock meeft van alle de Natien van de Wereldt , die aldaer hadden hare Koopmanfchap ende gelt. Ende niet tegenftaen-de dat de voorfz Spaengiaerden by den Rade van State (by den welcken doen ter tijdt,midts de doot van den voorfz grooten Commandeur te voren ge-fchiet, het gouvernement van den Lande was, uyt lafte ende Commiffie van den voorfz Coningh van
Spaen-

Spaengien aenveert) ten by-syne van Hieronymo de Rhoda, om heur overlast, force ende gheweldt 't welck sy deden, verklaert ende ghekondight waren voor Vyanden van den Lande, heeft den selven Rhoda uyt syne auctoriteyt (ofte soo het te presumeren is, uyt kracht van seeckere secrete Instructie die hy van Spaengien hebben mochte) aenghenomen Hooft te wesen van de voorsz Spaengiaerden ende heure Adherenten: ende (sonder aensien van den voorseyden Rade van Staten) te ghebruycken den name ende auctoriteyt van den Coningh, te contreseyten synen Zegel, hem openbaerlijck te dragen als Gouverneur ende Lieutenant van den Coningh: waer deur de Staten zijn geoorsaeckt geweest ten selven tyde met mynen voorsz Heere den Prince, ende de Staten van Hollant ende Zeelandt t'accorderen: welck Accoordt by den voorsz Raede van State, als wettige Gouverneurs van den Lande, is gheapprobeert, ende goet gevonden gheweest, om gelijcker handt ende eendrachtelijck de Spaengiaerden, des gemeynen Landts Vyanden, te mogen aenvechten, ende uyt den Lande verdryven: niet latende nochtans, als goede Ondersaten, binnen middelen tyden by diversche ootmoedige Remonstrantien nessens den voorsz Coningh van Spaengien, met aller vliet, ende alle bequame middelen moghelick wesende, te vervolgen, ende bidden dat den Coningh, ooge ende regard nemende op de troublen ende inconvenienten die alreede in dese Landen geschiet waren, en noch apparentelick stonden te geschieden, soude willen de Spaengiaerden doen vertrecken uyt 't Landt, en straffen de gene die oorsake geweest hadden van het saccageren ende bederven van syne principale Steden, ende onuytspreeckelijcke overlasten die syne arme Ondersaten geleden hadden, tot een vertroostinge van de ghene dien 't overkomen was, ende tot een exempel van andere: Maer den Coningh, al was 't dat hy met woorden hen gheliet oft tegens synen dancke ende wille 't selve geschiet ware, ende dat hy van meyninge was te straffen de Hoofden daer af, ende voortaen op de ruste van den Lande met alle goedertierenheydt (als een Prince toebehoort) te willen ordre stellen, heeft nochtans niet allenlick geen Justitie oft straffe over de selve laten doen, maer ter contrarien genoegh met der daet blijckende, dat met sijnen consente ende voorgaende Rade van Spaegnien 't selve geschiet was, is by op-gehouden Brieven korts daer naer bevonden, dat aen Roda ende andere Capiteynen (oorsake van 't voorsz quaet) by den Coningh selve geschreven wort, dat hy niet allenlick haer feyt goet vondt, maer haer daer af prees, ende beloofde te recompenseren, besonder den voorsz Roda, als hem gedaen hebbende eenen sonderlingen dienst, ghelijck hem oock tot sijnder wederkomste in Spaegnien, ende alle andere (sijne Dienaers van de voorsz tyrannie in dese Landen geweest hebbende) met der daet heeft bewesen. Heeft oock ten selven tyde (meynende des te meer d'oogen vande Ondersaten te verblinden) den Coningh in dese Landen gesonden voor Gouverneer sijnen Bastardt Broeder, Don Johan van Oostenrijck, als wesende van synen bloede, de welcke onder 't decksel van goet te vinden ende t'approberen 't Accoordt tot Gent ghemaeckt, het toeseggen van de Staten voor te staen, de Spaegniaerden

te doen vertrecken, ende d'Aucteurs van de gewelden ende desordren in dese voorsz Landen geschiet, te doen straffen, ende ordre op de ghemeyne ruste vande Landen ende hare oude vryheyt te stellen, sochte de voorsz Staten te scheyden, ende 't een Landt voor, 't ander naer, t'onder te brengen, soo korts daer na door de gehengenisse Godts (Vyandt van alle tyrannye) ontdeckt is door opgehouden en geintercipieerde Brieven, daer by bleeck dat hy van den Coningh last hadde om hem te reguleren na de Instructie ende bescheet dat hem Roda soude geven, tot meerder gheveynstheyt, verbiedende datse malkanderen niet en souden sien ofte spreken, ende dat hy hem soude nessens de principale Heeren minlick dragen, ende de selve winnen, tot der tijdt toe dat hy deur haer middel ende assistentie soude mogen Hollandt ende Zeelandt in sijn geweldt krijgen, om dan voorts met den anderen te doen na synen wille. Ghelijck oock Don Johan, niet tegenstaende hy de Pacificatie van Gent, ende seecker Accoordt tusschen hem ende de Staten van alle de Landen doen gemaeckt, hadde solemnelick in presentie van alle de voorsz Staten belooft ende beswooren t'onderhouden, contrarie van dien alle middelen socht om de Duytsche Soldaten, die doen ter tijdt alle de principaelste Sterckten ende Steden hadden in bewaringe, door middel van hare Colonellen, die hy hadde tot synen wille ende devotie, met groote beloften te winnen, ende soo de selve Sterckten ende Steden te krygen in sijn ghewelt, gelijck hy den meestendeel alreede ghewonnen hadde, ende de Plaetsen hielt voor hem toeghedaen, om door dien middel de gene die hen t'soecken soude willen maecken, om den voorschreven Heer Prince, en die van Hollant en Zeelandt Oorloge te helpen aendoen, faytelick daer toe te bedwingen, en alsoo een straffer en crueler Inlandtsche Oorloge te verwecken, dan oyt te voren hadde geweest: 't Welck (ghelijck 't gene dat geveynsdelick ende tegens de meyninge uytwendighlick gehandelt wort, niet lange en kan bedeckt blyven) uytbrekende eer hy volkomelick syne intentie gheeffectueert hadde, heeft 't selve nae syn voornemen niet konnen volbrengen, maer nochtans een nieuwe Oorloge in stede van Vrede (daer hy hem t'syner komste af vanteerde) verweckt, noch jegenwoordelick duerende. Alle 't welck ons meer dan genoegh Wettige oorsaecke gegeven heeft om den Coningh van Spangien te verlaten, ende een ander machtigh en goedertieren Prince, om de voorsz Landen te helpen beschermen en voor te staen, te versoecken: Te meer, dat in alsulcken disordre ende overlast de Landen bet dan twintigh Jaren van heuren Coningh zijn verlaten geweest, ende getracteert niet als Ondersaten, maer als Vyanden, heur soeckende heur eygen Heer met kracht van Wapenen t'onder te brengen: Hebbende oock naer de aflyvicheyt van Don Johan, deur den Baron van Selle, onder het decksel van eenige bequame middelen van Accoorde voor te houden, genoegh verklaert de Pacificatie van Gent, die Don Johan uyt synen name besworen hadde, niet te willen advoyeren, ende alsoo dagelijcks swaerder conditien voor-geslagen. Dien niet tegenstaende hebben niet willen laten by schriftelicke en ootmoedige Remonstrantien, met intercessie van de princi-

principaelſte Princen van Chriſtenrijck, ſonder op-
houden te verſoecken met den voorſz Coningh te
concilieren ende accorderen, hebbende oock leſt-
mael lange tijdt onſe Geſanten ghehadt te Colen,
hoopende aldaer, deur tuſſchen ſpreecken van de
Keyſerlijcke Majeſteyt, ende de Keur-Vorſten die
daer mede gemoeyt waren, te verkrijgen eenen ver-
ſeeckerden Pays, met eenige gracelijcke vryheydt,
beſonder vande Religie (de conſcientie ende Gode
principalick rakende) maer hebben by experientie
bevonden, dat wy met de ſelve Remonſtrantien ende handelingen niet en koſten yet vanden Coningh
verwerven, maer dat de ſelve handelingen ende
communicatien alleenlick voor geſlagen werden,
ende dienden om de Landen onderlinge twiſtigh
te maecken, ende te doen ſcheyden d'een van den
anderen, om des te gevoegelicker de een voor ende
d'ander naer onder te brengen, ende heur eerſte
voornemen nu met aller rigeur tegens haer te wer-
ke te ſtellen: 't welck naederhandt wel openbaerlick ghebleken is by ſeecker Placaet van proſcrib-
tien by den Coningh laten uytgaen, by den welcken wy ende alle de Officieren ende Ingheſetenen
van de voorſz geunieerde Landen, ende heure par-
tye volgende (om ons tot meerder deſperatie te
brengen, alomme odieus te maken, de traffique ende handelinge te beletten) verklaert worden voor
Rebelle, ende over ſulcx verbeurt te hebben lijf ende goet: Settende daer en boven op het lijf vanden
voorſz Heer Prince, groote ſomme van Penningen:
ſoo dat gantſchelick van alle middele van reconci-
liatie wanhopende, ende oock van alle andere re-
medie ende ſecours verlaten weſende, hebben, volgende de Wet der natueren, tot beſchermeniſſe en-
de bewaerniſſe van onſen ende den anderen Landt-
ſaten, Rechten, Privilegien, oude herkomen ende
vryheden van ons Vaderlandt, van het leven ende
eere, van onſe Huyſvrouwen, Kinderen ende Nakomelingen, op datſe niet en ſouden vallen inde ſla-
vernye van de Spangaerden, verlatende met rechte
den Coningh van Spangien, andere middelen bedwongen geweeſt voor te wenden, die wy tot onſe
meeſte verſeeckeringe, ende bewaerniſſe van onſe
Rechten, Privilegien ende Vryheden voorſz hebben
te rade gevonden.

DOEN TE WETEN: Dat wy 't ghene
voorſz overgemerckt, ende door den uyterſten noot
als voren, gedrongen zijnde, by gemeynen Accoorde, deliberatie ende overdragen, den Coningh van
Spangien verklaert hebben, ende verklaren midts
deſen, iſo jure vervallen van ſyne Heerſchappye,
Gerechtigheydt ende Erſſeniſſe van de voorſeyde
Landen: ende voortaen nu egeene meyninge te
zijn den ſelven te kennen in eenige ſaecken den
Prince, ſyne Hoogheyt, Juriſdictie ende Domeynen
van deſe voorſeyde Landen rakende, ſynen name
als Overheer meer te gebruycken, of by yemanden
te laten gebruyckt te worden: Verklarende oock
dien volgende alle Officiers, Juſticiers, Smalle
Heeren, Vaſſalen, ende alle andere Ingeſetene van
den voorſeyden Lande, van wat conditie oft quali-
teyt die zijn, voortaen ontſlagen van den Eede die
ſy den Coningh van Spangien, als Heere van deſe
voorſz Landen geweeſt hebbende, mogen eenighſins gedaen hebben, oft in hem ghehouden weſen.

Ende gemerckt uyt oorſaecken voorſz den meeſten
deel van de geunieerde Landen, by gemeynen Accoorde ende conſente van heure Leden, hebben
hun begeven gehadt onder de Heerſchappye ende
Gouvernemente van den Doorluchtigen Prince,
den Hertogh van Anjou, op ſeeckere Conditien ende Poincten met ſyne Hoogheyt aenghegaen ende
geſloten: Dat oock de Doorluchtigheydt van den
Eertz-Hertoge Matthias het Gouvernement generael van den Lande, in onſe handen heeft gereſig-
neert, ende by ons is geaccepteert geweeſt, Ordonneren ende bevelen allen Juſticiers, Officiers ende
andere die 't ſelve eenighſins aengaen ende raken
mach, dat ſy voortaen den Name, Tytel, groote
ende kleyne Zegelen, contre-Zegelen, ende Cachetten van den Coningh van Spangien verlaten,
ende niet meer en gebruycken: Ende dat in plaetſe
van dien, ſoo lange de Hoogheyt vanden voorſz
Hertogh van Anjou, om noodelicke affairen, het
welvaren van deſe voorſz Landen rakende, noch van-
hier abſent is (voor ſo vele de Landen met de Hoogheyt van den voorſz Hertoge van Anjou ghecontracteert hebbende, aengaet) ende anderſints d'andere by maniere van voorraedt ende proviſie ſullen
aennemen ende gebruycken den Tytel ende name
van 't Hooft ende Landt-raedt: Ende middeler tijt
dat 't ſelve Hooft ende Raden volkomelick ende
dadelick genoemt, beſchreven ende in oeffeninge
van hunnen Staet getreden ſullen zijn, onſen voorſz
name. Welverſtaende dat men in Hollandt ende
Zeelandt ſal, als hier voormaels, ghebruycken den
name van den hoogh-gheboren Vorſt den Prince
van Orangien, ende de Staten van de ſelve Landen, tot der tijdt toe den voorſz Landt-raedt dadelick ſal ingeſtelt weſen, ende ſullen hun als dan reguleren achtervolgende de conſenten by hunlieden
op de Inſtructie van den Landt-raedt ende Con-
tractie met ſyne Hoogheyt aenghegaen. Ende in
plaetſe van des voorſz Coninghs Zegel, ſullen voortaen ghebruycken ſal onſen grooten Zegel, contre-
Zegel ende Cachetten, in ſaecken raeckende de
ghemeyne Regeeringe, daer toe den Landt-raedt,
volgende heure Inſtructie, ſal geauthoriſeert weſen:
maer in ſaecken raeckende de Policie, adminiſtra-
tie van Juſtitie, ende andere particuliere, in elck
Landt beſonder, ſal gebruyckt worden by de Pro-
vinciale ende andere Raden den name, Tytel ende
Zegel vanden Lande reſpectivelick, daer 't ſelve
valt te doen, ſonder ander: al op de pene van nul-
liteyt van de Brieven, Beſcheyden ofte Depeſchen,
die contrarie van 't gene voorſz is, gedaen ofte ge-
zegelt ſullen weſen. Ende tot beter ende ſeecker-
der volkominge ende effectuatie van 't gene voorſz
is, hebben geordonneert ende bevolen, ordonneren
ende bevelen midts deſen, dat alle des Coninghs
van Spangiens Zegelen, in deſe voorſchreve geunieerde Landen weſende, terſtondt na de publicatie
van deſen, gebrocht ſullen moeten worden in handen van de Staten van elcke vande voorſchreve
Landen reſpectivelick, ofte den genen die daer toe
by de ſelve Staten ſpecialick ſullen weſen ghecom-
mitteert ende geauthoriſeert, op pene van arbitrale
correctie. Ordonneren ende bevelen daer en boven, dat voortaen in egeenderhande maniere van
de voorſz gheunieerde Landen ſal gheſlagen worden den naem, tytel ofte wapenen vanden voorſz

C   Coningh

Coningh van Spangien, maer alſulcken ſlagh ende forme als geordonneert ſal worden tot eenen nieuwen gouden ende ſilveren Penningh met ſyne gedeelten. Ordonneren ende bevelen inſgelijcks den Preſident ende andere Heeren van den Secreten Rade, midtſgaders alle andere Cantſeliers. Preſidenten, ende Heeren van den Raede Provinciäel, ende alle de Preſidenten oft eerſte Reecken-meeſters, ende andere van allen de Reecken-kameren in de voorſz Landen reſpective weſende, ende alle andere Officiers ende Juſticiers, dat ſy (als heur ontſlagen houdende van den Eede die ſy den Coningh van Spangien hebben reſpectivelick naer luyt heurer Commiſſien ghedaen) ſchuldigh ende ghehouden ſullen weſen in handen van de Staten des Landts daer onder ſy reſpective reſorteren, ofte heure ſpeciale Ghecommitteerde, te doen eenen nieuwen Eedt, daer mede ſy ons ſweeren ghetrouwigheyt tegens den Coningh van Spangien, ende alle ſyne Aenhangers, alles naervolgende het formulier daer op by de Generale Staten gheraemt. Ende ſal men den voorſz Raden, Juſticiers ende Officiers geſeten onder de Landen (met de Hoogheyt van den Hertogh van Anjou ghecontracteert hebbende van onſent wegen) geven Acte van continuatie in hunne Officien, ende dat by maniere van proviſie, tot de aenkomſte toe van ſyne voorſz Hoogheyt, in plaetſe van nieuwe Commiſſien, inhoudende caſſatie van hare voorgaende: Ende de voorſz Raden, Juſticiers ende Officiers geſeten in de Landen, met ſyne voorſeyde Hoogheyt niet gecontracteert hebbende, nieuwe Commiſſien onder onſen name ende Zegel: 't en ware nochtans dat d'Impetranten van hare voorſz eerſte Commiſſien wederſproocken ende achterhaelt werden van con-

traventie der Privilegien des Landts, onbehoorlickheyt, ofte andere diergelijcke ſaecken. Ontbieden voorts den Preſident ende Luyden van den Secreten Rade, Cantelier van 't Hertoghdom van Brabandt, midtſgaders den Cancelier van het Vorſtendom van Gelre, ende van het Graefſchap van Zutphen, Preſident ende Luyden van den Rade in Vlaenderen, Preſident ende Luyden van den Rade in Hollandt, Rentmeeſteren ofte de hooge Officieren van Beooſt ende Beweſter-Scheldt van Zeelandt, Preſident ende Rade in Vrieſlant, den Schoutet van Mechelen, Preſident ende Luyden van den Rade van Utrecht, ende alle andere Juſticieren ende Officieren wien dat aengaen mach, hare Stadthouders, ende een yeghelick van hen-lieden beſonder, ſoo hem toebehooren ſal, dat ſy deſe onſe Ordonnantie verkondigen ende uytroepen over alle het bedrijf van hare Juriſdictie, ende daer men ghewoonlick is publicatie ende uytroepinge te doen, ſoo dat niemandt des cauſe van ignorantie pretenderen en mach: Ende de ſelve Ordonnantie doen onderhouden ende achtervolgen onverbrekelick: ende ſonder infractie, daer toe rigoureuſelick bedwingende de Overtreders in de maniere voorſz, ſonder verdragh ofte diſſimulatie: Want wy tot welvaren van den Lande alſoo hebben bevonden te behooren. Ende van des te doen, ende wat daer aen kleeſt, geven wy u, ende elcken van u, die 't aengaen mach, volkomen macht, auctoriteyt ende ſonderlingh bevel. Des t'oorkonden, hebben wy onſen Zegel hier aen doen hangen. Gheghieven in onſe Vergaderinge in 's Graven-Hage, den 26. Julii Anno 1581. Op de Plijeque ſtont geſchreven, Ter Ordonnantie van de voornoemde Staten. Ende getecckent, *I. van Aſſeliers.*

---

4. Artijckelen ende Conditien *van't verdragh, geſloten by ſijn Princelicke Excellentie, ende den Wel-gebooren Heere, Graef Wilhelm van Naſſauw, by advijs van de Heeren Raden van State, uyt name der Heeren Staten Generael der Vereenighde Nederlanden, met de Stadt Groeningen, ende 't Garniſoen, daer binnen gheweeſt hebbende, op't overgeven der ſelve Stadt.* Geaccordeert den 22 Iulii, Anno 1594.

I.

I N den eerſten, dat alle Offenſien, injurien, miſdaden, ende alle wegen van ſeyte ende dadelicke wercken, gedaen, geſchiet ende volbracht, van den beginne der troublen, ſoo wel in d'eerſte als de laetſte troublen, alteratien ende beroerten, gevallen, hoe oock die onder de belegeringe der Stadt Groeningen tegenwoordelick gheſchiet, tot wat plaetſen ende manieren dat het oock zy, ſoo in't generael als particulier, ſoo binnen als buyten, ſullen weſen, zyn ende blyven vergeven ende vergeten, ende gehouden als niet gheſchiet, ſulcks dat tot genen tyde eenigh vermaen, mentie, moleſtatie, actie ofte onderſoeck, met recht ofte buyten recht, daerom gedaen, gemaeckt, ofte yemant te laſte geleydt ſal mogen worden: op pene dat de Contraventeurs gereputeert, ghéacht ende geſtraft ſullen worden, als perturbateurs ende ver-

ſtoorders van de ghemeene ruſte ende vrede.

II.

Sullen die van de Magiſtraet ende Ingeſetene van Groeningen aennemen ende beloven, ghelijck ſy aennemen ende belooven by deſen, hen in de Unie van de generale Nederlandtſche Provintien te reunieren, ende de Heeren Staten Generael der ſelve Geunieerde Provintien aen te hangen, ghehouw ende getrouw te zijn. Ende dat den volgende die van Groeningen als een mede-Lidtmaet neffens de Provintien malkanderen als goede Bondtgenooten, in goeder trouwe, ende ongeveynſdelicke, vaſte ende onverbreeckelicke vriendtſchap onder malkanderen, onderhouden ſullen, ende in alle tyden ende in alle occurrentien malkanderen byſtaen, om te wederſtaen, daer uyt te houden ende te verdrijven, alle de Spangiaerden ende hare Adherenten, gebruyckt ende ghepooght hebbende, boven alle recht, redene ende billigheyt, de Onderſaten te verdrucken ende te verderven, ende

te regeren. Welcke volgende den Coningh, zedert alle middelen gesocht heeft dese voorsz Landen te brengen uyt heure oude vryheyt, in een slavernye onder 't gouvernement vande Spaengiaerden: hebbende eerst, onder 't dexsel vande Religie, willen inde principaelste en machtichste Steden stellen nieuwe Bisschoppen, de selve begiftigende en doterende met toevoeginge en incorporatie vande rijckste Abdyen, en hem bysettende de negen Canoniken, die souden wesen van synen Rade, waer af de drye soude besonderen last hebben over d'Inquisitie: door de welcke incorporatie de selve Bisschoppen (die souden mogen gheweest hebben, soo wel Vreemdelingen als Ingeborene) souden hebben gehadt d'eerste plaetsen en voysen in de Vergaderinge van de Staten van de voorsz Landen, ende geweest syne Creaturen, staende tot sijnen bevele ende devotie: Ende deur de voorsz toegevoeghde Canoniken de Spaensche Inquisitie ingebrocht, de welcke in dese Landen altijdt soo schrickelick ende odieus, als de uyterste slavernye selve, gheweest is, soo een yegelijck is kennelijck: Soo dat de voorsz Keyserlicke Majesteyt de selve t'anderen tyden den Landen voorgeslagen hebbende, deur die Remonstrantie diemen aen syne Majesteyt daer tegens gedaen heeft (thoonende d'affectie die hy syne Ondersaten was toedragende) die heeft laten varen: Maer niet tegenstaende diversche remonstrantien, soo by particuliere Steden ende Provintien, als oock van eenige principale Heeren vanden Lande, namentlick den Heere van Montigny, ende den Grave van Egmont, tot dien eynde by consente van de Hartoginne van Parma, doen ter tijdt Regente over de selve Landen, by advijse van den Rade van State ende generaliteyt na Spaegnien tot distincte reysen gesonden, mondelinge gedaen: ende dat oock den voorsz Coningh van Spaegnien de selve mondelinge goede hope hadde ghegheven van, naevolgende hen versoeck, daer inne te versien, heeft ter contrarien corts daer naer by Brieven scherpelick bevolen de voorsz Bisschoppen, op sijn indignatie, terstont t'ontfangen, ende te stellen in de possessie van heure Bisdommen, ende geincorporeerde Abdyen: de Inquisitie te wercke te stellen daerse te vooren was, ende d'Ordonnantie van het Concilie van Trenten (die in vele Poincten contrarieerde de Privilegien vande voorsz Landen) t'achtervolgen. 't Welck gecomen zijnde ter ooren vande gemeynte, heeft met redenen oorsake gegeven van een groote beroerte onder haer, ende eenen aftreck van de goede affectie die sy als goede Ondersaten den voorsz Coningh van Spangien ende sijne voorsaten altijdt toegedragen hadden, besonder aenmerckende dat hy niet alleenlick en sochte te tyranniseren over hunne Persoonen ende goet, maer oock over heure conscientien, waer van sy verstonden niemant, dan aen Gode alleene, gehouden te wesen reeckeninge te geven oft te verantwoorden: Waer deur, ende uyt medelyden van de voorsz gemeynte, de principaelste vanden Adel vanden Lande hebben inden Jare 1566. seker Remonstrantie overgegeven, versoeckende dat, om de Gemeynte te stillen, ende alle oproer te verhoeden, sijne Majesteyt soude de voorsz poincten, ende besonder noopende de rigoreuse ondersoeckinge ende straffe over de Religie willen versoeten, daer inne thoonende de liefde en-

de affectie die hy tot sijne Ondersaten, als een goedertieren Prince was dragende. Ende om 't selve al naerder ende met meerder authoriteyt den voorsz Coningh van Spaegnien te kennen te geven, ende te verthoonen hoe nootlick het was voor het Lants welvaren, ende om 't selve te houden in ruste, sulcke nieuwigheden af te doen, ende het rigeur vande contraventie vanden Placate op de saecken vande Religien gemaeckt, te versoeten, ter begeerte vande voorsz Gouvernante, Raede van Staete, ende van de Staten Generael van alle de Landen, als Gesanten zijn nae Spaengien gheschickt gheweest den Marckgrave van Bergen, ende den voorsz Heere van Montigny: in stede van de welcke ghehoor te geven, ende te versiene op de inconvenienten die men voor gehouden hadde (die midts het uytstel van daer inne in tijdts te remedieren soo den noot uyteyschte, alreede onder de Gemeynte meest in alle de Landen begost waren hen te openbaren) heeft deur opruyen van den voorsz Spaenschen Raedt, de Persoonen de voorsz Remonstrantie gedaen hebbende, doen verklaren rebel, ende schuldigh van het Crijm læsæ Majestatis, ende alsoo strafbaer in Lijf ende Goet: Hebbende daer-enboven de voorsz Heeren Gesanten namaels (meynende dese voorsz Landen deur 't geweldt van den Hertoge van Alve geheelijck gebrocht te hebben onder sijn subjectie ende tyrannye) tegens alle gemeyne Rechten, oock onder de wreedste ende tyrannighste Princen altydt onverbreeckelijck onderhouden, doen vangen, dooden, ende heure goeden confisqueren. Ende al was 't alsoo dat meest de beroerte in dese voorsz Landen, deur toedoen van de voorsz Regente ende heure Adherenten in 't voorsz Jaer 1566. op-gestaen, was geslist, ende vele die de vryheyt des Landts voor stonden, verjaeght, en d'andere verdruckt ende t'onder gebrocht, soo dat den Coningh egheen oorsake ter wereldt meer en hadde, om de voorsz Landen met gewelt ende wapenen t'overvallen: nochtans om sulcken oorsaecke die den voorseyden Spaenschen Raedt langen tijdt gesocht ende verwacht hadde (soo opentlijck de opgehouden ende geintercipieerde Brieven van den Ambassadeur van Spaegnien Alana, in Vranckrijck wesende, aen de Hertoginne van Parma doen ter tijdt geschreven, dat uytwijsden) om te niete te mogen doen alle des Landts Privilegien, dat nae heuren wille by de Spaegniaerden tyrannighlijck te mogen gouverneren, als de Indien, ende nieuwe geconquesteerde Landen, heeft deur ingeven ende rade van de selve Spaegniaerden (thoonende de kleyne affectie die hy syne goede Ondersaten was toedragende, contrarie van 't gene hy haer, als haer Prince, Beschermer, ende goede Herder schuldich was te doen) nae dese Landen, om de selve t'overvallen, geschickt met groote heyr-kracht den Hertogh van Alva, vermaert van strafheyt ende crudeliteyt, een van de principale Vyanden van de selve Landen, vergeselschapt, om als Raden neffens hem te wesen, met Persoonen van gelijcker natuere ende humeuren. Ende al was het soo dat hy hier in de Landen sonder slach ofte stoot is gekomen, ende met alle reverentie ende eere is ontfangen van de arme Ingesetene, die niet anders en verwachteden dan alle goedertierentheyt ende clementie, gelijck den Coningh hen-lieden dickwils ende menichmael

Dominion of New Zealand

Located 1,200 miles east of Australia in the South Pacific Ocean, New Zealand was first discovered by the Dutch in 1642. British influence was established after the explorations by Captain James Cook in 1769. New Zealand sovereignty was transferred to the British in 1840. In 1853 New Zealand was granted self-government and achieved dominion status in a September 9, 1907 British Proclamation. The Statute of Westminister in 1947 recognized autonomy within the Commonwealth.

NEW ZEALAND

BRITISH PROCLAMATION

DECLARING THAT THE COLONY OF NEW ZEALAND

SHALL BE CALLED AND KNOWN BY THE TITLE OF

THE DOMINION OF NEW ZEALAND

LONDON

SEPTEMBER 9, 1907

Edward R. & I.

 Whereas We have on the Petition of the Members of the Legislative Council and House of Representatives of Our Colony of New Zealand determined that the title of the Dominion of New Zealand shall be substituted for that of the Colony of New Zealand as the designation of the said Colony, We have therefore by and with the advice of Our Privy Council thought fit to issue this Our Royal Proclamation, and We do ordain, declare, and command that on and after the 26th day of September, 1907, the said Colony of New Zealand and the territory belonging thereto shall be called and known by the title of the Dominion of New Zealand. And We hereby give our Commands to all Public Departments accordingly.

 Given at Our Court at Buckingham Palace, this 9th day of September, in the year of our Lord, 1907, and in the 7th year of Our Reign.

God save the King.

Republic of Nicaragua

The Republic of Nicaragua is a Central
American country bounded to the north by Honduras,
to the east by the Caribbean Sea, to the south by
Costa Rica, and to the west by the Pacific Ocean.
Nicaragua was explored and colonized by the
Spanish beginning in 1502. The Mosquito Coast
became a British protectorate in the middle of the
17th century. In 1786 Great Britain recognized
Spanish title to the entire area which became part
of the audencia of Guatemala. On September 15,
1821, following the overthrow of Spanish rule in
Mexico, a revolutionary junta at Guatemala City
declared the independence of all Central America.
Along with other Central American states,
Nicaragua united with Mexico. On July 11, 1823,
Nicaragua split from Mexico and joined the United
Provinces of Central America. After years of
internal strife, the Union dissolved and in 1838
Nicaragua became a separate independent state.

ACT OF SEPTEMBER 15, 1821

DECLARATION OF INDEPENDENCE

National Palace of Guatemala: fifteenth of September, eighteen hundred twenty one.

The desire for Independence from the Government of Spain being clearly and openly expressed by word of mouth and in writing by the people of this Capital; and having in our possession by the last mail official letters from the cabildos of Ciudad Real, Comitan and Tuxtlas [all in what is Mexico today] in which they inform us that they have proclaimed and sworn said Independence, and invite us to do the same; and the honorable Provincial Deputation having been convened to discuss this grave matter, there met in one of the Chambers of this Palace the said Provincial Deputation, the most excellent Archbishop of Guatemala, the Territorial Courts of Justice, the heads of the Church, and other public functionaries; the letters referrred to having been read, discussed and meditated on, and the matter having been given thought; and heard the clamor of the people in the streets and those congregated in the plazas, patios and half of this palace, raising their voices to cry "long live Independence," it was agreed by the Deputation and the members of the honorable cabildo:

1. That Independence from Spain being the general will of the people, and without prejudice to what the future Congress may decide in regard to independence, the Jefe Politico orders that it be published in order to preclude the dreadful consequences should the general public take this matter in their hands and proclaim it de facto.

2. Notice should be promptly sent to the Provinces, by special mail, so that without delay, they proceed to elect representatives or deputies, and that these convene in this Capital to form a Congress which shall debate the question of general and absolute independence, and to establish, in the event independence be agreed upon, the form of government and to draw up a constitution.

3. To expedite the appointment of deputies this should be done by the same electoral committees that were elected or appointed to choose the representatives to the Spanish Assembly.

4. That the number of deputies be in the proportion of one to each fifteen thousand inhabitants, without excluding those originating in Africa.

5. That the same Electoral Committee of the Provinces, taking into consideration the latest census, determine, on this basis, the number of deputies or representatives to be elected.

6. That in view of the seriousness and urgency of this matter, elections be held in such manner that by the 1st of March of the next year, 1822, all of the deputies be able to gather here in this Capital.

7. That, meanwhile, no changes are to be made among the established authorities, all are confirmed in their positions and will continue to carry out their respective duties in accordance with the Constitution, Decrees and Laws now in force, until the Congress, under reference, determine what is most just and beneficial.

8. That the Jefe Politico, Brigadier don Gabino Gainza, continue as Supreme Political and Military Commander, that he have the rank and the attributes which seem most appropriate to the circumstances; that a Provisional Junta be formed for Consultative purposes, and that this be made up of the Provincial Deputation and of others whom we appoint hereunder.

9. That this Provisional Consultative Junta consult the Jefe Politico in all matters of finance and government which are deemed worthy of his attention.

10. That the Catholic Religion, which we have professed in past ages and which we shall continue to profess in coming ages, be conserved pure and unchanged, keeping alive in Guatemala the religious spirit with which it has always been distinguished, extending due respect to the Ecclesiastic Ministers and guaranteeing them protection of both their

property and their persons.

11.   That instructions be sent to all the
honorable Prelates of the Religious Communities
asking them to cooperate in maintaining the peace
and tranquility which is the primary necessity of
peoples when they pass from one government to another ti tge end that those being united in their
fervor for independence be also united in all other
matters, submerging individual desires and passions
that can create dissention with fatal consequences.

12.   That the cabildo being charged by its
very nature with the maintenance of order and tranquility, take the most active measures to maintain
these unperturbed in this Capital and the nearby
towns.

13.   That the Jefe Politico publish the desires
of the people, the opinions of the authorities and
the corporations, the measures taken by this Government, the causes and the circumstances which induced
them, at the request of the people, to declare
Independence and swear fealty to the American government that be established.

14.   That the same oath be taken by the Provincial
Junta, the cabildo, the Archbishop, the Tribunals,
the political and military chiefs, the Regular Prelates, the religious communities, the Chiefs and
employees of the tax administration, Authorities,
corporations and troops of the respective garrisons.

15.   That the day be set on which the people
should make the proclamation and swear the oath of
independence by common agreement between the Jefe
Politico and the cabildo.

16.   That the cabildo have a medal struck to
commemorate throughout the ages the memory of the
15th of September, eighteen hundred twenty-one, on
which Guatemala proclaimed its independence.

17.   That this act be printed and the declaration
distributed to the honorable Provincial Deputations,
Constitutional Magistrates, and other ecclesiastical,
regular, secular and military authorities, so that
in conformity with the sentiments declared by the
People they may work in agreement with all that is

expressed therein.

18.   That the Jefe Politico designate a day for a Mass of Thanksgiving in the presence of the Provincial Junta and all authorities, corporations and Chiefs, with artillery salute and three days of illumination.

Tanslated by Sarah J. Campbell

Declaration of Independence
of
The United Provinces of Central America

THE SUPREME EXECUTIVE AUTHORITY OF THE UNITED
PROVINCES OF CENTRAL AMERICA.

Whereas the National Constituent Assembly
of the said Provinces has decreed as follows:
The Representatives of The United Provinces
of Central America, assembled by virtue of the
Convocation issued from this City on the 15th
September, 1821, and renewed on the 29th March of
the present Year, for the important object of
deciding on the Independence and Liberty of the
People we represent -- upon their reciprocal Union --
upon their Government -- and upon the other Points
contained in the memorable Act of the said 15th
September, which was then adopted by the majority
of the Inhabitants of this extensive Territory,
and to which all the rest have since adhered, who
are now represented in this General Assembly:
After examining, with all the care and
consideration which are required by the delicacy
and importance of the Objects on which we are
called together, the said Acts of September, 1821,
and of the 5th of January, 1822; and also the
Decree of the Provisional Government of this
Province, dated the 29th of March last; with all
other Documents relating to the specific Objects
of our assembling:
Having before us all the information
necessary to ascertain the state of the population,
riches, resources, local situation, extent, and other
circumstances of the People who occupy the Territory
formerly called the Kingdom of Guatemala:
And having discussed the subject, and
received the Reports of the different Commissions
which have laboured to collect and present to this
Assembly all possible information on the above
points; considering all that may be necessary to the
establishment of a New State; and also considering:--
First -- That Independence of the Spanish
Government has been and is necessary in the situation
of that Nation, and that of all the Nations of America;
that it was and is just in itself, and essentially
consonant to the sacred rights of nature; that it
was imperiously demanded by the lights of the Age,
the necessities of the New World, and all the

dearest interests of the People who inhabit it:

That Nature itself resists the dependence of this part of the Globe, separated by an immense Ocean from that which was its Metropolis, and with which it is impossible to maintain the immediate and frequent communication indispensible between the People of the same State:

That the experience of more than three hundred Years has convinced America that Her felicity was altogether incompatible with the nullity to which She was reduced by the sad condition of a Colony to a small part of Europe:

That the arbitrary manner in which She was governmed by the Spanish Nation, and the conduct always pursued by It since the Conquest, excited in the People the most ardent desire to re-conquer their usurped rights:

That, impelled by these just sentiments, all the Provinces of America threw off the yoke which had oppressed them for the space of three Centuries: That those of the ancient Kingdom of Guatemala gloriously proclaimed their Independence towards the close of 1821; and that the determination to preserve and maintain it is the general and uniform resolve of all its Inhabitants.

Secondly -- Considering also, that the incorporation of these Provinces with the extinguished Mexican Empire, was effected, only de facto, at the end of 1821 and the beginning of 1822, and was a hasty decision extorted by vicious and illegal means:

That it was neither granted nor pronounced, by legitimate organs or means: That in consequence the National Representatives of the Mexican State never expressly accepted it, nor could of right accept it; and that the orders dictated and expedited by Don Augustin Iturbide, respecting this Union are null:

That the said Union was, and is, contrary to the interests and sacred rights of the People we represent, and opposed to their will, and that the concurrence of circumstances so powerful and irresistible, requires that the Provinces of the ancient Kingdom of Guatemala should be constituted of themselves, and separately from the Mexican State.

We, therefore, the Representatives of the said Provinces, in their names, with their authority, and conformably to their wishes, solemnly declare:

"1. That the said Provinces, represented in this Assembly, are free and Independent of Old Spain, of Mexico, and of every other Power, whether in the Old or the New World, and that they are not, and ought not to be, the patrimony of any Person or Family.

"2. That on consequence they are, and form, a Sovereign Nation, with the Right freely to exercise and enjoy such Acts, Contracts, and Functions, as are exercised and enjoyed by the other Free People of the Earth.

"3. That the abovenamed Provinces represented in this Assembly, and the others of those forming the Ancient Kingdom of Guatemala, which shall spontaneously unite themselves, shall, henceforth, without prejudice to the Constitution about to be formed, be called, The United Provinces of Central America.

"And we command that this Declaration, and the Act of our Installation, shall be published with due solemnity in this Town of Guatemala, and in all and each of the Towns represented in this Assembly; and that they be printed and circulated; that they be communicated to the Provinces of Leon, Granada, Costarrica, and Chiapas; and that they be communicated to the Governments of Spain and Mexico, and to the other Independent States of both Americas, in the form and manner which may be determined upon.

Given in Guatemala, 1st July, 1823."

[Here follow the Signatures of forty-three Deputies.]

Let this be communicated to the Supreme Executive Power, to be printed, published, and circulated -- Guatemala, July 10, 1823.

JOSE MATIAS DELGADO, President
JUAN FRANCISCO SOSA, Deputy Secretary
MARIANO GALVEZ, Deputy Secretary

By the Supreme Executive Authority.

We therefore Order it to be obeyed, fulfilled, and executed, in all its Parts. The Secretary of Dispatch is required to cause it to be printed, published, and circulated.

PEDRO MOLINA, President
JUAN VINCENTE VILLA-CORTA
ANTONIO RIVERA

National Palace of Guatemala,
    July 11, 1823.

NICARAGUA

1838

The Constituent Assembly issued a decree on April 7 in Chinandega, ordering the deputies to adjourn to Leon to continue their sessions there.

On April 30, the Constituent Assembly of Nicaragua declared that the State was free and independent.

The Federal Congress made the following decree:

"1. The States shall be free to constitute themselves in whatever way they consider appropriate, while preserving the representative, popular, and republican form of government.

"2. Article 12 of the Federal Constitution of November 22, 1824, shall be repealed and replaced by the preceding article."

The Constituent Assembly of Nicaragua has taken into consideration this decree of the Federal Congress, and has issued another, the resolution of which states: "The State of Nicaragua consents to and approves the decree of the Federal Congress of May 30 past, insofar as it does not contradict the pronouncement made by the same State in the decree of November 30.

Translated by Sarah J. Campbell

Republic of Niger

A West African country, the Republic of
Niger is bounded to the north by Libya, to the
south by Nigeria, and to the northwest by Algeria.
Following French conquest in the 19th century
Niger became a French military colony in 1900, a
colony in 1922, and an overseas territory in 1946.
After a referendum Niger joined the French
Community as a Republic on December 18, 1958. A
law passed by the French Republic on June 4, 1960,
made it possible for Niger to become independent
without leaving the Community. Following agreements signed in July, 1960 the Republic of Niger
declared its independence in August 1960. Decree
No. 60-123 and Law No. 60-45 are those documents
by which Niger achieved independence.

REPUBLIC OF NIGER

LAW NO. 60-45

raising the State of Niger into an independent
and sovereign

Republic

In view of the Constitution of the Republic
of Niger, dated March 12, 1959;

In view of the Constitution of the
Communauté;

In view of Law No. 60-31 of July 27, 1960,
approving the private agreement of July 11, 1960,
accepted by the Republic of Niger and the French
Republic, transferring powers held at the level of
the Communauté, promulgated by Decree No. 60-147
P.C.M. of the same day;

In view of Law No. 60-43 of July 29, 1960,
raising the Legislative Assembly into a National
Assembly, promulgated by Decree No. 60-150 of
July 30, 1960;

The National Assembly has deliberated and
adopted the constituional law the terms of which
follows:

Article 1. The State of Niger is an independent and sovereign Republic.

Article 2. The rank, prerogatives and powers
of the Head of State shall be conferred upon the
President of the Council of Ministers.

Article 3. This constitutional law shall be
executed as a law of the State.

Niamey, August 1, 1960.

The President of the Legislative Assembly of
Niger,

BOUBOU HAMA.

DECREE NO. 60-123 P.C.M., promulgating Law No.
6-45 of August 1, 1960, raising the State of Niger
into an

             independent and sovereign Republic.

    The President of the Council of Ministers,

    In view of the Constitution of the Republic
of Niger,

    DECREES:

    Article 1. National Assembly Law No. 60-45
of August 1, 1960, raising the State of Niger
into an independent and sovereign Republic, is
promulgated and shall be executed as a law of
the Republic of Niger.

    Article 2. This decree shall be published
in the Journal Officiel of the Republic of Niger.

    Niamey, August 6, 1960.

                      HAMANI DIORI.

Translation by Sarah J. Campbell.

LOI N° 60-45
érigeant l'Etat du Niger en une République
indépendante et souveraine

Vu la Constitution de la République du Niger, en date du 12 mars 1959 ;

Vu la Constitution de la Communauté ;

Vu la loi n° 60-31 du 27 juillet 1960, approuvant l'accord particulier du 11 juillet 1960, intervenu entre la République du Niger et la République Française et portant transfert des compétences détenues au niveau de la Communauté, promulguée par décret n° 60-147 p.c.m. du même jour ;

Vu la loi n° 60-43 du 29 juillet 1960, érigeant l'Assemblée Législative en Assemblée Nationale, promulguée par décret n° 60-150 du 30 juillet 1960 ;

L'Assemblée Nationale a délibéré et adopté la loi constitutionnelle dont la teneur suit :

Article premier. — L'Etat du Niger est une République indépendante et souveraine.

Art. 2. — Le rang, les prérogatives et les pouvoirs de Chef d'Etat sont conférés au Président du Conseil des Ministres.

Art. 3. — La présente loi constitutionnelle sera exécutée comme loi de l'Etat.

Niamey, le 1ᵉʳ août 1960.

Le Président de l'Assemblée Législative du Niger,
BOUBOU HAMA.

Décret n° 60-163 p.c.m., *promulguant la loi n° 60-45 du 1ᵉʳ août 1960, érigeant l'Etat du Niger en une République indépendante et souveraine.*

Le Président du Conseil des Ministres,

Vu la Constitution de la République du Niger,

Décrète :

Article premier. — Est promulguée et sera exécutée comme loi de la République du Niger, la loi de l'Assemblée Nationale n° 60-45 du 1ᵉʳ août 1960, érigeant l'Etat du Niger en une République indépendante et souveraine.

Art. 2. — Le présent décret sera publié au *Journal officiel* de la République du Niger.

Niamey, le 6 août 1960.

HAMANI DIORI.

THE REPUBLIC OF THE NIGER

A Modern Democratic State

IN THE Referendum of September 28, 1958, the people of Niger returned a 78% vote in favor of the Constitution drawn up by General de Gaulle's Government, offering the Overseas Territories of the French Republic a choice between several possible statuses.

On December 14, 1958, the R.D.A. party (African Democratic Rally) won a majority of the seats in the newly elected Territorial Assembly, which immediately formed itself into a Constituent Assembly and on December 18 chose the status of member State of the Community.

At the same time, it called on Mr. Hamani Diori, deputy to the French National Assembly and secretary general of the Niger branch of the R.D.A., to form a Government.

After adopting the Constitution of the Republic of the Niger on February 25, 1959, the Constituent Assembly became the Legislative Assembly.

The last stage was reached after adoption by the French Parliament and by the Senate of the Community of the Constitutional Law of June 4, 1960. This law transformed the original Community based on common institutions into a contractual association, which made it possible for a State to become independent without thereby leaving the Community.

Following the signature with the French Republic on July 11, 1960 of agreements providing for the unconditional international sovereignty of the four member States of the *Council of the Entente,* the Republic of the Niger proclaimed its independence on August 3, 1960. The form of its future relationship with the French Republic is to be determined by subsequent negotiations.

Under French sponsorship, Niger was admitted to the United Nations on September 20, 1960.

Flags were displayed at every home in honor of independence day.

527

Republic of Nigeria

The Republic of Nigeria is a West African
country bounded to the north east by Chad, the
north by Niger, and to the south by the Gulf of
Guinea. Establishing themselves in the mid 1800's
the Royal Niger Company received a royal charter
over Nigeria. The charter was revoked in 1900
when the country was divided into the Protectorates
of Southern Nigeria and Northern Nigeria. From
1912 Great Britain attempted to amalgamate the
two. In 1914 the two became the Colony and
Protectorate of Nigeria. A rising nationalist
movement, though marked by its lack of unity,
resulted in a series of constitutions from 1947
through 1957 which gave greater internal autonomy
yet sought to centralize the government. After
the establishment of a national government, Great
Britain announced its willingness to grant independence. On October 1, 1960, independence was granted
by the Nigerian Independence Act.

Nigeria Independence Act, 1960

An Act to Make Provision For, And In Connection With, The Attainment By Nigeria Of Fully Responsible Status Within The Commonwealth.

29 July 1960

BE IT ENACTED by the Queen's most Excellent Majesty, by and with the advice and consent of the Lords Spiritual and Temporal, and Commons, in this present Parliament assembled, and by the authority of the same, as follows:--

1. --(1) On the first day of October, nineteen hundred and sixty (in this Act referred to as "the appointed day"), the Colony and the Protectorate as respectively defined by the Nigeria (Constitution) Orders in Council, 1954 to 1960, shall together constitute part of Her Majesty's dominions under the name of Nigeria.

(2) No Act of the Parliament of the United Kingdom passed on or after the appointed day shall extend, or be deemed to extend, to Nigeria or any part thereof as part of the law thereof, and as from that day--

(a) Her Majesty's Government in the United Kingdom shall have no responsibility for the government of Nigeria or any part thereof; and

(b) the provisions of the First Schedule to this Act shall have effect with respect to legislative powers in Nigeria.

(3) Without prejudice to subsection (2) of this section, nothing in subsection (1) thereof shall affect the operation in Nigeria or any part thereof on and after the appointed day of any enactment, or any other instrument having the effect of law, passed or made with respect thereto before that day.

2.--(1) As from the appointed day, the British Nationality Acts, 1948 and 1958, shall have effect as if--

      (a)   in subsection (3) of section one of the said Act of 1948 (which provides for persons to be British subjects or Commonwealth citizens by virtue of citizenship of certain countries) the word "and" in the last place where it occurs were omitted, and at the end there were added the words "and Nigeria";

      (b)   in the First Schedule to the British Protectorates, Protected States and Protected Persons Order in Council, 1949, the words "Nigeria Protectorate" were omitted:

      Provided that a person who immediately before the appointed day is for the purposes of the said Acts and Order in Council a British protected person by virtue of his connection with the Nigeria Protectorate shall not cease to be such a British protected person for any of those purposes by reason of anything contained in the foregoing provisions of this Act, but shall so cease upon his becoming a citizen of Nigeria under the law thereof.

Nigeria Independence Act, 8 & 9, Eliz. 2, c. 55
    (1960).

Kingdom of Norway

After centuries of independence Norway joined
Denmark and Sweden in the Union of Kalmar in 1387.
When the Union was dissolved in the sixteenth
century Norway came under Danish rule.   Danish
rule continued until 1814 when the country passed
to Sweden.   This change did not occur without
resistance by the Norwegians, who declared
independence in the Norwegian Constitution of
May 17, 1814.   A treaty between Norway and Sweden
eventually provided for Swedish recognition of
this action.

The Constitution of Norway

of

17 May 1814

A. Form of Government and Religion

1. The Kingdom of Norway is a free, independent, indivisible and inalienable realm. Its form of government is a limited and hereditary monarchy.

Translation by the Royal Norwegian Ministry of Foreign Affairs.

Sultanate of Oman

Located at the southeastern corner of the Arabian peninsula, Oman has remained an independent country. An 1862 reciprocal treaty between Great Britain and France recognized the independence of Muscat and Oman, but until the official statement of Sultan Qabis Bin Said on July 24, 1970, the status of Oman was unclear.

SULTANATE OF OMAN

ANGLO-FRENCH TREATY ON MUSCAT INDEPENDENCE

MARCH 10, 1862

Her Majesty the Queen of the United Kingdom
of Great Britain and Ireland and His Majesty the
Emperor of the French, taking into consideration
the importance of maintaining the independence of
His Highness the Sultan of Muscat and of His Highness the Sultan of Zanzibar, have thought it right
to engage reciprocally to respect the independence
of these Sovereigns.

The Undersigned, Her Britannic Majesty's Ambassador Extraordinary and Pleniotentiary at the
Court of France, and the Minister Secretary of
State for Foreign Affairs of His Majesty the
Emperor of the French, being furnished with the
necessary powers, hereby declare, in consequence,
that their said Majesties take reciprocally that
engagement.

In witness whereof, the Undersigned have
signed the present Declaration, and have affixed
thereto the seals of their arms.

Done at Paris, the 10th March, 1862.

(L.S.) COWLEY.
(L.S.) E. THOUVENEL.

Consolidated Treaty Series (1861-1862), Vol. 125,
p. 35.

STATEMENT BY SULTAN QABUS BIN SAID

BROADCAST TO THE PEOPLE OF OMAN

JULY 24, 1970

I address you in my capacity as the Sultan
of Muscat and Oman, having succeeded my father to
the throne on the 23rd July, 1970 - 18th Jamadi
Al-Awal, 1390 h.

I observed with mounting concern and intense
indignation my father's inability to govern. My
family and my armed forces have vowed their obedience and sincerity. The former Sultan has left
the Sultanate. I promise you to dedicate myself
to the speedy establishment of a modern government in no time. My first aim will be the abolition of all unnecessary restrictions that over-
burdened you.

My people, I shall work as promptly as possible to ensure a better life in a better future.
Each and every one of you should participate in
that duty. Our country in the past had the glory
and the might, and if we work in co-operation and
unity we shall be able to restore our past glory
and to obtain our prominent place in the Arab
world. I will take the necessary legal steps to
ensure the recognition of foreign powers, and I
am looking forward to the immediate support and
the long-range cordial co-operation with all nations, especially with our neighbors, with whom
we will conduct consultations for the future of
our area.

My friends, I urge you to continue your every-
day activities and I shall reach Muscat in the next
few days, and my main goal is the following.

My people, I and my new government hope to
achieve our mutual goal.

My people and brothers, yesterday we were completely in the dark but, with the aid of God, tomorrow a new dawn will arise for Muscat and Oman and

its people.

May God preserve us and crown our efforts with success.

Translation by Attia Abdel Moneim Attia.

Islamic Republic of Pakistan

Pakistan arose from the desire of the Moslems
in India to have their own nation. Conflict
between Moslems and Hindus increased in the 1930's
and during World War II. As a result, when independence in the shape of dominion status came on
August 15, 1947, pursuant to the Indian Independence
Act, two dominions, India and Pakistan, were
created. Pakistan became a republic in 1956 and
left the Commonwealth in 1972. In 1971, East
Pakistan (Bangladesh) declared itself independent
of Pakistan.

An Act to make provision for the setting up in India of two independent Dominions, to substitute other provisions for certain provisions of the Government of India Act, 1935, which apply outside those Dominions, and to provide for other matters consequential on or connected with the setting up of those Dominions.

[18th July 1947.]

BE it enacted by the King's most Excellent Majesty, by and with the advice and consent of the Lords Spiritual and Temporal, and Commons, in this present Parliament assembled, and by the authority of the same, as follows :—

1.—(1) As from the fifteenth day of August, nineteen hundred and forty-seven, two independent Dominions shall be set up in India, to be known respectively as India and Pakistan.

(2) The said Dominions are hereafter in this Act referred to as "the new Dominions", and the said fifteenth day of August is hereafter in this Act referred to as "the appointed day".

2.—(1) Subject to the provisions of subsections (3) and (4) of this section, the territories of India shall be the territories under the sovereignty of His Majesty which, immediately before the appointed day, were included in British India except the territories which, under subsection (2) of this section, are to be the territories of Pakistan.

India Independence Act, 10&11 George 6, c.30 (1947)

Republic of Panama

A Central American country, Panama is bounded
on the north by the Caribbean Sea, on the east by
Columbia, on the south by the Pacific Ocean, and
on the west by Costa Rica. Settled by the Spanish
in 1509, Panama became a royal audiencia in 1542
under the viceroyalty of Peru. In 1717 the viceroyalty
passed to Columbia. Panama remained loyal to Spain
until 1821 when it became free and adhered to
Columbia. A separatist movement which began in
1886, resulted in a bloodless revolt on November 3,
1903, and independence on November 4, 1903.

PANAMA

ACT OF NOVEMBER 3, 1903

(Presidency of the Honorable Council Member Brid)

In the city of Panama, at 9:50 P.M. on the night of Tuesday, November 3, 1903, the Municipal Council of the District met in extraordinary solemn session, in the presence of its members: General Rafael Aizpuru, Agustin Arias Feraud, Demetrio H. Brid, Jose Maria Chiari R., Manuel J. Cucalon P., Enrique Linares and Manuel Maria Mendez.

As the session opened, the President declared to the members of the Council that at that moment, at once solemn and of great excitement, a considerable group of citizens of the capital had proclaimed the Independence of the Isthmus, with the consent of the residents of the towns and cities comprising it. And, for that reason, he wished to know whether the current representatives of the rights of the people were disposed to follow and to second that political movement under an oath to sacrifice their interests and their lives, and even the future of their children if that were necessary.

The Council swore a solemn oath to accept and support that movement, in virtue of which Council Member Aizpuru presented the following proposal:

"The Municipality of Panama, in view of the spontaneous movement of the people of the Isthmus, particularly of the city of Panama, declaring its independence from the Colombian metropole and wishing to be established as its own free and independent Government, accepts and supports said and consequently,

RESOLVES:

To convene in an Open Meeting the people in general and all Civil, Military and Ecclesiastical public corporations tomorrow at three in the afternoon in the Presidential Palace of the Republic of Panama.

In the discussion, the same speaker, Aizpuru, took the floor to express the view that this motion was entirely in agreement with the oath already sworn. He said that the independence of the Isthmus was a transcendent fact and that it would resound among our children just like the oath which the nobility swore within these same walls on November 28, 1821, on the emancipation of the Isthmus from the Government of Spain to unite spontaneously with Gran Colombia. Today, he said, they proclaim their independence from the Colombian Government to reap the best of fruits: independence; and that this independence was absolutely indispensable in reaching the goal of happiness.

Said motion being submitted to a vote, the result was unanimous approval, which circumstance was recorded by Council Member Cucalon P.

Immediately afterwards, Council Member Brid, leaving the Presidential chair, signed this other motion:

"That the following telegram be sent to His Excellency the President of the United States, Washington: 'The Municipality of Panama is celebrating at this moment a solemn session uniting with the movement for separation of the Isthmus of Panama from the rest of Colombia, and hopes for recognition by that Government for our cause.'"

Upon discussion this motion, this same Council Member, Brid, declared that he had been moved to make that motion by the vision of the future, and because the current popular movement depended upon the devoted support of the Isthmus. He added that such support must necessarily have a guide and that this guide was the direct protection of the United States.

Being put to a vote, this was also approved by unanimous vote, with a request that it be recorded by the same Council Member making the motion.

The object of the convention having terminated, and Council Member Brid again occupying the post of President, he ratified the oath sworn by the Council Members and invoked the name of God and Country as witnesses of this solemn act.

Whereupon the meeting ended at ten o'clock at night.

PRESIDENT   SECRETARY
/signed/ Demetrio H. Brid.   /signed/ Ernesto J. Goti

Act of November 3, 1903 - Documentacion Historica de los dias Independentistes

Translated by Sarah J. Campbell.

ACTA DEL 3 DE NOVIEMBRE DE 1903

(Presidencia del Honorable Concejal Brid)

En la ciudad de Panamá, a las nueve cincuenta minutos de la noche del martes tres de Noviembre de mil novecientos tres, se reunió el Consejo Municipal del Distrito, en sesión extraordinaria y solemne con la asistencia de sus miembros, señores: General Rafael Aizpuru, Agustín Arias Feraud, Demetrio H. Brid, José María Chiari R., Manuel J. Cucalón P., Enrique Linares y Manuel María Méndez.

Abierta la sesión el señor Presidente manifestó a los señores miembros del Concejo, que en este solemne momento y de gran exitación, un grupo respetable de ciudadanos de esta capital habían proclamado la Independencia del Istmo, con el beneplácito de los pueblos de su comprensión y de la ciudadanía y, que con tal motivo, deseaba saber si los actuales representantes de los derechos del pueblo estaban dispuestos a adherirse y secundar ese movimiento político bajo juramento de sacrificar sus intereses y vidas, y hasta el porvenir de sus hijos si fuere necesario.

El Concejo prestó el solemne juramento de aceptar y sostener ese movimiento, y en tal virtud el Concejal señor Aizpuru presentó la siguiente proposición:

"La Municipalidad de Panamá en vista del movimiento espontáneo de los pueblos del Istmo, y particularmente de la ciudad de Panamá, declarando su independencia de la metrópoli Colombiana y deseando establecerse en Gobierno propio independiente y libre, acepta y sostiene dicho movimiento y en consecuencia, RESUELVE:

Convocar a Cabildo Abierto al pueblo en general y a todas las corporaciones públicas Civiles, Militares y Eclesiásticas para mañana a las tres de la tarde en el Palacio Presidencial de la República de Panamá"

Puesta en discusión, el mismo proponente Vocal Aizpuru, usó de la palabra para expresar que esa moción estaba de acuerdo en un todo con el juramento prestado anteriormente y que la independencia del Istmo era un hecho trascendental, que tendría eco entre nuestros hijos, pues así como en este mismo recinto nuestros Próceres juraron la emancipación del Istmo del Gobierno de España el 28 de Noviembre de 1821, para agregarse espontáneamente a la Gran Colombia, hoy proclaman su independencia del Gobierno Colombiano para recoger óptimos frutos y que esa independencia era absolutamente indispensable para llegar a la meta de la felicidad.

Sometida a votación a proposición aludida, resultó aprobada por unanimidad, circunstancia que se hace constar a solicitud del Concejal Cucalón P.

Acto continuo el Concejal señor Brid, separado de la silla Presidencial, suscribió esta otra proposición:

"Envíese el siguiente telegrama a Su Excelencia el Presidente de los Estados Unidos, Washington: "La Municipalidad de Panamá celebra en este momento sesión solemne adhiriéndose movimiento separación Istmo de Panamá resto de Colombia, y espera reconocimiento de ese Gobierno para nuestra causa".

Al discutirse esta proposición, el mismo Concejal Brid hizo presente que le había movido a hacer esa moción, la visión del porvenir, y porque el actual movimiento popular contaba con el decidido apoyo del Istmo pero que necesariamente ese apoyo debía tener una guia y que esa era la la protección directa de los Estados Unidos.

Puesta en votación fue igualmente aprobada por unanimidad de votos, que pidió se hiciera constar el mismo Concejal proponente.

Terminado el objeto de la convocatoria, y vuelto a ocupar el Concejal Brid el puesto de Presidente, ratificó el juramento prestado por los señores Concejales, e invocó el nombre de Dios y de la Patria como testigos de este acto solemne.

Con la cual terminó la sesión a las diez de la noche.

EL PRESIDENTE,

(Fdo.) Demetrio H. Brid.

EL SECRETARIO,

(Fdo.) Ernesto J. Gotl.

Papua New Guinea

Papua New Guinea is comprised of the eastern
half of the island of New Guinea and a large number of neighboring South Pacific islands. Following World War II it was administered by Australia
as a United Nations Trust Territory. Papua New
Guinea became autonomous in domestic affairs on
December 1, 1973. The United Nations General
Assembly acceded to Papua New Guinea independence
in its resolution of December 13, 1974. Independence was obtained on September 16, 1975, by virtue
of Australian legislation.

PAPUA NEW GUINEA

[Australia Enactment]

AN ACT

Relating to the attainment of Independence by

Papua New Guinea

[Assented to 9 September 1975]

WHEREAS certain territories and islands formerly constituting the Possession of British New Guinea and placed by the Crown under the authority of Australia were administered by Australia under the Papua Act 1905-1940 as the Territory of Papua:

AND WHEREAS, in accordance with a Mandate under the Covenant of the League of Nations, certain territories and islands, being former German possessions, were administered by Australia under the New Guinea Act 1920-1935 as the Territory of New Guinea:

AND WHEREAS the Territory of Papua and the Territory of New Guinea were, for a period, administered jointly by Australia under the Papua-New Guinea Provisional Administration Act 1945-1946:

AND WHEREAS Australia's administration of the Territory of Papua became subject to Chapter XI of the Charter of the United Nations:

AND WHEREAS, in accordance with Chapter XII of that Charter, the General Assembly of the United Nations on 13 December 1946 approved the terms of a Trusteeship Agreement for the Territory of New Guinea, submitted to it by the Government of Australia, in substitution for the terms of the Mandate, which Agreement designates the Government of Australia as the sole

Authority to exercise the administration of the
Territory of New Guinea:

AND WHEREAS the Papua and New Guinea Act
1949 provided for the administration of the
Territory of Papua and the Territory of New
Guinea by Australia in an administrative union,
by the name of the Territory of Papua and New
Guinea, whilst maintaining the identity and
status of the Territory of New Guinea as a Trust
Territory and the identity and status of the
Territory of Papua as a Possession of the Crown:

AND WHEREAS on 18 November 1963 a House of
Assembly was established by the Papua and New
Guinea Act 1963 to make laws for the peace, order
and good government of the Territory of Papua
and New Guinea:

AND WHEREAS, by virtue of the Papua New
Guinea Act 1971, the Territories governed in the
administrative union became together known as
Papua New Guinea:

AND WHEREAS on 9 July 1974 the House of
Assembly resolved that Papua New Guinea move to
independent nation status:

AND WHEREAS the General Assembly of the
United Nations on 13 December 1974 noted that
resolution and resolved that, on the date on
which Papua New Guinea became independent, the
Trusteeship Agreement would cease to be in force:

AND WHEREAS on 18 June 1975 the House of
Assembly nominated 16 September 1975 as the date
on which Papua New Guinea is to become independent:

AND WHEREAS on 16 September 1975 Papua New
Guinea is to become an independent sovereign
state by the name of the Independent State of
Papua New Guinea, having a constitution established, adopted and given to themselves by the
people of Papua New Guinea acting through their
Constituent Assembly:

BE IT THEREFORE ENACTED by the Queen, the
Senate and the House of Representatives of

Australia, as follows:--

1. This Act may be cited as the Papua New Guinea Independence Act 1975.

2. This Act shall come into operation on the day on which it receives the Royal Assent.

3. (1) In this Act--

"Independence Day" means 16 September 1975;

"Papua New Guinea" has the same meaning as in the Papua New Guinea Act 1949-1975.

(2) In this Act, a reference to an Act or to an Imperial Act includes a reference to an instrument made under an Act or an Imperial Act.

4. On the expiration of the day preceding Independence Day, Australia ceases to have any sovereignty, sovereign rights or rights of administration in respect of or appertaining to the whole or any part of Papua New Guinea.

5. On the expiration of the day preceding Independence Day--

(a) the Acts specified in the Schedule are repealed; and

(b) every Act, and every Imperial Act, extending to the whole or any part of Papua New Guinea as part of the law of Papua New Guinea ceases so to extend.

6. (1) The Governor-General may make regulations making provision for or in relation to matters arising out of or connected with the attainment of the independence of Papua New Guinea, including regulations making modifications or adaptations of any Act.

(2) Regulations under sub-section (1) made before Independence Day shall not have effect before that day.

No. 98 of 1975

PAPUA NEW GUINEA

UNITED NATIONS GENERAL ASSEMBLY RESOLUTION 3284

(XXIX) OF 13 DECEMBER 1974 ON THE QUESTION

OF PAPUA NEW GUINEA

In resolution 3284 (XXIX), concerning Papua
New Guinea, the General Assembly,

"1. Resolves, in agreement with the administering Power, that on the date on which Papua New Guinea shall become independent the Trusteeship Agreement for the Territory of New Guinea, approved by the General Assembly on 13 December 1946, shall cease to be in force;

"2. Requests the administering Power to notify the Secretary-General of the date on which Papua New Guinea will accede to independence and on which the Trusteeship Agreement shall cease to be in force."

Papua New Guinea Act 1975

No. 97 of 1975

AN ACT

Relating to the Pocklington Reef Islands.

[*Assented to 9 September 1975*]

WHEREAS the Pocklington Reef Islands, being all of the islands lying between the parallels 10 degrees 30 minutes and 11 degrees South Latitude and between the meridians 155 and 156 degrees East Longitude, . are territory acquired by Australia:

5   AND WHEREAS those islands are adjacent to the Territory of Papua:

AND WHEREAS it is desirable to make provision for the government of those islands as part of Papua New Guinea:

BE IT THEREFORE ENACTED by the Queen, the Senate and the House of Representatives of Australia, as follows:—

10   **1.** (1) This Act may be cited as the *Papua New Guinea Act* 1975.   Short title and citation.

(2) The *Papua New Guinea Act* 1949–1974* is in this Act referred to as the Principal Act.

(3) The Principal Act, as amended by this Act, may be cited as the *Papua New Guinea Act* 1949–1975.

---

* Act No. 9, 1949, as amended by No. 80, 1950; No. 41, 1954; No. 15, 1957; Nos. 4 and 47, 1960; No. 20, 1963; No. 104, 1964; No. 84, 1966; Nos. 25 and 157, 1968; Nos. 58 and 123, 1971; No. 74, 1972; Nos. 69 and 120, 1973; No. 216, 1973 (as amended by No. 20, 1974); and Nos. 56 and 161, 1974.

16375/75—Recommended retail price 5c

2. This Act shall come into operation on the day on which it receives the Royal Assent.

3. After Part III of the Principal Act the following Part is inserted:—

" PART IIIA—POCKLINGTON REEF ISLANDS

" 12A. (1) In this section, ' Pocklington Reef Islands ' means all of 5
the islands lying between the parallels 10 degrees 30 minutes and 11 degrees South latitude and between the meridians 155 degrees and 156 degrees East longitude.

" (2) The Pocklington Reef Islands shall be deemed to be annexed to, and to form part of, the Territory of Papua for all purposes, including the 10
purposes of this Act and of all laws in force in the Territory of Papua immediately before the commencement of this section.

" (3) The laws in force in the Pocklington Reef Islands immediately before the commencement of this section, other than laws that were, at that time, also in force in the Territory of Papua, shall, upon the com- 15
mencement of this section, cease to be in force in the Pocklington Reef Islands.".

4. Section 52A of the Principal Act is amended—

(a) by omitting from sub-section (1) the definition of " off-shore area "; and 20

(b) by inserting after sub-section (1) the following sub-section:—

" (1A) A reference in this section to the off-shore area is a reference to the sea-bed and subsoil beneath—

(a) the waters of—

(i) the territorial sea appertaining to the Territory of 25
Papua; and

(ii) the territorial sea appertaining to the Territory of New Guinea; and

(b) the superjacent waters of the continental shelf of each of those Territories, 30

but, for the purposes of this sub-section, those waters shall not be taken to include waters to which, immediately before the commencement of this sub-section, the *Petroleum (Submerged Lands) Act* 1967–1974 applied.".

Republic of Paraguay

Paraguay is located in south central South America. The first permanent settlement was in 1537 by the Spanish. After joining the Spanish in defeating the United Provinces, the people of Paraguay rebelled and declared their independence from Spain on June 20, 1811. Two years later Paraguay declared independence from Argentina. It was not until November 26, 1842, that a formal declaration was made.

In this city of Assumption, in the Republic
of Paraguay, on the 26th of November, 1842, there
being united in general extraordinary Congress,
by special convocation of the Consuls who legally
form the supreme Government, citizens Carlos
Antonio Lopez and Mariano Roque Alonzo, 400 deputies; in the exercise of the powers we hold, in
the fulfilment of our duty, and with the constant
and decided wishes of our fellow citizens, and
with those which inspire us in this act--Consid-
ering:

That our emancipation and independence,
during the period of more than 30 years, is a
solemn and incontestable fact;

That during this lengthened period and ever
since the Republic of Paraguay separated herself,
by her own efforts, from the Spanish metropolis
for ever, she likewise separated herself de facto
from every foreign Power, desirous ever since
with one will to belong to herself alone and to
form as she has formed a free and independent
nation under the Republican system, and that no
motive whatever shall appear to contradict this
explicit declaration;

That this right inherent to every free State
has been recognized to other provinces of South
America by the Argentine Republic, and it does
not appear just to suppose that it would be denied
to Paraguay where, besides the just titles on
which she founds her right, nature has lavished
her gifts with prodigality to render her a powerful nation, populous, and fertile in resources in
every branch of industry and commerce;

That so many previous sufferings and privations consecrated with resignation to the independence of our Republic and to save ourselves
from the abyss of civil war, are also strong
proofs of the indubitable general will of the
people of the Republic for its emancipation and
independence from every foreign Power and dominion;

That in accordance with these principles and the general desire of the Republic, and that nothing may be wanting in the fundamental basis of our political existence, confiding in Divine Providence, we solemnly declare:

1stly. The Republic of Paraguay, in that of La Plata, is for ever in fact and in right a nation free and independent of every' foreign Power.

2ndly. Never at any time shall it be the patrimony of a person or of a family.

3rdly. Henceforward the Government that shall be called to preside over the destinies of the nation shall be sworn in presence of the Congress to defend and preserve the integrity and independence of the territory of the Republic, without which they shall not take command. The existing Government to be excepted as having taken the oath at their installation.

4thly. The military, civil, and ecclesiastical employees shall be sworn to the tenor of this declaration immediately on its publication.

5thly. No citizen can hereafter fill any public office until he shall have taken the oath prescribed in the preceding Article.

6thly. The supreme Government shall communicate officially this solemn declaration to the surrounding Governments and to that of the Argentine Confederation, and shall give account to the Sovereign Congress of the results.

7thly. That this be communicated to the Executive Power of the Republic in order to its being published throughout the territory of the Republic with all possible solemnity and to its being duly fulfilled.

Done in the Hall of Congress, signed with our hand and countersigned by our Secretary.
                    CARLOS ANTONIO LOPEZ.

34 British and Foreign State Papers, pp. 1320-1 (1845-6).

Republic of Peru

Peru was settled by Spain in 1531 with authority
firmly established by 1548.   One of the most
powerful colonies, Peru remained loyal until July 15,
1821, when General Jose de San Martin proclaimed
independence.   Peru's independence was complete in
1826, with the capture of Culla.

ACT OF THE INDEPENDENCE OF PERU

LIMA

JULY 15, 1821

The Senors who compose the same, having yesterday assembled in the Most Excellent Senate, with the Most Excellent and Most Illustrious Senor the Archbishop of this Holy Metropolitan Church, the Prelates of the religious Convents, Titulars of Castile, and various neighbours of this Capital, for the purpose of fulfilling what had been provided in the Official Letter of the Most Excellent Senor the General in Chief of the Liberator Army of Peru, D. Jose de San Martin, dated Yesterday, the contents of which were read; and the same being reduced to what Persons of known probity, learning, and patriotism, who inhabit this Capital, would express, if the general opinion for Independence had been resolved on, which vote would serve as a guide to the said General for proceeding to take the Oath: All the Senors, agreeing for themselves, and satisfied of the opinion of the Inhabitants of the Capital, declared, that the general will was decided for the Independence of Peru of the Spanish Dominion, and of any other Foreign Dominion whatever, and that they would proceed to its sanction by means of the corresponding oath. It was compared with a certified Copy of this Act to the same most Excellent Senor, and the Senors signed it.

> THE COUNT OF SAN ISIDRO.
> BARTOLOME, Archbishop of Lima.
> FRANCISCO DE ZARATE.
> SIMON RAVAGO.
> FRANCISCO XAVIER DE ECHAGUE.
> MANUEL DE ARIAS.
> The Count DE LA VEGA DEL REN.
> FR. GERONIMO CAVERO.
> JOSE IGNACIO PALACIOS.
> ANTONIO PADILLA, Syndic, Proc. Gen.

British and Foreign State Papers, Vol. 9, pp. 393-4 (1821-1822).

GACETA DEL GOBIERNO

DE LIMA INDEPENDIENTE.

DEL MIERCOLES 1 DE AGOSTO DE 1821.

Año II. de la independencia del Perú

y I. de la de lima.

Proclamacion y juramento de la Independencia.

Desde la aclamacion pública del 15 de Julio anunciada en la gaceta núm. 1. la qual subscribieron el mismo dia, y han continuado subscribiendo en los posteriores las primeras y mas distinguidas personas de este vecindario, quedaron los votos de esta capital uniformados con la voluntad general de los pueblos libres del Perú. Nadie hubo que no ansiase desde entónces por el momento de consolidar la base de la independencia del modo mas solemne y extraordinario, qual correspondia á un pueblo soberano en el acto de recuperar el goce de los derechos imprescriptibles de su libertad civil. Destinóse al efecto la mañana del 28 de este mes : y ordenado todo por el Excmo. Ayuntamiento conforme á las disposiciones de S. E. el Señor General en Gefe Don Jose de San Martin, salió este de palacio à la plaza mayor, junto con el Excmo. Señor Teniente General Marques de Montemira, Gobernador político y militar, y acompañàndole el E. M. y demas generales del Exercito Libertador. Precedia una lucida y numerosa comitiva compuesta de la Universidad de San Márcos con sus quatro colegios : los prelados de las casas religiosas : los gefes militares : algunos Oidores, y mucha parte de la principal nobleza con el Excmo. Ayuntamiento: todos en briosos caballos ricamente enjaezados. Marchaba por detras la guardia de caballería y la de alabardéros de Lima : los hùsares que forman la escolta del Excmo. Señor General en Gefe : el batallon numero ocho con las banderas de Buenos-Ayres y de Chile, y la artillerìa con sus cañones respectivos.

En un espacioso tablado aseadamente prevenido en medio de la plaza mayor (lo mismo que en las demas de la ciudad) S. E. el General en Gefe enarboló el pendon en que está el nuevo escudo de armas de esta (*) recibièndole de mano del Señor Gobernador que le llevaba desde palacio : y acallado el alborozo del inmenso concurso, pronunció estas palabras que permanecerán esculpidas en el corazon de todo peruano eternamente : el Perú es desde este momento libre e independente por la voluntad general de los pueblos, y por la Justicia de su causa que Dios defiende.

(*) *Es un sol que se eleva por el oriente sobre los cerros extendidos á lo largo de la ciudad y el Rimac que baña sus faldas: el cual escudo orlado de laurel ocupa el medio de la bandera que se divide en quatro ángulos, dos agudos encarnados, y dos obtusos blancos.*

Batiendo despues el pendon, y en el tono de un corazon anegado en el placer puro y celestial que solo puede sentir un sér benéfico, repetia mucha veces: VIVA LA PATRIA: VIVA LA LIBERTAD: VIVA LA INDEPENDENCIA: expresiones que como eco festivo resonáron en toda la plaza, entre el estrépito de los cañones, el repique de todas las campanas de la ciudad, y las efusiones de alborozo universal, que se manifestaba de diversas maneras, y especialmenre con arrojar desde el tablado y los balcones, no solo medallas de plata con inscripciones que perpetuen la memoria de este dia; (**) sino tambien toda especie de monedas pródigamente derramadas por muchos vecinos y señoras: en que se distinguió el ilustre Colegio de Abogados. (***)

En seguida procedió el acompañamiento por las calles públicas, repitiendo en cada una de las plazas el mismo acto con la misma ceremonia y demas circunstancias, hasta volver á la plaza mayor en donde le esperaba el inmortal è intrèpido Lord Cochrane en una de las galerias del palacio: y alli terminó. Mas no cesáron las aclamaciones generales ni el empeño de significar cada qual el intimo regocijo que no podia contener deutro del pecho.

Manifestó este con especialidad el Excmo. Ayuntamiento, disponiendo en las salas capitulares un magnifico y exquisito Desert la noche de aquel dia. La asistencia de quantos intervinieron en la proclamacion de la mañana; el concurso numeroso de los principales vecinos: la gala de las señoras: la música: el bayle: sobre todo, la presencia de nuestro Libertador, que se dexó ver alli mezclado entre todos con aquella popularidad franca y afable con que sabe cautivar los corazones.—todo cooperaba á hacer resaltar mas y mas el esplendor de una solemnidad tan gloriosa.

Al siguiente dia 29, reunida en la iglesia catedral la misma distinguida concurrencia entre un numeroso gentío de todas clases, y con asistencia del Excmo. é Illmo. Señor Arzobispo; entonó la música el *Te Deum*, y celebróse una misa solemne en accion de gracias: y en ella pronunció la correspondiente oracion el P. Lector Fr. Jorge Bastante, franciscano.

Concluido este deber religioso, cada individuo de las corporaciones así eclesiásticas como civiles en sus respectivos departamentos prestáron *á Dios y á la patria* el debido juramento de *sostener y defender con su opinion, persona y propiedades la* INDEPENDENCIA DEL PERÚ *del gobierno español y de qualquiera otra dominacion extrangera*: con lo qual finalizó este primer acto de ciudadanos libres cuya dignidad hemos recuperado.

Por último, para complemento de tan extraordinaria solemnidad, S. E. el Señor General en Xefe dió una liberal muestra de su justa satisfacion, y de su afecto á esta capital, haciendo que

<hr>

(**) *Se representa en ellas por el anverso un sol con esta letra al rededor:* LIMA LIBRE JURÓ SU INDEPENDENCIA EN 28 DE JULIO DE 1821. *y por el reverso un laurel de que está circundada esta inscripcion:* BAJO LA PROTECCION DEL EXERCITO LIBÉRTADOR DEL PERÚ MANDADO POR SAN MARTIN.
(***) *El Colegio de abogados con inumerables vecinos de distincion y algunos xefes de oficinas, no pudiendo cabalgar en el acompañamiento por la escacez de caballos provenida de las repetidas requisiciones con que los arrebató á sus dueños el exército español ántes de su fuga — se contentáron con satisfacer sus deseos, presenciándose en pié al rededor de los varios tablados en que se efectuó la proclamacion.*

todos los vecinos y señoras concurriesen aquella noche al palacio: en donde se repitiéron, si no es que superáron, junto con la esplendidez del refresco, los mismos regocijos que la noche anterior en el cabildo.

Aquí seria de desear que pudiese describirse la magnificencia de esta y de las demas funciones, como igualmente la costosa decoracion de caprichosas iluminaciones, geroglíficos, inscripciones, arcos (*) banderas, tapicerías y otras mil invenciones con que en tales casos sé ostenta el público regocijo, y en las quales compitió á porfía este vecindario. Baste decir que todos y cada qual se excediéron à sì mismos, hallando el interes del bien comun recursos, en donde las exôrbitantes exâcciones del extinguido gobierno y la ruina de las propiedades parecia no haber dexado ni medios para la precisa subsistencia. ¡ Tanto distan del obsequio tributado involuntariamente al despotismo las espontaneas efusiones de alegrìa en un pueblo entusiasmado por la posesion de una felicidad inexplicable !

CALLAO.

Parte del Señor General D. Juan Gregorio de las Heras al Señor General en Gefe.

EXCMO. Señor. Tengo el honor de anunciar á V. E. el bizarro hecho de algunos soldados y oficiales del benémerito cuerpo de húsares que hacen la escolta de V. E.

Desde ayer tenia emboscadas en las casas de Bellavista diez y seis hombres con un oficial, con el objeto de si los enemigos echaban algunas descubiertas algo adelantadas de infanterìa ò de caballeria, lograr cortarlas. No se pudo lograr esto el primer dia: y como hoy á pesar de algunos tiradores que se les echàron, no quisièron los enemigos abandonar la posicion que media entre la puerta del castillo Real Felipe y una pequeña casa que se halla á la inmediacion del foso y al frente de una laguna;—nuestros húsares al mando de su sargento mayor comandante y el capitan D. Pedro Roulet, se decidièron á cargarlos á sable en mano, como lo verificàron, mezclándose entre quarenta infantes y diez y seis caballos enemigos: de los que quedàron en el campo entre muertos y heridos lo ménos veinte; teniendo que huir los restantes à la fortificacion, donde solo pudièron salvarse. Nuestra pèrdida solo ha consistido en un sargento muerto, y heridos levemente dicho capitan Roulet y un soldado.

Yo recomiendo à V. E. el valor y decision del expresado Sargento mayor capitan Roulet, y tropa del cuerpo de húsares; que con tanta bizarrìa han sabido comportarse al frente de sus compañeros de armas, haciendo convencer á nuestros enemigos de la nulidad è impotencia de su situacion,----Dios guarde á V. E. muchos años. Hacienda de Baquíjano Julio 26 de 821.—Excmo. Señor.—Juan Gregorió de las Heras.—Excmo. Señor D. Josè de San Martin, Capitan General y en Xefe del Exèrcito Libertador.

(*) *Señalóse con especialidad el arco triunfal que erigió el tribunal del Consulado, de primorosa estructura y con magníficos adornos, inscripciones y emblemas. Sobre él se veia una soberbia estatua equèstre del Libertador del Perú con sable en mano.*

A consequencia de esta intrépida accion, S. E. el Señor General en Xefe, se ha servido decretar los premios siguientes. 1. Al comandante de húsares Don Eugenio Necochea y al Capitan Raulet, el ascenso de un grado sobre el que obtenian. 2. A todos los individuos que componian la partida en la referida accion, el uso de un escudo de distincion en el brazo izquierdo con un letrero que diga: A LOS BRAVOS DEL CALLAO. 3. A la tropa, dos pesos de sueldo mensal sobre el que obtenian.

Otro del mismo.

EXCMO. Señor.—La comunicacion de V.E. para el gobierno del Callao que V. E. se sirviò derigirme con oficio de ayer noche, ha sido remitida esta mañana.

De à noche acà se nos han pasado siete soldados enemigos; y de ellos dos esta mañana, que habiendo salido de guerrilla, con toda bizarría echàron à correr de las filas enemigas, y sostenidos por otra guerrilla nuestra lográron el salvarse.—Dios guarde à V. E. muchos años,—Baquìjano y Julio 27 de 1821. Excmo. Señor.—Juan Gregorio de las Heras.—Excmo. Señor Capitan General y en Xefe del Exèrcito Libertador.

Articulo de Oficio.

Por órdenes expresas del Excmo. Señor General en Gefe, Protector del Perú, y en combinacion con sus planes, mandò retirar la division del coronel Mìller, que se hallaba en Moquegua. Esta se embarcò en Arica el 22. del corriente, y ha llegado al puerto de Pisco con la fuerza de 963. hombres de todas armas.

El General Arenàles consequènte con los mismos planes de S. E, y en virtud de òrdenes que tenia, se ha replegado à esta parte de la Cordillera, cubriendo con la division de su mando la quebrada de san Mateo y demas avenidas. La expresada division se compone de los batallones de Numancia, num. 7. y num. 2. de Chile, 1. de cazadores del Perú, y 1. de cazadores de los Andes; y de los 4. esquadrones de granaderos à caballo con la total fuerza de 4384 hombres.

El resto de las tropas que habian quedado en Huaura, y los convalecientes de los hospitales han verificado su embarque en Supe, en número de 631. hombres: los que deberàn desembarcar de hoy á mañana en Ancon. Los batallones num, 4. y 5 de Chile, y num. 11. de los Andes, con tres esquadrones de cazadores à caballo y otro de húsares de la escolta con un tren de diez piezas cubren el sitio del Callao.

Las guerrillas de Vidal, Quiros, Ninavilca, Cordero y otras con un cuerpo de caballerìa, fuertes de 600. hombres, persiguen al General La Serna, y protegen la espantosa desèrcion que và sufriendo Ellas le han quitado infinidad de cargas. El resto de las partidas al mando del comandante Villar marchan sobre las provincias de Yauyos y Xauxa, para hostilizar al enemigo.

Tal es el verdadero estado de las cosas: lo qual dexa à la capital à cubierto de todo insulto, y debe calmar la inquietud de algunos tímidos, al mismo tiempo que conozcan su impotencia los mal intencionados.

Mañana saldrá un suplemento con noticia individual de la accion de la esquadra patriótica en la bahìa del Callao el dia 24 de Julio.

Por D. Manuel Peña.

Republic of The Philippines

Discovered by Magellan, the Republic of the Philippines was conquered by Spain in the sixteenth century. On June 12, 1898, during the Spanish-American War, the Philippines declared their independence. After several years of fighting the Philippines were ceded to the United States. In 1934, the United Congress passed a law providing for Philippine independence after a transitional period. On July 4, 1946, the Philippines became independent by action of the American Congress.

REPUBLIC OF THE PHILIPPINES

CAVITE DECLARATION OF JUNE 12, 1898

In the town of Cavite Vicjo, in this province of Cavite, on the twelfth day of June eighteen hundred and ninety-eight, before me, Don Ambrosio Rianzares Bautista, Auditor of War and Special Commissioners appointed to proclaim and solemnize this act by the Dictatorial Government of these Philippine Islands, for the purposes and by virtue of the circular addressed by the Eminent Dictator of the same Don Emilio Aguinaldo y Famy, the undersigned being assembled, among whom figure commanders of his army and the representatives of other who have not been able to attend and notable residents of various towns of the same, taking into consideration, that their inhabitants being already weary of bearing the ominous yoke of Spanish domination, on account of the arbitrary arrests and harsh treatment practiced by the Civil Guard to the extent of causing death with the connivance and even with the express orders of their commanders, who sometimes went to the extreme of ordering the shooting of prisoners under the pretext that they were attempting to escape, in violation of the provisions of the Regulations of their Corps, which abuses were unpunished and on account of the unjust deportations, especially those decreed by General Blanco, of eminent personages and of high social position, at the instigation of the Archbishop and friars interested in keeping them out of the way for their own selfish and avaricious purpose, deportations which are quickly brought about by a method of procedure more execrable than that of the Inquisition and which every civilized nation rejects on account of a decision being rendered without a hearing of the persons accused, the people determined to start an insurrectionary movement in August, eighteen hundred and ninety-six, for the purpose of recovering the independence and sovereignty of which Spain deprived them through the Adelantado Miguel Lopez de Legaspi, who continuing the course followed by his pre-

decessor Hernando de Magallanes, who arrived upon
the shores of Cebu, and occupied that Island by
virtue of the treaty of friendship which he celebrated with its King Tupas, although he was killed
in the battle which took place on said shores, to
which he was provoked by King Kalipulako de Maktan,
who was suspicious of his bad intentions; he landed
on the Island of Bohol, entering also into the
celebrated blood compact of friendship with its
King Sikatuna, for the purpose, after taking Cebu
by force of arms, because the successor of Tupas
did not permit him to occupy it, of coming to
Manila, the capital, as he did, likewise winning
the friendship of its Kings Soliman and Lakandula
and afterwards taking possession of it and thus
of the entire Archipelago for Spain, by virtue of
an order of King Philip II: that in view of these
historical data, because in international law the
prescription established by the laws legalizing
even the fraudulent acquisition of the property
of individuals is not recognized, there can be no
doubt as to the legality of such a movement as the
one that was quited but not entirely quenched by
the pacification proposed by Pedro A. Paterno with
Don Emilio Aguinaldo as President of the Republican
government established in Biac-na-bato, and accepted by the Governor-General, Don Fernando Primo
de Rivera, under conditions which were established,
some in writing and others verbally, among them
a general amnesty for all deported and sentenced;
that by reason of nonfulfillment of some of these
conditions after the destruction of the Spanish
squadron by the North American one and the bom-
bardment of Cavite, Don Emilio Aguinaldo returned
to start a new revolution, and hardly had he given
the word to commence, on the thirty-first of last
month, when several towns anticipated the movement, and on the twenty-eighth between Imus and
Cavite Viejo here was engaged and captured force
of one hundred and seventy-eight, commanded by a
major of marine infantry. This movement spread
like an electric spark through the other towns
not only of this province, but also in Bataan,
Pampanga, Batangas, Bulacan, Laguna and Morong,
some of them with seaports. So complete is the
triumph of our arms, truly marvelous and unparalleled in the history of Colonial revolutions,
that in the first province mentioned there remain

to be surrendered only the detachments at Naic
and Indang; in the second there are none at all,
in the third, resistance by the Spanish forces
is localized in the town of San Fernando, where
the greater part are concentrated the remainder
being in Macabebe, Sesmoan and Guagua; in the
fourth only in the city of Lipa; in the fifth, in
the capital and Calumpit; and in the remaining
two, only in their respective capitals. The city
of Manila will soon be completely beseiged by our
forces, and also the posts in the province of
Nueva Ecija, Tarlac, Pangasinan, Union, Zambales
and several others in the Visayan islands, where
insurrection has broken out in several of their
towns, having started in some almost at the
moment of completing that pacification, and in
others even before that, wherefore the independence of our territory and the recovery of our
sovereignty are assured. And summoning as a
witness of the rectitude of our intentions, the
Supreme Judge of the Universe, and under the protection of the Mighty and Humane North American
Nation, we proclaim and solemnly declare, in the
name and by the authority of the inhabitants of
all these Philippine Islands, that they are and
have the right to be free and independent; that
they are released from all obedience to the crown
of Spain; that every political tie between the
two is and must be completely severed and annulled;
and that, like all free and independent states,
they have complete authority to make war, conclude
peace, establish treaties of commerce, enter into
alliances, regulate commerce, and execute all
other acts and things that Independent States
have the right to do. Reposing firm confidence
in the protection of Divine Providence, we mutually pledge for the support of this declaration,
our lives, our fortunes, and our most sacred
possession, which is our honor. We acknowledge,
approve and confirm together with the orders
that have been issued therefrom, the Dictatorship
established by Don Emilio Aguinaldo, whom we
honor as the Supreme Chief of this Nation, which
this day commences to have a life of its own, in
the belief that he is the instrument selected by
God, in spite of his humble origin, to effect the
redemption of this unfortunate people, as fore-
told by Doctor Jose Rizal in the magnificent

verses which he composed when he was preparing to
be shot, liberating them from the Yoke of Spanish
domination in punishment of the impunity with
which their Government allowed the commission of
abuses by its subordinates; and for the unjust
executions of said Rizal and others who were
sacrificed to please the greedy body of friars
in their insatiable desire to seek revenge upon
and exterminate all those who are opposed to
their Macciavellian purposes, which tramples upon
the penal code prescribed for these islands; and
for the sake of those persons who, though merely
suspected, were convicted by the Commanders of
detachments at the instigation of the friars
without form or semblance of a trial and without
the spiritual consolation afforded by our sacred '
religion; and likewise for the hanging for the
same motives of the eminent native Filipino
priests Doctor Jose Burgos, Mariano Gomez and
Jacinto Zamora, whose innocent blood was shed
through the intrigues of those so-called religious orders which pretended that a military insurrection had broken out on the night of January 21st, 1872, in the Fort of San Felipe in the
town of Cavite, accusing said martyrs of starting
it, so as to prevent the execution of the decree-
sentence issued by the Council of State in the
appeal in administrative litigation (contencioso
administrativo) interposed by the Secular Clergy
against the Royal Orders where in it was directed
that the parishes under them in the jurisdiction
of this Archbishopic should be turned over to
the Recoletos in exchange for those controlled
by the Recoletos in Mindanao, which were to be
transferred to the Jesuits. These were revoked
completely, and the return of those parishes was
ordered. The papers were filed in the Colonial
Department, to which they were sent some time
during the last months of the preceding year,
for the preparation of the respective Royal Provision. That was what caused the tree of Liberty
to bud in this land of ours, the iniquitious
measures employed to suppress it only causing it
to grow more and more, until, the last drop
having been drained from the cup of our afflictions, the former insurrection broke out at
Caloocan, extended to Santa Mesa, and continued
its course to the adjoining places in this province, where the unequalled heroism of its in-

habitants met with failure in the battles with General Blanco, and continued the struggle against the great hosts of General Polavieja for the period of three months, without any of the war material that we now possess, but commencing with arms peculiar to the country, such as the bolo, sharpened bamboo, and arrow. Moreover we confer upon our renowned Dictator, Don Emilio Aguinaldo, all the powers necessary for the due administration of his Government, including the prerogatives of pardon and amnesty. And finally, it was unanimously resolved that this Nation, independent from this day, must use the same flag used heretofore, whose design and colors and described in the accompanying drawing, with design representing in natural colors the three arms referred to. The white triangle represents the distinctive emblem of the famous Katipunan Society, which by means of its compact of blood urged on the masses of the people to insurrection; the three stars represent the three principal Islands of this Archipelago, Luzon, Mindanao and Panay, in which this insurrectionary movement broke out; the sun represents the gigantic strides that have been made by the sons of this land on the road of progress and civilization, its eight rays simbolizing the eight provinces of Manila, Cavite, Bulacan, Pampanga, Nueva Ecija, Bataan, Laguna and Batangas, which were declared in a state of war almost as soon as the first insurrectionary movement was initiated; and the colors blue, red and white, commemorate those of the flag of the United States of North America, in manifestation of our profound gratitude towards that Great Nation for the disinterested protection she is extending to us and will continue to extend to us. And grasping that flag, I displayed it to the assemblage, and all swore solemnly to recognize it and defend it to the last drop of our blood. In witness thereof, I commit the proceedings to writing in this act, which is signed with me by all those concurring in this act, as well as by the only foreigner, a North American subject, Mr. L. M. Johnson, Colonel of Artillery, who attended the meeting, to all of which I certify.   (Signed) AMBROSIO RIANZARES.

John R. M. Taylor, <u>Philippine Insurgent Records</u>, Vol. III, Exhibit 28.

PROCLAMATION 2695

INDEPENDENCE OF THE PHILIPPINES

BY THE PRESIDENT OF THE UNITED STATES OF AMERICA

A PROCLAMATION

WHEREAS the United States of America by the Treaty of Peace with Spain of December 10, 1898, commonly known as the Treaty of Paris and by the Treaty with Spain of November 7, 1900, did acquire sovereignty over the Philippines, and by the Convention of January 2, 1930, with Great Britain did delimit the boundary between the Philippine Archipelago and the State of North Borneo; and

WHEREAS the United States of America has consistently and faithfully during the past forty-eight years exercised jurisdiction and control over the Philippines and its people; and

WHEREAS it has been the repeated declaration of the legislative and executive branches of the Government of the United States of America that full independence would be granted the Philippines as soon as the people of the Philippines were prepared to assume this obligation; and

WHEREAS the people of the Philippines have clearly demonstrated their capacity for self-government; and

WHEREAS the Act of Congress approved March 24, 1934, known as the Philippine Independence Act, directed that, on the 4th day of July immediately following a ten-year transitional period leading to the independence of the Philippines, the President of the United States of America should by proclamation withdraw and surrender all rights of possession, supervision, jurisdiction, control, or sovereignty of the United States of America in and over the territory and people of the Philippines, except certain reservations therein or thereafter authorized to be made, and, on behalf of the United States of America, should recognize the independence of the Philippines:

NOW, THEREFORE, I, HARRY S. TRUMAN, President of the United States of America, acting under and by virtue of the authority vested in me by the aforesaid act of Congress, do proclaim that, in accord with and subject to the reservations provided for in the applicable statutes of the United States,

The United States of America hereby withdraws and surrenders all rights of possession, supervision, jurisdiction, control, or sovereignty now existing and exercised by the United States of America in and over the territory and people of the Philippines; and,

On behalf of the United States of America, I do hereby recognize the independence of the Philippines as a separate and self-governing nation and acknowledge the authority and control over the same of the government instituted by the people thereof, under the constitution now in force.

IN WITNESS WHEREOF, I have hereunto set my hand and caused the seal of the United States of America to be affixed.

DONE at the City of Washington this Fourth day of July in the year of our Lord, nineteen hundred and forty-six, and of the Independence of the United States of America the one hundred and seventy-first.

[SEAL]

HARRY S. TRUMAN

By the President:

DEAN ACHESON,
Acting Secretary of State.

[F. R. Doc. 46-11843; Filed, July 8, 1946;
11:42 a. m.]

Polish People's Republic

The birth of Poland as an independent
European state took place some time during the
10th century. As with several other European states
it is virtually impossible to point out to any
particular date, year or occurrence marking the
beginning of Polish statehood.

In 1795 Poland lost its independent political
existence as a state ("the third partition of
Poland"); since then Polish territory was under
the governments of Russia, Austria and Prussia.
The resurrection of the Polish Republic was
effected gradually during the stormy years of
World War I. Under the circumstances it is
difficult to indicate a precise and objective date
of the commencement of the new Polish statehood.
Nevertheless there is some kind of a national
consensus, that the first year of independence
was 1918 and that the major occurrence which took
place at that time was the assumption of military
and political power by Joseph Pilsudski, a fighter
for national independence, actually a national
hero at the time.

Note by Stanislaw Pomorski

Portuguese Republic

Invaded by the Arabs in the eighth century,
Portugal gradually developed into a nation as a
result of invasions by various liberating forces.
Though Spain recognized Portuguese independence in
1143, the date generally accepted for independence
is May 23, 1179, when Pope Alexander III published
a papal bull entitled "Manifesto Probatum." In
1580 Portugal and Spain formed a dual monarchy
under the King of Spain. The union dissolved in
1640 with Portugal losing many of its overseas
territories.

ALEXANDER III TO ALPHONSO, KING OF PORTUGAL

LATERAN, MAY 23, 1179

Alexander, bishop and servant of the servants of God to the dearest son in Christ, Alphonso illustrious king of Portugal and to his heirs, in perpetuity.

It has been attested by manifest evidence that through painful wars and military conflicts you, the bold destroyer of enemies of the Christian name and diligent defender of the Christian faith, have, like a good son and Catholic prince, performed manifold services for your mother, the holy Church, and have left behind a name worthy to be remembered and an unparalleled example for posterity. It is right that what heavenly dispensation has chosen from on high for the governance and salvation of people, the apostolic see cherishes with deepest affection and is anxious to answer effectively just demands. Thus mindful of your person, distinguished for prudence, endowed with justice and responsive to the government of people, we take under the protection of St. Peter you and the kingdom of Portugal with that full respect and honor which befit kings, and moreover all those places which you have snatched from the hands of the Saracens with divine assistance and in which Christian princes cannot assert rights for themselves, we grant to your excellency and confirm by apostolic authority. So that you may be kindled more fervently to obedience to St. Peter, prince of the apostles and the Holy Roman church, these we have determined to grant to your aforesaid heirs and shall defend them in addition to what has been conferred, God willing, on behalf of the apostolic office entrusted to us. Therefore it is important for you, dearest son, to remain humble and devout in respect and obedience to your mother, the Holy Roman church, and to devote yourself to its advantage and the possibilities of the Christian faith in such a way that the

apostolic see will rejoice in such a devout and
renowned son and find peace in his devotion. As
proof that the aforesaid kingdom exists under the
jurisdiction of St. Peter, you have agreed for
the sake of more tangible obedience to pay two
marks of gold each year to us and our successors.
This payment you and your successors will take
care to assign for our use and that of our successors to the archbishop of Braga.

We determine therefore that no man may mo-
lest your person or your heirs or the aforesaid
kingdom, or to seize its possessions or to keep
and diminish what has been taken away, or to
weary with other disturbances.

> Alexander, bishop of the Catholic Church.
> John, cardinal priest of St. John and St.
>   Paul tit. Pamachius.
> John, cardinal priest tit. St. Mark.
> Peter, cardinal priest tit. St. Susannah.
> Viceranus, cardinal priest of St. Stephan
>   on the Caelian hill.
> Cintius, cardinal priest tit. St. Cecilia.
> Luigo, cardinal priest tit. St. Clement.
> Anduin, cardinal priest tit. Holy Cross in
>   Jerusalem.
> Matthew, cardinal priest tit. St. Marcellus.
> Rubald, bishop of Ostia.
> Theodinus, bishop of Porta and St. Rufine.
> Peter, bishop of Tusculum.
> Laborahs, cardinal of St. Mary's in Porticu.
> Rainerius, cardinal S. George ad Velum
>   Aureum.
> Gratian, cardinal of SS. Cosma and Damiani.
> John, cardinal of St. Angeli.
> Raineris, cardinal of St. Madrian.
> Matthew, cardinal of Santa Marie Nuova.
> Bernard, cardinal of St. Nicholas in Carcere
>   Tulliano.
> Dated Laterna, x. Kal. May.

Translation by Professor Ernest McDonnell

State of Qatar

The State of Qatar is on the western coast
of the Persian Gulf bordering with Saudi Arabia.
Under Persian rule until the 19th century, Qatar
entered into a general maritime truce with Great
Britain in 1868. A definitive treaty in 1916
reserved foreign affairs and defense to Great
Britain but allowed internal autonomy. A Treaty
of Friendship and an Exchange of Notes entered into
on September 3, 1971 between Great Britain and the
State of Qatar provide for complete independence.

STATE OF QATAR

TREATY OF FRIENDSHIP

BETWEEN THE UNITED KINGDOM OF GREAT BRITAIN AND

NORTHERN IRELAND AND THE STATE OF QATAR

The United Kingdom of Great Britain and Northern Ireland and the State of Qatar;

Considering that the State of Qatar has resumed full international responsibility as a sovereign and independent State;

Determined that their long standing and traditional relations of close friendship and co-operation shall continue henceforth;

Desiring to give expression to this intention in the form of a Treaty of Friendship;

Have agreed as follows:.

Article 1

The relations between the United Kingdom of Great Britain and Northern Ireland and the State of Qatar shall continue to be governed by a spirit of close friendship. In recognition of this, the Contracting Parties, conscious of their common interest in the peace and stability of the region, shall:

(a) consult together on matters of mutual concern in time of need;
(b) settle all their disputes by peaceful means in conformity with the provisions of the Charter of the United Nations.

Article 2

The Contracting Parties shall encourage educational, scientific and cultural co-operation between the two States in accordance with arrangements to be agreed. Such arrangements could cover

580

among other things:

    (a) the promotion of mutual understanding of their respective cultures, civilisations and languages;

    (b) the promotion of contacts among professional bodies, universities and cultural institutions in their countries;

    (c) the encouragement of educational, scientific and cultural exchanges.

Article 3

The Contracting Parties shall maintain the close relations already existing between them in the field of trade and commerce. Representatives of the Contracting Parties shall meet from time to time to consider means by which such relations can be further developed and strengthened, including the possibility of concluding treaties or agreements on matters of mutual concern in this respect.

Article 4

The present Treaty shall enter into force on the date of signature and shall remain in force for a period of ten years. Unless, twelve months before the expiry of the said period of ten years, either Contracting Party shall have given notice to the other of its intention to terminate the Treaty, this Treaty shall remain in force thereafter until the expiry of twelve months from the date on which notice of such intention is given.

In witness whereof the undersigned have signed this Treaty.

Done in duplicate in Geneva the third day of September 1971 A.D., corresponding to the thirteenth day of Rajab 1391 H., in the English and Arabic languages, both texts being equally authoritative.

Cmd. Paper 4850 (1972).

Rhodesia

A South African country, Rhodesia is bounded on the north by Zambia, on the east by Mozambique, and on the north by the Republic of South Africa. First explored by the Portuguese in the 15th century, Rhodesia became a self-governing British colony under a charter from the British South African Company in 1899 and by a 1929 amendment. Objecting to continual British influence and its protection of African interests, the minority ruled government declared its independence from Great Britain on November 11, 1965. Despite international economic sanctions, Rhodesia has maintained its independent status.

RHODESIA

Whereas in the course of human affairs history has shown that it may become necessary for a people to resolve the political affiliations which have connected them with another people and to assume amongst other nations the separate and equal status to which they are entitled:

And whereas in such event a respect for the opinions of mankind requires them to declare to other nations the causes which impel them to assume full responsibility for their own affairs:

Now therefore, we, the Government of Rhodesia, do hereby declare ﹔

That it is an indisputable and accepted historic fact that since 1923 the Government of Rhodesia have exercised the powers of self-government and have been responsible for the progress, development and welfare of their people;

That the people of Rhodesia having demonstrated their loyalty to the Crown and to their kith and kin in the United Kingdom and elsewhere through two world wars, and having been prepared to shed their blood and give of their substance in what they believed to be the mutual interests of freedom-loving people, now see all that they have cherished, about to be shattered on the rocks of expediency;

That the people of Rhodesia have witnessed a process which is destructive of those very precepts upon which civilisation in a primitive country has been built; they have seen the principles of Western democracy, responsible government and moral standards crumble elsewhere; nevertheless, they have remained steadfast;

That the people of Rhodesia fully support the requests of their Government for sovereign independence but have witnessed the consistent refusal of the Government of the United Kingdom to accede to their entreaties;

That the Government of the United Kingdom
have thus demonstrated that they are not prepared
to grant sovereign independence to Rhodesia on
terms acceptable to the people of Rhodesia, thereby
persisting in maintaining an unwarrantable jurisdiction over Rhodesia, obstructing laws and treaties
with other states and the conduct of affairs with
other nations and refusing assent to laws necessary
for the public good; all this to the detriment of
the future peace, prosperity and good government
of Rhodesia;

That the Government of Rhodesia have for a
long period patiently and in good faith negotiated
with the Government of the United Kingdom for the
removal of the remaining limitations placed upon
them and for the grant of sovereign independence;

That in the belief that procrastination and
delay strike at and injure the very life of the
nation, the Government of Rhodesia consider it essential that Rhodesia should attain, without delay,
sovereign independence, the justice of which is beyond question;

Now therefore, we, the Government of Rhodesia,
in humble submission to Almighty God who controls
the destinies of nations, conscious that the people
of Rhodesia have always shown unswerving loyalty
and devotion to Her Majesty the Queen and earnestly
praying that we and the people of Rhodesia will not
be hindered in our determination to continue exercising our undoubted right to demonstrate the same
loyalty and devotion, and seeking to promote the
common good so that the dignity and freedom of all
men may be assured, do, by this Proclamation, adopt,
enact and give to the people of Rhodesia the Constitution annexed hereto.

GOD SAVE THE QUEEN.

Given under Our Hand at Salisbury, this
eleventh day of November in The Year of Our Lord
one thousand nine hundred and sixty-five.

Rhodesian Commentary, Supplement, November 1975.

Proclamation

Whereas in the course of human affairs history has shown that it may become necessary for a people to resolve the political affiliations which have connected them with another people and to assume amongst other nations the separate and equal status to which they are entitled:

And Whereas in such event a respect for the opinions of mankind requires them to declare to other nations the causes which impel them to assume full responsibility for their own affairs:

Now Therefore, We, The Government of Rhodesia, Do Hereby Declare:

That it is an indisputable and accepted historic fact that since 1923 the Government of Rhodesia have exercised the powers of self-government and have been responsible for the progress, development and welfare of their people;

That the people of Rhodesia having demonstrated their loyalty to the Crown and to their kith and kin in the United Kingdom and elsewhere through two world wars, and having been prepared to shed their blood and give of their substance in what they believed to be the mutual interests of freedom-loving people, now see all that they have cherished about to be shattered on the rocks of expediency;

That the people of Rhodesia have witnessed a process which is destructive of those very precepts upon which civilization in a primitive country has been built; they have seen the principles of Western democracy, responsible government and moral standards crumble elsewhere; nevertheless they have remained steadfast;

That the people of Rhodesia fully support the requests of their Government for sovereign independence but have witnessed the consistent refusal of the Government of the United Kingdom to accede to their entreaties;

That the Government of the United Kingdom have thus demonstrated that they are not prepared to grant sovereign independence to Rhodesia on terms acceptable to the people of Rhodesia, thereby persisting in maintaining an unwarrantable jurisdiction over Rhodesia, obstructing laws and treaties with other states and the conduct of affairs with other nations and refusing assent to laws necessary for the public good; all this to the detriment of the future peace, prosperity and good government of Rhodesia;

That the Government of Rhodesia have for a long period patiently and in good faith negotiated with the Government of the United Kingdom for the removal of the remaining limitations placed upon them and for the grant of sovereign independence;

That in the belief that procrastination and delay strike at and injure the very life of the nation, the Government of Rhodesia consider it essential that Rhodesia should attain, without delay, sovereign independence, the justice of which is beyond question;

Now Therefore, We The Government of Rhodesia, in humble submission to Almighty God who controls the destinies of nations, conscious that the people of Rhodesia have always shown unswerving loyalty and devotion to Her Majesty the Queen and earnestly praying that we and the people of Rhodesia will not be hindered in our determination to continue exercising our undoubted right to demonstrate the same loyalty and devotion, and seeking to promote the common good so that the dignity and freedom of all men may be assured, *Do, By This Proclamation,* adopt, enact and give to the people of Rhodesia the Constitution annexed hereto.

God Save The Queen

Given under Our Hand at Salisbury, this .... day of November in the Year of Our Lord one thousand nine hundred and sixty-five.

Prime Minister

Deputy Prime Minister

Ministers

587

Socialist Republic of Romania

Abandoned by the Romans in 270, Romania
was subjected to repeated invasions by the Visigoths
Huns, Lombards, and Avars for several centuries.
In the fifteenth century, the Romanian principalities, Walachia, and Moldavia became Turkish
tributaries. Except for Phanariot rule from 1711
until 1821, Romania remained under Turkish domination. On May 9, 1877, a proclamation of independence
was passed by the Romanian Senate and Chamber of
Deputies following a speech by the Minister of
Foreign Affairs, Michail Kogalniceahu. Independence
was exacted from the Turks by the Russians on March
3, 1878. The Treaty of Berlin, on July 13, 1878,
recognized internationally the independence of
Romania.

SOCIALIST REPUBLIC OF ROMANIA

MOTION PASSED ON MAY 9, 1877

BUCHAREST

The Chambers, satisfied with the government's explanations

- officially acknowledge that there is a state of war between Romania and Turkey, that our relations with the Porte are broken and that Romania is now officially established as absolutely independent;

- and, relying on the justice of the guaranteeing powers, resumes the agenda.

SPEECH BY MICHAEL KOGALNICEAU

The Chamber and the Senate acknowledge that
we are in a state of war, they acknowledge that
we are released from our bonds with the Sublime
Porte and that relations first were broken by the
Sublime Porte. Being in a state of war with our
bonds broken, what are we now? We are independent;
we are an independent nation. But, gentlemen,
does our work stop here? Does our mission end
here? We have reached the aim we have pursued
not only at the present time, but over many centuries and especially so, since 1848. First of
all, let us ask ourselves: What were we before
war was declared? Have we ever been a Turkish
province? Have we ever been vassals of Turkey?
Did we ever have the Sultan as suzerain? Foreigners may have said this; we ourselves never
said it. The Sultan has not been our suzerain.
We have not been vassals. There has been something, that is true. There has been a sui
generis relation, feeble when Romanians were
strong and strong when Romanians were feeble.
We must now prove that we are a living nation,
able to make sacrifices to keep this country and
its rights for our children.

Therefore, I have not the slighest hesita-
tion and fear to state in front of this nation's
representatives that we are a free and independent
nation.

Monitorul Official, no. 118, pp. 3449-53,
May 27, 1877.
Unofficial translation by Leonard C. Meeker.

Republic of Rwanda

Located in east central Africa and bounded
on the west by Zaire, the Republic of Rwanda
became part of German East Africa in the 19th
century. After World War I, Rwanda, along with
neighboring Burundi, was administered by Belgium.
Ruanda-Urundi became a United Nations trust territory after World War II, still administered
by Belgium. Following internal tensions the
National Rwandan Congress declared independence
on January 28, 1961.

REPUBLIC OF RWANDA

2ND TELEGRAM ADDRESSED TO THE

RESIDENT GENERAL AND TO THE RESIDENT OF RWANDA

BY THE "NATIONAL RWANDAN CONGRESS AND THE

PERMANENT INSTITUTIONS"

JANUARY 28, 1961

In view of the equivocal attitudes expressed
by Belgium and the U.N. concerning Rwanda's legislative elections, in view of decisions which are
both arbitrary and contrary to decisions of our
colleagues Kisenyi and Ostende, in view of the
gravity of the situation and responding to the
wishes of the majority of the Rwandan populations
to see their country progressing in unity, harmony,
and authentic democracy, the Rwandan people, cou-
rageously taking hold of their grave responsibilities, convened in a national congress at Gitarama
on January 28, 1961, have solemnly decided and
established the following in the higher interest
of the Nation, for the final pacification of both
our country and its permanent institutions: the
abolition of the Mwami form of government and the
deposition of Kigeri V Ndahindurwa, the solemn
proclamation of the Republic of Rwanda, the election of a president, the formation of a permanent
government, the election of the second house of
the Legislative Assembly, the creation of a
Supreme Court; all future democratic institutions
shall be established only in accordance with the
will of the Rwandan Nation as freely expressed
by a mandatory vote of citizens. STOP.

We are happy to cooperate in good faith and
in a friendly manner with Belgium and all Free
Nations. The National Rwandan Congress and the
permanent democratic institutions, which comprise
the government, invite the Belgian Government and
all local Trusteeships to continue to execute
their responsibilities faithfully. STOP.

As a consequence we insist that a conference be convened in the next few weeks with Belgium, the U.N., and Rwanda, to deal with the problem of Rwanda's Independence. STOP.

NATIONAL RWANDAN CONGRESS AND THE

PERMANENT INSTITUTIONS

Rwanda Politique 1958-60, pp. 386-7.
Translation by Sarah J. Campbell.

2° Télégramme adressé au Résident Général et au Résident du Rwanda par le « Congrès National Rwandais et Institutions définitives »

28 janvier 1961

Vu attitudes équivoques Belgique-ONU concernant élections législatives Rwanda, suite décisions arbitrairement contraires aux conclusions colloques Kisenyi-Ostende, devant gravité situation et répondant aux vœux majorité populations Rwandaises voir progresser pays dans unité, harmonie et démocratie authentique, prenant courageusement ses graves responsabilités le peuple Ruandais réuni solennellement et librement en congrès national à Gitarama, le vingt-huit janvier de l'an de salut mil neuf cent soixante et un, a décidé et établi solennellement, dans l'intérêt supérieur de la Nation et pour la pacification définitive pays, institutions démocratiques définitives suivantes : abolition forme Mwami de gouvernement et déposition de Kigeri V Ndahindurwa, proclamation solennelle république Rwandaise, élection président de la république, promulgation constitution Rwandaise, formation gouvernement définitif, élection second degré Assemblée législative, création Cour suprême, toutes institutions démocratiques établies selon volonté nation rwandaise librement exprimée par voie mandataires naturels stop.

Heureux collaborer loyalement et amicalement avec Belgique et toutes Nations Libres, Congrès National Rwandais et Institutions démocratiques définitives, invitons Gouvernement belge et tutelle locale prendre loyalement ses responsabilités stop.

Exigeons en conséquence prochaines semaines conférence organisée Belgique-O.N.U.-Rwanda pour traiter problème Indépendance Rwanda stop.

CONGRES NATIONAL RWANDAIS ET INSTITUTIONS DEFINITIVES

Le Président de la République : MBONYUMUTWA
Le Président de la Cour suprême NZEYIMANA
Le Président de l'Assemblée législative J GITERA
Le Premier Ministre KAYIBANDA

Democratic Republic of Sao Tome
and Principe

Sao Tome and Principe is a country made up
of two islands of the coast of West Africa.
Discovered by Portugal in 1470 the islands became
an overseas province in 1522. Except for a brief
period of Dutch rule in the 1600's the province
remained a Portuguese province until the 1970's.
A rising nationalist movement led by the Liberation
Movement of Sao Tome' and Principe exacted a November 26, 1974 agreement providing for the right to
self determination. A transitional government
took over the following month until the guaranteed
date of independence, July 12, 1975.

DEMOCRATIC REPUBLIC OF SAO TOME AND PRINCIPE

AGREEMENT BETWEEN PORTUGAL AND

THE LIBERATION MOVEMENT OF SAO TOME AND PRINCIPE

1.   The Portuguese Government reaffirms the rights of the people of Sao Tome and Principe to self-determination and independence, according to Portuguese Constitutional Law 7/74 of 26 July 1974 and the relevant United Nations resolutions.

2.   The Portuguese Government recognizes the Libration Movement of Sao Tome and Principe as its only interlocutor and as the legitimate representative of the people of Sao Tome and Principe.

3.   The Liberation Movement of Sao Tome and Principe and the Portuguese Government, aware of the need to ensure, under the best possible conditions, the transmission of powers to the future independent State of Sao Tome and Principe, agreed on establishing the outline and the time-table for decolonization and, for that purpose, the High Commissioner and a Transitional Government are established.

Kingdom of Saudi Arabia

The Kingdom of Saudi Arabia is located on
the Arabian Peninsula in southwest Asia and is
bounded to the north by Jordon. Saudi Arabia
began to develop into a nation in the early 18th
century when the Wahhabis, Islamic fundamentalists,
started a reform movement in central Arabia. After
taking much of the Arabian peninsula, the movement
was crushed by the Turks. The movement again
started in 1902 under Abd al-Aziz Ibn Saud. By the
beginning of World War I Ibn Saud had conquered
most of the other central Arabian tribes. British
influence in the Arabian peninsula had increased
through the 19th century and by World War I all
foreign affairs were conducted through them. A
December 26, 1915, treaty between the principality
of Abd al-Aziz Ibn Saud and Great Britain recognized
Ibn Saud as leader but limited freedom of action as
well as limiting sovereignty. During the next ten
years Ibn Saud, through conquests, built the Wah-
habi principality into a state stretching from the
Persian Gulf to the Red Sea. On May 20, 1927, a
treaty between the parties recognized what was
already apparent; Saudi Arabia as an Independent
State. A kingdom was formed in 1932 comprising
all the conquests, and the name Saudi Arabia was
taken.

Treaty between His Britannic Majesty and His Majesty the King of the Hijāz and of Najd and its Dependencies, signed at Jiddah, the 20th May, 1927.

His Majesty the King of Great Britain, Ireland and the British Dominions beyond the Seas, Emperor of India, on the one part ; and His Majesty the King of the Hejaz and of Nejd and its Dependencies, on the other part ;

Being desirous of confirming and strengthening the friendly relations which exist between them and of consolidating their respective interests, have resolved to conclude a treaty of friendship and good understanding, for which purpose His Britannic Majesty has appointed as his plenipotentiary Sir Gilbert Falkingham Clayton, and His Majesty the King of the Hejaz and of Nejd and its Dependencies has appointed His Royal Highness the Amir Faisal ibn Abdul-Aziz, his son and Viceroy in the Hejaz, as his plenipotentiary.

His Highness the Amir Faisal ibn Abdul-Aziz and Sir Gilbert Falkingham Clayton, having examined their credentials and found them to be in good and due form, have accordingly agreed upon and concluded the following articles:

Art. 1. His Britannic Majesty recognizes the complete and absolute independence of the dominions of His Majesty the King of the Hejaz and of Nejd and its Dependencies.

Art. 2. There shall be peace and friendship between His Britannic Majesty and His Majesty the King of the Hejaz and of Nejd and its Dependencies. Each of the high contracting parties undertakes to maintain good relations with the other and to endeavour by all the means at its disposal to prevent his territories being used as a base for unlawful activities directed against peace and tranquillity in the territories of the other party.

Art. 3. His Majesty the King of the Hejaz and of Nejd and its Dependencies undertakes that the performance of the pilgrimage will be facilitated to British subjects and British-protected persons of the Moslem faith to the same extent as to other pilgrims, and announces that they will be safe as regards their property and their person during their stay in the Hejaz.

Art. 4. His Majesty the King of the Hejaz and of Nejd and its Dependencies undertakes that the property of the aforesaid pilgrims who may die within the territories of His Majesty and who have no lawful trustee in those territories shall be handed over to the British Agent in Jeddah or to such authority as he may appoint for the purpose, to be forwarded by him to the rightful heirs of the deceased pilgrims ; provided that the property shall not be handed over to the British representative until the formalities of the competent tribunals have been complied with and the dues prescribed under Hejazi or Nejdi laws have been duly collected.

Art. 5. His Britannic Majesty recognizes the national (Hejazi or Nejdi) status of all subjects of His Majesty the King of the Hejaz and of Nejd and its Dependencies who may at any time be within the territories of His Britannic Majesty or territories under the protection of His Britannic Majesty.

Similarly, His Majesty the King of the Hejaz and of Nejd and its Dependencies recognizes the national (British) status of all subjects of His Britannic Majesty and of all persons enjoying the protection of His Britannic Majesty who may at any time be within the territories of His Majesty the King of the Hejaz and of Nejd and its Dependencies ; it being understood that the principles of international law in force between independent Governments shall be respected.

Art. 6. His Majesty the King of the Hejaz and of Nejd and its Dependencies undertakes to maintain friendly and peaceful relations with the territories of Kuwait and Bahrain, and with the Sheikhs of Qatar and the Oman Coast, who are in special treaty relations with His Britannic Majesty's Government.

Art. 7. His Majesty the King of the Hejaz and of Nejd and its Dependencies undertakes to co-operate by all the means at his disposal with His Britannic Majesty in the suppression of the slave trade.

Art. 8. The present treaty shall be ratified by each of the high contracting parties and the ratifications exchanged as soon as possible. It shall come into force on the day of the exchange of ratifications and shall be binding during seven years from that date. In case neither of the high contracting parties shall have given notice to the other six months before the expiration of the said period of seven years of his intention to terminate the treaty it shall remain in force and shall not be held to have terminated until the expiration of six months from the date on which either of the parties shall have given notice of the termination to the other party.

Art. 9. The treaty concluded between His Britannic Majesty and His Majesty the King of the Hejaz and of Nejd and its Dependencies (then Ruler of Nejd and its then Dependencies) on the 26th December, 1915, shall cease to have effect as from the date on which the present treaty is ratified.

Art. 10. The present treaty has been drawn up in English and Arabic. Both texts shall be of equal validity; but in case of divergence in the interpretation of any part of the treaty the English text shall prevail.

Art. 11. The present treaty shall be known as the Treaty of Jeddah.

Signed at Jeddah on Friday, May 20th, 1927 (corresponding to the 18th Zul Qa'da, 1345).

Cmd. Paper 2951 (1927).

Republic of Senegal

Located in western Africa, the Republic of
Senegal lies on the Atlantic Ocean south of Mauritania. Although Portuguese and Dutch trading
stations were established in Senegal during the 15th
and 17th centuries, it wasn't until the 19th
century that Senegal came under European control.
Beginning in 1854 the foundation for French colonial
administration had been laid. By the end of the
1880's most of western Senegal had become a French
Protectorate. In 1895 Senegal was made a French
colony, becoming an overseas territory in 1946.
The relationship between Senegal and France
was changed by a constitutional referendum on September 28, 1958, in which the Senegalese elected to join
the French Community. In 1959 Senegal joined with
Sudan in forming the Mali Federation. Senegal
withdrew from the federation on August 20, 1960,
and declared its independence in a new constitution
on August 25, 1960. France recognized the independence by an exchange of letters beginning on
September 16, 1960.

SENEGAL

SPECIAL AGREEMENT

TRANSFERRING JURISDICTION OF THE COMMUNITY

April 4, 1960

The Government of the French Republic, on the one hand,

The Governments of the Republic of Senegal and the Sudanese Republic, grouped within the Federation of Mali, on the other hand, agree on the following:

The jurisdictions instituted by Article 78 of the Constitution of October 4, 1958, are transferred, so far as they are applicable, to the Republic of Senegal and to the Sudanese Republic, grouped within the Federation of Mali, dating from the fulfillment by the contracting Parties of the procedure provided for in Article 87 of said Constitution.

Paris, April 4, 1960.

For the Government of the French Republic,
MICHEL DEBRE.

For the Government of the Sudanese Republic,
MODIBO KEITA.

For the Government of the Republic of Senegal,
MAMADOU DIA.

Translated by Sarah J. Campbell

SENEGAL

DECREE NO. 60-628 OF JUNE 30, 1960,

PUBLISHING SPECIAL AGREEMENTS SIGNED APRIL 4, 1960,

BETWEEN THE GOVERNMENT OF THE FRENCH REPUBLIC,

AND THE GOVERNMENTS OF THE REPUBLIC OF SENEGAL

AND THE SUDANESE REPUBLIC GROUPED WITHIN THE

FEDERATION OF MALI

The President of the Republic,

Upon the report of the Prime Minister and the Secretary of State for relations with the States of the Community,

In view of the Constitution, especially Articles 86 and 87,

In view of Law No. 60-569 of June 17, 1960, approving the special agreements signed April 4, 1960, between the Government of the French Republic and the Governments of the Republic of Senegal and the Sudanese Republic, grouped within the Federation of Mali,

Decrees:

Article 1. The special agreements signed April 4, 1960, between the Government of the French Republic and the Governments of the Republic of Senegal and the Sudanese Republic, grouped within the Federation of Mali, will be published in the Journal Officiel of the French Republic.

Article 2. The Prime Minister and the Secretary of State for relations with the States of the Community shall be responsible for the execution of this decree.

Paris, June 30, 1960.

C. DE GAULLE
President of the Republic

Secretary of State for
   Relations with the
   Community,
Jean FOYER

Prime Minister,
Michel DEBRE

Translated by Sarah J. Campbell

REPUBLIC OF SENEGAL

PRESIDENT OF THE COUNCIL

Dakar, September 16, 1960

To Mr. Michel DEBRE,
Prime Minister of the French Republic

Mr. Prime Minister,

I have the honor of informing you that the
Government of the Republic of Senegal considers
that, by virtue of the principles of international
law relative to the succession of States, the Republic of Senegal is replacing, so far as they are
applicable, the rights and obligations resulting
from the cooperation agreements dated June 22,
1960, between the French Republic and the Federation of Mali, without excluding adaptations which,
by mutual agreement, may be recognized as necessary.

I would be grateful if you would inform me
that this view is shared by the Government of the
French Republic.

Very respectfully yours,

Signed: MAMADOU DIA.

Translated by Sarah J. Campbell

THE PRIME MINISTER

Paris, September 19, 1960

To Mr. MAMADOU DIA,
President of the Council of the Republic of Senegal

Mr. President,

By letter dated September 16, you wished to address to me the following communication:

"I have the honor of informing you that the Government of the Republic of Senegal considers that, by virtue of the principles of international law relative to the succession of States, the Republic of Senegal is replacing, so far as they are applicable, the rights and obligations resulting from the cooperation agreements dated June 22, 1960, between the French Republic and the Federation of Mali, without excluding adaptations which, by mutual agreement, may be recognized as necessary.

"I would be grateful if you would inform me that this view is shared by the Government of the French Republic."

I have the honor of informing you that the Government of the French Republic shares the view of the Republic of Senegal.

Very respectfully yours,

Signed: MICHEL DEBRE

Translated by Sarah J. Campbell

Décret n° 60-628 du 30 juin 1960 portant publication des accords particuliers signés le 4 avril 1960 entre le Gouvernement de la République française et les Gouvernements de la République du Sénégal et de la République soudanaise groupées au sein de la Fédération du Mali.

Le Président de la République,

.Sur le' rapport du Premier ministre et du secrétaire d'État aux relations avec les États de la Communauté,

Vu la Constitution, et notamment ses articles 86 et 87 ;

Vu la loi n° 60-569 du 17 juin 1960 portant approbation des accords particuliers signés le 4 avril 1960 entre le Gouvernement de la République française et les Gouvernements de la République du Sénégal et de la République soudanaise groupées au sein de la Fédération du Mali,

Décrète :

Art. 1er. — Les accords particuliers signés le 4 avril 1960 entre le Gouvernement de la République française et les Gouvernements de la République du Sénégal et de la République soudanaise groupées au sein de la Fédération du Mali seront publiés au Journal officiel de la République française.

Art. 2. — Le Premier ministre et le secrétaire d'État aux relations avec les États de la Communauté sont chargés de l'exécution du présent décret.

Fait à Paris, le 30 juin 1960.

C. DE GAULLE.

Par le Président de la République :

Le Premier ministre,

Michel DEBRÉ.

Le secrétaire d'État
aux relations avec les États de la Communauté,
Jean FOYER.

ACCORD PARTICULIER

PORTANT TRANSFERT DES COMPÉTENCES DE LA COMMUNAUTÉ

Le Gouvernement de la République française, d'une part,

Les Gouvernements de la République du Sénégal et de la République soudanaise, groupées au sein de la fédération du Mali, d'autre part,

sont convenus de ce qui suit :

Les compétences instituées par l'article 78 de la Constitution du 4 octobre 1958 sont, pour ce qui les concerne, transférées à la République du Sénégal et à la République soudanaise, groupées au sein de la fédération du Mali, dès l'accomplissement par les Parties contractantes de la procédure prévue à l'article 87 de ladite Constitution.

Fait à Paris, le 4 avril 1960.

Pour le Gouvernement de la République française :
Michel DEBRÉ.

Pour le Gouvernement de la République soudanaise :
Modibo KEITA.

Pour le Gouvernement de la République du Sénégal :
Mamadou DIA.

ACCORD

CONCERNANT LES DISPOSITIONS TRANSITOIRES EN MATIÈRE DE JUSTICE
ENTRE LA RÉPUBLIQUE FRANÇAISE ET LA FÉDÉRATION DU MALI

Le Gouvernement de la République française, d'une part,

Les Gouvernements de la République du Sénégal et de la République soudanaise, groupées au sein de la Fédération du Mali, d'autre part,

sont convenus de ce qui suit :

Article 1er

Jusqu'à l'installation des juridictions suprêmes de la Fédération du Mali, les
recours en cassation formés contre les décisions rendues par les juridictions
maliennes de l'ordre administratif et de l'ordre judiciaire seront portés devant
les formations ordinaires du Conseil d'État et de la cour de cassation, siégeant
à Paris, lesquelles statueront en outre sur les recours formés à la date d'entrée
en vigueur du présent accord.

En cas de cassation, l'affaire sera renvoyée devant une juridiction de la Fédération du Mali; la juridiction de renvoi statuera dans les conditions et formes
ordinaires en ces matières.

Article 2

Les décisions rendues par les juridictions siégeant en France ou au Mali continueront, jusqu'à la fin de la période transitoire prévue à l'article 1er, à être
exécutées sur le territoire de l'autre État selon la procédure appliquée lors de
l'entrée en vigueur de l'accord portant transfert des compétences de la Communauté.

Article 3

A la fin de la période transitoire prévue à l'article 1er, alinéa 1, un accord
entre la République française et la Fédération du Mali déterminera les conditions
dans lesquelles seront réglées les instances pendantes devant le Conseil d'État
et la Cour de Cassation.

Article 4

La transmission et la remise des actes judiciaires et extrajudiciaires, la transmission et l'exécution des commissions rogatoires, la comparution des témoins
en matière pénale, les formalités relatives à l'inscription au casier judiciaire
et à la demande des extraits de casier judiciaire, les inscriptions et les formalités
relatives à l'état civil, les dispenses de législation seront réglées, jusqu'à signature d'un accord entre les parties, selon la procédure en vigueur avant le transfert
des compétences communes.

Article 5

Le présent accord entrera en vigueur simultanément avec l'accord en date de
ce jour portant transfert des compétences de la Communauté, pour ce qui les

concerne, à la République du Sénégal et à la République soudanaise, groupées au sein de la Fédération du Mali.

Fait à Paris, le 4 avril 1960.

Pour le Gouvernement de la République française :

Michel Debré.

Pour le Gouvernement de la République soudanaise :

Modibo Keita.

Pour le Gouvernement de la République du Sénégal :

Mamadou Dia.

Décret n° 61-536 du 17 mai 1961 portant publication d'un échange de lettres entre la République française et la République du Sénégal

Le Président de la République,

Sur le rapport du Premier ministre et du secrétaire d'État aux relations avec les États de la Communauté,

Vu la Constitution, et notamment les articles 52 à 55;

Vu la loi n° 60-569 du 17 juin 1960 portant approbation des accords particuliers signés le 4 avril 1960 entre le Gouvernement de la République française et les Gouvernements de la République du Sénégal et de la République soudanaise groupées au sein de la Fédération du Mali;

Vu la loi n° 60-682 du 18 juillet 1960 portant approbation des accords particuliers signés le 22 juin 1960 entre la République française et la Fédération du Mali,

Décrète :

Art. 1er. — L'échange de lettres entre le Premier ministre de la République française et le président du conseil des ministres de la République du Sénégal en date des 16 et 19 septembre 1960, qui est annexé au présent décret, sera publié au Journal officiel de la République française.

Art. 2. — Le Premier ministre et le secrétaire d'État aux relations avec les États de la Communauté sont chargés de l'exécution du présent décret.

Fait à Paris, le 17 mai 1961.

C. de Gaulle.

Par le Président de la République :

Le Premier ministre,
Michel Debré.

Le secrétaire d'État aux relations avec les États de la Communauté,
Jean Foyer.

611

RÉPUBLIQUE DU SÉNÉGAL

Dakar, le 16 septembre 1960.

LE PRÉSIDENT DU CONSEIL

—

A Monsieur Michel Debré,
Premier ministre de la République française.

Monsieur le Premier ministre,

J'ai l'honneur de porter à votre connaissance que le Gouvernement de la République du Sénégal estime qu'en vertu des principes du droit international relatif à la succession d'États la République du Sénégal est, pour ce qui la concerne, substituée aux droits et obligations résultant des accords de coopération, en date du 22 juin 1960, entre la République française et la Fédération du Mali, sans préjudice des adaptations qui, d'un commun accord, seraient reconnues nécessaires.

Je vous serais obligé de bien vouloir me faire savoir que tel est également le sentiment du Gouvernement de la République française.

Je vous prie d'agréer, monsieur le Premier ministre, l'expression de mes sentiments de très haute considération.

Signé : Mamadou DIA.

LE PREMIER MINISTRE

Paris, le 19 septembre 1960.

—

A Monsieur Mamadou Dia,
président du Conseil de la République du Sénégal.

Monsieur le Président,

Par lettre en date du 16 septembre, vous avez bien voulu m'adresser la communication suivante :

« J'ai l'honneur de porter à votre connaissance que le Gouvernement de la République du Sénégal estime qu'en vertu des principes du droit international relatif à la succession d'États la République du Sénégal est, pour ce qui la concerne, substituée aux droits et obligations résultant des accords de coopération, en date du 22 juin 1960, entre la République française et la Fédération du Mali, sans préjudice des adaptations qui, d'un commun accord, seraient reconnues nécessaires.

« Je vous serais obligé de bien vouloir me faire savoir que tel est également le sentiment du Gouvernement de la République française. »

J'ai l'honneur de vous faire savoir que le Gouvernement de la République française partage le point de vue de la République du Sénégal.

Je vous prie d'agréer, monsieur le Président, l'expression de mes sentiments de très haute considération.

Signé : Michel DEBRÉ.

ACCORD

CONCERNANT LES DISPOSITIONS TRANSITOIRES APPLICABLES JUSQU'À L'ENTRÉE
EN VIGUEUR DES ACCORDS DE COOPÉRATION ENTRE LA RÉPUBLIQUE FRAN-
ÇAISE ET LA FÉDÉRATION DU MALI.

———

Le Gouvernement de la République française, d'une part

Les Gouvernements de la République du Sénégal et de la République soudanaise, groupées au sein de la Fédération du Mali, d'autre part,

sont convenus de ce qui suit :

Article 1er

Jusqu'à l'entrée en vigueur des accords de coopération, les dispositions pré-
vues aux articles ci-après seront applicables.

Article 2

La République française continue d'assurer la protection diplomatique des ressortissants maliens à l'étranger.

Article 3

Les forces armées françaises continuent d'assurer les missions qui leur sont
actuellement assignées selon les règles et procédures applicables à la date de la
signature du présent accord.

Le comité de défense franco-malien, prévu à l'accord de coopération en matière
de défense, sera constitué sans délai pour préparer la mise sur pied des forces
armées maliennes.

Article 4

Les régimes actuels des échanges et de l'émission monétaire, les modalités de
coopération au sein de la zone franc, le statut du domaine, l'organisation générale
des transports extérieurs et communs et des télécommunications continueront
d'être appliqués.

Article 5

Le présent accord entrera en vigueur simultanément avec l'accord en date de
ce jour portant transfert des compétences de la Communauté, pour ce qui les
concerne, à la République du Sénégal et à la République soudanaise, groupées au
sein de la Fédération du Mali.

Fait à Paris, le 4 avril 1960.

Pour le Gouvernement de la République française :
Michel DEBRÉ.

Pour le Gouvernement de la République soudanaise :
Modibo KEITA.

Pour le Gouvernement de la République du Sénégal :
Mamadou DIA.

———

Republic of Seychelles

Although appearing on Portuguese navigational charts as early as 1505, the first European expedition to the Seychelles was made by the French Governor of Mauritius in 1742. The islands remained a Mauritian dependency under French control until 1815 when they were ceded to Great Britain by the Treaty of Paris following the defeat of Napoleon. Mauritius also became a British possession. Separate administrations were established for Mauritius and the Seychelles in 1888, and in 1903 the Seychelles became a separate British Crown Colony. Independence was granted by Great Britain on May 27, 1976, pursuant to the Seychelles Independence Act, to be effective on June 29.

Seychelles Act 1976

1976 CHAPTER 19

An Act to make provision for, and in connection with, the attainment by Seychelles of fully responsible status as a Republic within the Commonwealth.

[27th May 1976]

BE IT ENACTED by the Queen's most Excellent Majesty, by and with the advice and consent of the Lords Spiritual and Temporal, and Commons, in this present Parliament assembled, and by the authority of the same, as follows:—

1.—(1) On and after 29th June 1976 (in this Act referred to as " the appointed day ") Her Majesty's Government in the United Kingdom shall have no responsibility for the government of Seychelles.

(2) No Act of the Parliament of the United Kingdom passed on or after the appointed day shall extend, or be deemed to extend, to Seychelles as part of its law.

2. Her Majesty may by Order in Council (to be laid before Parliament after being made) make provision for the constitution of Seychelles as a Republic on the appointed day.

Seychelles Independence Act 1976, c.19

Republic of Sierra Leone

Located on the coast of West Africa, the
Republic of Sierra Leone is bounded to the north and
east by the Republic of Guinea, and to the south by
Liberia..Originally several dozen independent
political units, Sierra Leone became a crown
colony to Great Britain in1808. In 1896, Great
Britain declared its protectorat over the interior
of the country. After World War II parlimentary
institutions were introduced to direct Sierra
Leone toward independent status. The Sierra Leone
Independence Act of 1961 granted independence
effective as of April 27, 1961. On that date a
new constitution was adopted, which was immediately
recognized by Great Britain.

An Act to make provision for, and in connection with, the attainment by Sierra Leone of fully responsible status within the Commonwealth.   [28th March, 1961]

BE it enacted by the Queen's most Excellent Majesty, by and with the advice and consent of the Lords Spiritual and Temporal, and Commons, in this present Parliament assembled, and by the authority of the same, as follows:—

1.—(1) On the twenty-seventh day of April, nineteen hundred and sixty-one (in this Act referred to as " the appointed day "), the Sierra Leone Colony and the Sierra Leone Protectorate (of which the combined area is that specified in the First Schedule to this Act) shall together constitute part of Her Majesty's dominions under the name of Sierra Leone.

(2) No Act of the Parliament of the United Kingdom passed on or after the appointed day shall extend, or be deemed to extend, to Sierra Leone as part of the law thereof, and as from that day—

 (a) Her Majesty's Government in the United Kingdom shall have no responsibility for the government of Sierra Leone ; and

 (b) the provisions of the Second Schedule to this Act shall have effect with respect to legislative powers in Sierra Leone.

(3) Without prejudice to subsection (2) of this section, nothing in subsection (1) thereof shall affect the operation in Sierra Leone or any part thereof on and after the appointed day of any enactment, or any other instrument having the effect of law, passed or made with respect thereto before that day.

Sierra Leone Independence Act, 9 & 10 Elizabeth 2, c.16 (1961)

Republic of Singapore

Singapore is made up of one major island and several small ones at the southern end of the Malay Peninsula. Established by the East Indian Company in 1819, the Republic of Singapore became part of the British Straights Settlement in 1867. During World War II the island was occupied by Japan. After the war it became a separate crown colony. In September 1964 Singapore joined the Federation of Malaysia. On August 7, 1965, severe internal conflict led to Singapore's separation from the federation effective August 9th. The Singapore Act 1966 recognized Singapore's status as an independent sovereign state within the Commonwealth.

No. 8206. AN AGREEMENT RELATING TO THE SEPARATION OF SINGAPORE FROM MALAYSIA AS AN INDEPENDENT AND SOVEREIGN STATE. SIGNED AT KUALA LUMPUR, ON 7 AUGUST 1965

An Agreement dated the 7th day of August, 1965, and made between the Government of Malaysia of the one part and the Government of Singapore of the other part.

Whereas Malaysia was established on the 16th day of September, 1963, by a federation of the existing states of the Federation of Malaya and the States of Sabah, Sarawak and Singapore into one independent and sovereign nation ;

And whereas it has been agreed by the parties hereto that fresh arrangements should be made for the order and good government of the territories comprised in Malaysia by the separation of Singapore from Malaysia upon which Singapore shall become an independent and sovereign state and nation separate from and independent of Malaysia and so recognised by the Government of Malaysia ;

Now therefore it is agreed and declared as follows :

Article I

This Agreement may be cited as the Independence of Singapore Agreement, 1965.

Article II

Singapore shall cease to be a State of Malaysia on the 9th day of August, 1965, (hereinafter referred to as "Singapore Day") and shall become an independent and sovereign state separate from and independent of Malaysia and recognised as such by the Government of Malaysia ; and the Government of Malaysia will proclaim and enact the constitutional instruments annexed to this Agreement in the manner hereinafter appearing.

Article III

The Government of Malaysia will declare by way of proclamation in the form set out in Annex A to this Agreement that Singapore is an independent and sovereign state separate from and independent of Malaysia and recognised as such by the Government of Malaysia.

Article IV

The Government of Malaysia will take such steps as may be appropriate and available to them to secure the enactment by the Parliament of Malaysia of an Act in the form set out in Annex B to this Agreement and will ensure that it is made operative as from Singapore Day, providing for the relinquishment of sovereignty and jurisdiction of the Government of Malaysia in respect of Singapore so that the said sovereignty and jurisdiction shall on such relinquishment vest in the Government of Singapore in accordance with this Agreement and the constitutional instruments annexed.

Article V

The parties hereto will enter into a treaty on external defence and mutual assistance providing that :

(1) the parties hereto will establish a joint defence council for purposes of external defence and mutual assistance ;

(2) the Government of Malaysia will afford to the Government of Singapore such assistance as may be considered reasonable and adequate for external defence, and in consideration thereof, the Government of Singapore will contribute from its own armed forces such units thereof as may be considered reasonable and adequate for such defence ;

(3) the Government of Singapore will afford to the Government of Malaysia the right to continue to maintain the bases and other facilities used by its military forces within Singapore and will permit the Government of Malaysia to make such use of these bases and facilities as the Government of Malaysia may consider necessary for the purpose of external defence ;

(4) each party will undertake not to enter into any treaty or agreement with a foreign country which may be detrimental to the independence and defence of the territory of the other party.

Article VI

The parties hereto will on and after Singapore Day co-operate in economic affairs for their mutual benefit and interest and for this purpose may set up such joint committees or councils as may from time to time be agreed upon.

Article VII

The provisions of Annex J and K of the Agreement relating to Malaysia dated the 9th day of July, 1963 are hereby expressly rescinded as from the date of this Agreement.

Article VIII

With regard to any agreement entered into between the Government of Singapore and any other country or corporate body which has been guaranteed by the Government of Malaysia, the Government of Singapore hereby undertakes to negotiate with such country or corporate body to enter into a fresh agreement releasing the Government of Malaysia of its liabilities and obligations under the said guarantee, and the Government of Singapore hereby undertakes to indemnify the Government of Malaysia fully for any liabilities, obligations or damage which it may suffer as a result of the said guarantee.

IN WITNESS WHEREOF, the undersigned, being duly authorised thereto, have signed this Agreement.

DONE this 7th day of August, 1965, in two copies of which one shall be deposited with each of the Parties.

ANNEX "A"

PROCLAMATION ON SINGAPORE

In the name of God, the Compassionate, the Merciful. Praise be to God, the Lord of the Universe, and may the benediction and peace of God be upon Our Leader Muhammad and upon all His Relations and Friends.

WHEREAS Malaysia was established on the 16th day of September, 1963, by a federation of the existing states of the Federation of Malaya and the States of Sabah, Sarawak and Singapore into one independent and sovereign nation ;

AND WHEREAS by an Agreement made on the 7th day of August in the year one thousand nine hundred and sixty-five between the Government of Malaysia of the one part and the Government of Singapore of the other part it was agreed that Singapore should cease to be a state of Malaysia and should thereupon become an independent and sovereign state and nation separate from and independent of Malaysia ;

AND WHEREAS it was also agreed by the parties to the said Agreement that, upon the separation of Singapore from Malaysia, the Government of Malaysia shall relinquish its sovereignty and jurisdiction in respect of Singapore so that the said sovereignty and jurisdiction shall on such relinquishment vest in the Government of Singapore ;

Now in the name of God the Compassionate, the Merciful, I, Tunku Abdul Rahman Putra Al-Haj Ibni Almarhum Sultan Abdul Hamid Halim Shah, Prime Minister of Malaysia, with the concurrence and approval of His Majesty the Yang di-Pertuan Agong of Malaysia, do hereby declare and proclaim that, as from the 9th day of August in the year one thousand nine hundred and sixty-five, Singapore shall cease to be a State of Malaysia and shall forever be an independent and sovereign state and nation separate from and independent of Malaysia, and that the Government of Malaysia recognises the present Government of Singapore as an independent and sovereign government of Singapore and will always work in friendship and co-operation with it.

Y. T. M. TUNKU ABDUL RAHMAN PUTRA AL-HAJ, K.O.M.

563 United Nations Treaty Series, pp. 90-99, (1965)

Singapore Act 1966

1966 CHAPTER 29

An Act to make provision in connection with the establishment of Singapore as an independent sovereign state within the Commonwealth.   [9th August 1966]

B E IT ENACTED by the Queen's most Excellent Majesty, by and with the advice and consent of the Lords Spiritual and Temporal, and Commons, in this present Parliament assembled, and by the authority of the same, as follows:—

1.—(1) Subject to the provisions of this Act, all law which, whether being a rule of law or a provision of an Act of Parliament or of any other enactment or instrument whatsoever, was in force immediately before 9th August, 1965 (being the day on which Singapore became an independent sovereign state separate from and independent of Malaysia) or, having been passed or made before that day comes or has come into force thereafter, shall, unless and until provision to the contrary is made by Parliament or some other authority having power in that behalf, have the same operation in relation to Singapore, and persons and things belonging to or connected with Singapore, as it would have, apart from this subsection, if Singapore had not become an independent sovereign state as aforesaid.

(2) The enactments specified in the Schedule to this Act (being enactments applicable to Commonwealth countries having fully responsible status) shall have effect in accordance with the provisions of that Schedule.

(3) Subsection (1) of this section applies to law of, or of any part of, the United Kingdom, the Channel Islands and the Isle of Man, and, in relation only to an enactment of the Parliament of the United Kingdom or any Order in Council made by virtue of any such enactment whereby any such enactment applies in relation to Singapore, to law of any other country or territory to which that enactment or Order extends.

(4) This section shall be deemed to have had effect from 9th August, 1965.

Singapore Independence Act, Elizabeth 2, c.29 (1966)

Somali Democratic Republic

The Somali Democratic Republic is located
on the east coast of Africa and is bordered to
the west by Ethiopia. Arab influence was predomin-
ate from the 10th century until the 19th century
when European domination began. During the late
19th century Great Britain established a protectorate in northern Somali while Italy controlled the
southern region. During World War II the British
occupied southern Somali. In 1950, this region
became a United Nations trust territory under
Italian administration. A Royal Proclamation
on June 23, 1960, terminated the protectorate of
Great Britain. On June 27, 1960, the former
British protectorate joined the Italian protectorate
in a Union. In 1969 the country was renamed the
Somali Democratic Republic.

SOMALI DEMOCRATIC REPUBLIC

ROYAL PROCLAMATION terminating Her Majesty's protection over the Somaliland Protectorate.--
London, 23rd June, 1960

ELIZABETH R.

Whereas the territories in Africa known as
the Somaliland Protectorate are under Our protection:

And whereas by treaty, grant, usage, sufferance and other lawful means We have power and
jurisdiction in the Somaliland Protectorate:

And whereas it is intended that the Somaliland Protectorate shall become an independent
country on the twenty-sixth day of June 1960
(hereinafter referred to as "the appointed day").

Now, therefore, We do hereby, by and with
the advice of Our Privy Council, proclaim and declare that, as from the beginning of the appointed day, Our protection over the territories known
as the Somaliland Protectorate shall cease, and
all treaties and agreements in force immediately
before the appointed day between Us or Our Government of the United Kingdom of Great Britain and
Northern Ireland and any of the Tribes of the
said territories, all Our obligations existing
immediately before that day towards the said
territories and all functions, powers, rights,
authority or jurisdiction exercisable by Us immediately before that day in or in relation to the
said territories by treaty, grant, usage, sufferance or otherwise, shall lapse.

Given at Our Court at Buckingham Palace this
twenty-third day of June in the year of our Lord
one thousand nine hundred and sixty, and in the
ninth year of Our Reign.

GOD SAVE THE QUEEN

LAW of Union between Somaliland and Somalia.--
     Hargeisa, 27th June, 1960

     Whereas the State of Somaliland achieved in-
dependence and ceased to be under British protection or within the jurisdiction and sovereignty
of Her Britannic Majesty on the 26th day of June,
1960, being Muharram 1st 1379, and

     Whereas the State of Somalia achieved its
independence and ceased to have the status of a
Trust Territory of the United Nations Organisation administered by the Republic of Italy on the
1st day of July, 1960, being Muharram 6th 1379,
and

     Whereas it is the will of the peoples of
Somaliland and Somalia that their States shall
unite and shall forever be united in the Somali
Republic.

     Now we the signatories hereof being the duly
authorised representatives of the peoples of
Somaliland and Somalia and having vested in us
the power to make and enter into this Law of
Union on behalf of our respective States and
peoples do hereby solemnly and in the name of God
the Compassionate and Merciful agree as follows:

     1. (a) The State of Somaliland and the State
of Somalia do hereby unite and shall forever remain united in a new, independent, democratic,
unitary republic the name whereof shall be the
Somali Republic.

     (b) The Capital of the Somali Republic shall
be Mogadishu.

     2. Subject to the express provisions of this
Act of Union the Union hereby constituted shall
be upon the following conditions:

     (1) That the component administrative units
of the Government of the Somali Republic until
more suitable administrative arrangements are
made, shall be firstly the region comprising the

627

territories contained in the boundaries of the presently existing State of Somaliland (hereinafter referred to as the Northern Region) and secondly those presently existing territories which comprise the six Regions of Mijertein, Mudugh, Hiran, Benadir, Upper Juba and Lower Juba all in Somalia (hereinafter collectively referred to as the second-named Regions).

(2) That the existing laws presently in force in the Northern Region and in the second-named Regions respectively shall remain in full force and effect within the respective territories where the same presently apply and shall not have force or effect beyond those respective territories where the same presently apply.

(3) That all persons now serving the Somaliland Government in the Northern Region and the Government of Somalia in the second-named Regions respectively shall continue to serve the Government of the Somali Republic upon terms not less favourable than those at present applicable to them.

(4) That the Courts as presently constituted in the aforesaid Northern Region and the aforesaid second-named Regions shall continue to exercise within their respective territories the jurisdiction which is conferred upon them by presently existing law and shall be Courts of the Somali Republic.

Republic of South Africa

European settlement began in 1652. The
Cape of Good Hope remained a Dutch possession
until 1795, when it was taken by the British.
After a brief period of renewed Dutch rule, the
colony was occupied by Britain in 1806. By the
terms of the Treaty of Paris in 1814, the Cape
of Good Hope passed to Great Britain. Following
the South African War of 1899-1902, the new
states that had been established by the Dutch
settlers, the Transvaal and the Orange Free State,
were joined with the older British colonies, to
form the Dominion of the Union of South Africa,
by a September 20, 1909, Act of Parliament. South
Africa became a republic outside the Commonwealth
in 1961.

An Act to constitute the Union of South Africa.

[20th September 1909.]

WHEREAS it is desirable for the welfare and future progress of South Africa that the several British Colonies therein should be united under one Government in a legislative union under the Crown of Great Britain and Ireland :

And whereas it is expedient to make provision for the union of the Colonies of the Cape of Good Hope, Natal, the Transvaal, and the Orange River Colony on terms and conditions to which they have agreed by resolution of their respective Parliaments, and to define the executive, legislative, and judicial powers to be exercised in the government of the Union :

And whereas it is expedient to make provision for the establishment of provinces with powers of legislation and administration in local matters and in such other matters as may be specially reserved for provincial legislation and administration :

And whereas it is expedient to provide for the eventual admission into the Union or transfer to the Union of such parts of South Africa as are not originally included therein :

Be it therefore enacted by the King's most Excellent Majesty, by and with the advice and consent of the Lords Spiritual and Temporal, and Commons, in this present Parliament assembled, and by the authority of the same, as follows : ,

PART I.

PRELIMINARY.

1. This Act may be cited as the South Africa Act, 1909.

2. In this Act, unless it is otherwise expressed or implied, the words "the Union" shall be taken to mean the Union of South Africa as constituted under this Act, and the words "Houses of Parliament," "House of Parliament," or "Parliament," shall be taken to mean the Parliament of the Union.

3. The provisions of this Act referring to the King shall extend to His Majesty's heirs and successors in the sovereignty of the United Kingdom of Great Britain and Ireland.

PART II.

THE UNION.

4. It shall be lawful for the King, with the advice of the Privy Council, to declare by proclamation that, on and after a day therein appointed, not being later than one year after the passing of this Act, the Colonies of the Cape of Good Hope, Natal, the Transvaal, and the Orange River Colony, hereinafter called the Colonies, shall be united in a Legislative Union under one Government under the name of the Union of South Africa. On and after the day appointed by such proclamation the Government and Parliament of the Union shall have full power and authority within the limits of the Colonies, but the King may at any time after the proclamation appoint a governor-general for the Union.

5. The provisions of this Act shall, unless it is otherwise expressed or implied, take effect on and after the day so appointed.

6. The Colonies mentioned in section four shall become original provinces of the Union under the names of Cape of Good Hope, Natal, Transvaal, and Orange Free State, as the case may be. The original provinces shall have the same limits as the respective Colonies at the establishment of the Union.

7. Upon any colony entering the Union, the Colonial Boundaries Act, 1895, and every other Act applying to any of the Colonies as being self-governing colonies or colonies with responsible government, shall cease to apply to that colony, but as from the date when this Act takes effect every such Act of Parliament shall apply to the Union.

An Act to Constitute the Union of South Africa,
9 Edward 7, c.9 (1909)

Union of Soviet Socialist Republic

First emerging as a nation of Slavic tribes
in the eight and ninth century, Russia developed
close ties with Byzantium in the 10th century.
Dissension among feudal princes and invasions by
nomadic tribes continued until the Tartar invasion
in the 13 century. The rule by the Tartars began
to decline in 1380 and by 1462 the first czar,
Ivan the Great, was in power. The Romanov family
rose to power in the 1600th century and continued
for almost 300 years. The first revolutionary
currents against the czarist rule came as early as
1825 with the return of soldiers from the Napoleonic
Wars. In 1898 the Russian Social Democratic
Party was formed promising that the "proletariat
will cast from itself the yoke of autocracy."
A 1905 revolution was put down. With military
defeat in World War I social unrest continued and
led to the February Revolution of 1917 and the
formation of the Provisional Government. The
Provisional Government was unable to solve the
country's problems and was overthrown on November
7, 1917 by the Bolsheviks led by Vladimir Lenin.
Under Lenin the Russian Socialist Federated Republic was formed on July 10, 1918.

TO THE CITIZENS OF RUSSIA!

The Provisional Government has been deposed. State power has passed into the hands of the organ of the Petrograd Soviet of Workers' and Soldiers' Deputies—the Revolutionary Military Committee, which heads the Petrograd proletariat and the garrison.

The cause for which the people have fought, namely, the immediate offer of a democratic peace, the abolition of landed proprietorship, workers' control over production, and the establishment of Soviet power—this cause has been secured.

Long live the revolution of workers, soldiers and peasants!

Revolutionary Military Committee
of the Petrograd Soviet of Workers'
and Soldiers' Deputies

10 a.m., October 25, 1917.

Rabochy i Soldat No. 8,
October 25 (November 7), 1917

Published according
to the newspaper text verified
with the manuscript

FOR BREAD AND PEACE

Two questions now take precedence over all other political questions—the question of bread and the question of peace. The imperialist war, the war between the biggest and richest banking firms, Britain and Germany, that is being waged for world domination, the division of the spoils, for the plunder of small and weak nations; this horrible, criminal war has ruined all countries, exhausted all peoples, and confronted mankind with the alternative—either sacrifice all civilisation and perish or throw off the capitalist yoke in the revolutionary way, do away with the rule of the bourgeoisie and win socialism and durable peace.

If socialism is not victorious, peace between the capitalist states will be only a truce, an interlude, a time of preparation for a fresh slaughter of the peoples. Peace and bread are the basic demands of the workers and the exploited. The war has made these demands extremely urgent. The war has brought hunger to the most civilised countries, to those most culturally developed. On the other hand, the war, as a tremendous historical process, has accelerated social development to an unheard-of degree. Capitalism had developed into imperialism, i.e., into monopoly capitalism, and under the influence of the war it has become state monopoly capitalism. We have now reached the stage of world economy that is the immediate stepping stone to socialism.

The socialist revolution that has begun in Russia is, therefore, only the beginning of the world socialist revolution. Peace and bread, the overthrow of the bourgeoisie, revolutionary means for the healing of war wounds, the complete victory of socialism—such are the aims of the struggle.

Petrograd, December 14, 1917.

Written in Russian
on December 14 (27), 1917
Signed: *Lenin*

First published in German
in May 1918 in the newspaper
Jugend-Internationale No. 11
Signed: *W. Lenin*

First published in Russian
(translated from the German)
in 1927 in the book *Transactions
of the Lenin Institute*, Vol. II

DECLARATION OF RIGHTS
OF THE WORKING AND EXPLOITED PEOPLE

The Constituent Assembly resolves:

1. Russia is hereby proclaimed a Republic of Soviets of Workers', Soldiers' and Peasants' Deputies. All power, centrally and locally, is vested in these Soviets.

2. The Russian Soviet Republic is established on the principle of a free union of free nations, as a federation of Soviet national republics.

Its fundamental aim being to abolish all exploitation of man by man, to completely eliminate the division of society into classes, to mercilessly crush the resistance of the exploiters, to establish a socialist organisation of society and to achieve the victory of socialism in all countries, the Constituent Assembly further resolves:

1. Private ownership of land is hereby abolished. All land together with all buildings, farm implements and other appurtenances of agricultural production, is proclaimed the property of the entire working people.

2. The Soviet laws on workers' control and on the Supreme Economic Council are hereby confirmed for the purpose of guaranteeing the power of the working people over the exploiters and as a first step towards the complete conversion of the factories, mines, railways, and other means of production and transport into the property of the workers' and peasants' state.

3. The conversion of all banks into the property of the workers' and peasants' state is hereby confirmed as one of the conditions for the emancipation of the working people from the yoke of capital.

4. For the purpose of abolishing the parasitic sections of society, universal labour conscription is hereby instituted.

5. To ensure the sovereign power of the working people, and to eliminate all possibility of the restoration of the power of the exploiters, the arming of the working people, the creation of a socialist Red Army of workers and peasants and the complete disarming of the propertied classes are hereby decreed.

1. Expressing its firm determination to wrest mankind from the clutches of finance capital and imperialism, which have in this most criminal of wars drenched the world in blood, the Constituent Assembly whole-heartedly endorses the policy pursued by Soviet power of denouncing the secret treaties, organising most extensive fraternisation with the workers and peasants of the armies in the war, and achieving at all costs, by revolutionary means, a democratic peace between the nations, without annexations and indemnities and on the basis of the free self-determination of nations.

2. With the same end in view, the Constituent Assembly insists on a complete break with the barbarous policy of bourgeois civilisation, which has built the prosperity of the exploiters belonging to a few chosen nations on the enslavement of hundreds of millions of working people in Asia, in the colonies in general, and in the small countries.

The Constituent Assembly welcomes the policy of the Council of People's Commissars in proclaiming the complete independence of Finland, commencing the evacuation of troops from Persia, and proclaiming freedom of self-determination for Armenia.[155]

3. The Constituent Assembly regards the Soviet law on the cancellation of the loans contracted by the governments of the tsar, the landowners and the bourgeoisie as a first blow struck at international banking, finance capital, and expresses the conviction that Soviet power will firmly pursue this path until the international workers' uprising against the yoke of capital has completely triumphed.

Having been elected on the basis of party lists drawn up prior to the October Revolution, when the people were not yet in a position to rise *en masse* against the exploiters, had not yet experienced the full strength of resistance of the latter in defence of their class privileges, and had not yet applied themselves in practice to the task of building socialist society, the Constituent Assembly considers that it would be fundamentally wrong, even formally, to put itself in opposition to Soviet power.

In essence the Constituent Assembly considers that now, when the people are waging the last fight against their exploiters, there can be no place for exploiters in any government body. Power must be vested wholly and entirely in the working people and their authorised representatives—the Soviets of Workers', Soldiers' and Peasants' Deputies.

Supporting Soviet power and the decrees of the Council of People's Commissars, the Constituent Assembly considers that its own task is confined to establishing the fundamental principles of the socialist reconstruction of society.

At the same time, endeavouring to create a really free and voluntary, and therefore all the more firm and stable, union of the working classes of all the nations of Russia, the Constituent Assembly confines its own task to setting up the fundamental principles of a federation of Soviet Republics of Russia, while leaving it to the workers and peasants of each nation to decide independently at their own authoritative Congress of Soviets whether they wish to participate in the federal government and in the other federal Soviet institutions, and on what terms. Published in *Pravda* No. 2 and *Izvestia* No. 2, January 4(17), 1918

V. I. Lenin, Collected Works, Vol. 26, Sept. 1917 - Feb. 1918, Progress Publishers, Moscow, 1964.

Written not later than
January 3 (16), 1918

Published in *Pravda* No. 2 and
Izvestia No. 2, January 4(17), 1918

Published according
to the manuscript

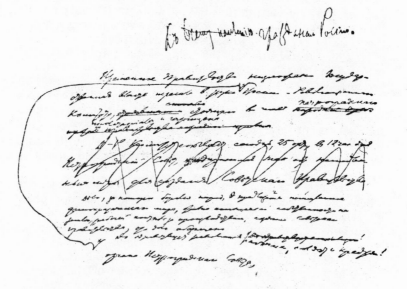

Facsimile of the manuscript of "To the Citizens of Russia!",
written by Lenin on October 25 (November 7), 1917
Reduced.

10 a.m., October 25, 1917.

Rabochy i Soldat No. 8,
October 25 (November 7), 1917

Published according
to the newspaper text verified
with the manuscript

Spanish State

Spain was originally settled by Iberians, Basques and Celts and then overrun by Carthaginian armies in the second century before Christ. The Romans defeated the Carthaginians, took effective control of the Iberian peninsula after the defeat of Carthage and ruled until the Visigoths took power in the Fifth Century A.D. This was followed by Muslim occupation of parts of the peninsula. The African muslims were not driven out of Iberia until after the joinder of the provinces of Aragon and Castile. The royal marriage of the King of Sicily (Prince of Aragon) to the heiress to the throne of Castille marked the beginning of the Kingdom of Spain, at the same time ending the period of foreign occupation. Thus, Spain may be said to have been formed on January 7, 1469, the date of the royal marriage agreement.

Our don Fernando, King of Sicily [King of Aragon] by the grace of God, who together with the Very Serene King (Juan II), our very honorable father, in the said kingdom of Sicily are co-regents and co-rulers, and first-born in all his kingdoms and lands, Governor General, Prince of Girona, Duke of Monblanc, Count of Ribagorza, Lord of the city of Balaguer; due to the fact we hope to contract matrimony, God willing, with the Most Serene Princess dona Isabella, first-born princess heir to the thrones and lordships of Castille and Leon: likewise, because in the times of such marriages the prince kings who hope to succeed through this line in the kingdoms and even lordships, it is the custom to swear to the agreed and written between both parts, the underwritten chapters and each thing and part of them with all the agreements and conditions contained in all and each of them to uphold, observe and guard!

1. Firstly, that as Catholic King and Lord we will be obedient and devout to the commands and exhortations of the Holy Apostolic See and to the Pope, and that we will entrust the prelates, and religious and ecclesiastical persons with the honor and reverence that is owed to the Holy Church and to the ecclesiastical liberty.

2. Item, that we will treat with all filial obedience, devotion, and reverence, King don Enrique, her brother, as if he were our father.

3. Item, that we will observe and make observe and administrate justice in all those mentioned Kingdoms and Lordships of Castille and Leon, in the Court as well as in the other cities, villages, and places in them, and that we will listen to and deal with clemency all who come to us for justice, as a good and Catholic King should, and that we will piously help the poor and the unfortunate.

4. Item, that for the comfort of the towns and their people we will give them hearings and we will treat them, in the dealing of justice as well

as all other things, with all the love and clemency that the good King owes his subjects.

5. Item, that we will keep and observe the institutions and the laudable practices, laws, decrees, and privileges of those mentioned kingdoms and lordships, and all the cities, villages, and place of these kingdoms, as the kings usually do when they take command over them.

6. Item, that we will treat all the lords, be they great or small and any others, well and with all the love, affection, and honor, as is hoped and expected that a good King do with his subjects.

7. Item, that we will observe and watch the peace made between said Lord King Enrique, her brother and her (F 1028), and that we will permit and allow that His Highness reign peacefully for all the days of his life without any hindrance as long as he complies with all that has been promised to her in the Capitulations of said peace.

8. Item, that we will keep and conserve in the Council of the ruling of those said kingdoms and in the other privileges, honors, and rights, the illustrious Archbishop of Toledo, Primate of the Spains, Mayor Chancellor of Castille, our very dear and loved uncle; and also the Archbishop of Seville and the illustrious and the magnificent Maestre of Santiago and the Count of Plasencia, who were instrumental in the good conclusion of said peace and in swearing the said Most Serene Princess, dona Isabella, as their heiress and successor; and the Bishop of Burgos and the other Grandees, Lords and Noblemen who would conform to her and our service, and that we will not do any royal or personal harm without due reason and without her expressed consent and will.

9. Item, that we will personally go to those said kingdoms to reside and be in them with the said Most Serene Princess, and that we will not wander or leave from them without her will and advice, and that we will not take her from said kingdoms without her consent and will.

10. Item, that if God gives us any offsprings, son or daughter, as no less is to be expected, that we will never separate them from her, nor will we take them from these said kingdoms; especially the first-born that we might have from her.

11. Item, that we will not anger nor will we do any favors to any city, village or fortress of these said kingdoms, neither de jure nor anything else pertaining to the Royal Crown, without the consent and will of the said Most Serene Princess; and that if the contrary is done, then be it had for naught.

12. Item, that all of the privileges, letters and any other writings that may be written, done or sent, either by her or by us, are to be signed jointly, so that they are all signed by hand by both, and that in the entitlement of those said kingdoms and lordships, both we and she are to entitle; and likewise in the other kingdoms and domains that we here have or shall have.

13. Item, that we will not place anybody in the Council of said kingdoms except Castillians and natives of said kingdoms, without consent and profound deliberation of the said Most Serene Princess.

14. Item, that we will allow the said Princess to receive and to take for herself all of the loyalty oaths of all and any city, village and site or fortress of the said kingdoms and lordships of Castille and Leon; and that we will not place nor send to said cities, villages, and sites, or fortresses, magistrates or examiners, or other officials, except those natives to those kingdoms and lordships, and that she will determine and decide.

15. Item, that we will not give occupancy of any fortress in the said kingdoms and lordships except to the natives and to whom the said Most Serene Princess chooses and wants to place in them, to serve both of them and the good of the kingdoms.

16. Item, that whenever the said Most Serene Princess may want to do any favor to any town or

site, either de jure or of anything else, that she
be able to do it without any impediment and that
we will observe such favor as if we had done it
ourselves; and that having her done any favor or
given her word and faith about it or that she may
give or give from here on, that we shall keep it and
obey it as she herself would.

17. Item, that whenever there is a vacancy in
an archbisopric, bishopric, priorship, abbey, or
benefice, that we will consult with her, as is most
suited for the service of God and the good of the
churches, and well being of the souls of all, and
the honor of said kingdoms, and that the ones who
are appointed, they be knowledgeable.

18. Item, that we will not take away the
favors granted until today, not only to cities,
towns, sites and fortresses, be the de jure or anything else; but also to any noblemen and any other
ecclesiastical person, and even secular that were
done by Your Most Serene King or any other relative
of his or ours or servant in those said kingdoms
and lordships and that we will do no change in all
or part of it for any reason or cause without the
consent and firm will of the said Most Serene
Princess; but that we will keep and maintain them
in such favors.

19. Item, that for any offense that the said
King our father, or any of his, might have suffered
during past times in those said kingdoms, and likewise any anger that the said King our father and
we, and any of his or ours, had for any person of
those said kingdoms, we will not take any actions
against them; moreover, for the service of God,
and the contemplation of the said Most Serene Princess, we pardon all, as did Our Lord in good and
proper example for us.

20. Item, that we will keep all the servants
and maids of the said Most Serene Princess in any
honor, position and office that are near her; and
that we will keep, love and respect them as she
herself does; and that we leave all the tenancies
of any city, town or place to whom she has granted
them; and likewise all of the offices of said
towns, cities and places that they now have or will

hold by her orders from here on.

21.   Item, that we will not make any movement in these kingdoms for any cause or reason without her consent and determined advice.

22.   Item, that after we in conjunction with the said Most Serene Princess, as one, have the Kingdoms and Lordships of Castílle and Leon under our power, that we be obligated to make war against the Moors, enemies of the Saintly Catholic Church, as did and have done the other Catholic Kings who preceded in the said kingdoms, that we be held to pay and that we shall pay the tenancies of the fortresses that border along the frontier with the Moors, as the other Kings have done and is the custom.

23.   Item, that we will not undertake any enterprise of war or confederation of peace with any king or neighboring lord or with nobleman or sire of those said kingdoms, whether they (the men) be ecclesiastical or secular, without the will and knowledge of the said Most Serene Princess and her determined advice, so that everything may be done, and is done for the service of God our Lord, the honor of both, and the good of the kingdoms.

24.   And our above-mentioned don Fernando, king in the places that the queens of Aragon have and are used to having as their dominions - such as Aragon, Borja, and Magallon; Valencia, Elche and Cribilen; and Sicily, Zaragoza and Catalonia; and those that after the said matrimony we hope to receive - that is all of the above-mentioned kingdoms and lordships of Castille and Leon and the rest - to rule, govern, and reign as one with her, as has been stated, with the will and consent of the said Most Serene King our father, we add in crex and betterment for her all of the said kingdoms and the other kingdoms and lordships that the King our father and we have, and likewise the Principalities, only; that there not be heads in such Principalities, which she will know how to choose and demand so that she can possess, have and reign in her lifetime, and so that she may take and does take, as Lady of them, all of the rents and rights, with all of the other high medium and low

jurisdictions, and that she place mayors or any
other officials, as long as they be natives and
not foreigners to them. And even if God should
send for us before her, after the matrimony has
been consummated, and even if we would not have any
offsprings from her, may God forbid, that she have
and possess them; as long as after her death all
of them, those in betterment as well the other domains, they return to us or our heirs to whom the
rights may belong.

25. And besides this, if by chance it may be
found that the Queen Mary, our aunt, wife of the
King, don Alfredo of Aragon, of glorious memory,
our uncle, or the Queen Juana, my lady mother,
whose soul may God have, had in their time more of
these places or other dominions in the said kingdoms and dominions, that they be, after the marriage takes place, given with all of the above
mentioned to the said Most Serene Princess, Donna
Isabella our our wife and woman that by then she
will be.

26. And likewise we promise and give to the
said Most Serene Princess in crex dowry and betterment, besides all of the above mentioned, as much
as the said Queen Maria obtained from the said
King Alfonso in crex and betterment above the dowry that she brought or was promised to her.

27. And more, within four months starting
after the above mentioned marriage between us and
the said Most Serene Princess has taken place and
has had the desired effect between us and the said
Most Serene Princess who will already be our wife
and woman by then, that we will send her 100,000
gold florins for the keeping of her honor and
position and any other necessities that could come
about; and that from now on, as her royal position
necessitates, we will keep and give her what is
due to her.

28. Item, that if the matters in Castille
came to rupture, may God forbid it, that we will
personally go there with 4,000 paid lances, while
the rupture lasts, and that the money for the said
4,000 lances we will carry with us, and that we be
held, for as long as the rupture in those said

kingdoms lasts, for the paying of the said 4,000 lances, and if while this is the will of the said Most Serene Princess, or that she would send for us, or in any other way that necessity might require, that we will go to her.

29. Item, that we will accordingly marry the maids that live and shall live with her, and as may be the will and pleasure of the said Most Serene Princess.

30. For greater surety, corroboration and firmness of the present writing, and of everything agreed in it and everything and part of it, that as is promised by us, by the faith and the word of the King, we promise and even swear to God and to Saint Mary, to the four Gospels, and on this sign of the cross + made with our right hand, that this which is written we shall maintain, uphold and observe, and that we will make, maintain, uphold and observe without any contradiction, and that we shall not go directly or indirectly, tacitly or secretly against it or part of it, at no time, in any way, or for any reason. In order to have, guard, keep and obey this, we oblige all of us and our fiscal and patrimonial property that we now have or will ever have.

31. About which we give testimony in this our Letter, signed with our name and that of the undersigned secretary, and sealed with our seal, that it was done in the town of Cervera on the seventh day of the month of January of the year of the birth of Our Lord of 1469, and the second year of the said our Kingdom of Sicily.

32. And that we, don John, by the grace of God, King of Aragon, of Navarra, of Sicily, of Valencia, of the Mallorcas, of Cerdena, of Corcica, Count of Barcelona, Duke of Atenas and of Neopatria, and still Count of Rosellon and of Cerdania, having seen and reviewed the present writing, and all of the chapters, agreements and conditions and pacts contained in it, done and signed by the Most Serene King of Sicily, don Ferdinand, our very dear and loved firstborn and governor general, and everything in it contained, we confess and know that the said King Ferdinand, our son, has granted, promised

and signed that writing and chapters.

And that we, accepting as we do, as acceptable, firm and valid, we promise by the faith and word of a King and we even swear to God and to Saint Mary, and to the four Gospels and to this sign of the cross made by our hand, to have for acceptable, firm, stable and valid all of the above mentioned and every and any part of it, and that we shall not go against it or part of it, now or ever. In testimony of which, we have done the present writing at the foot and end of said agreement, writing, and chapters, signed by our name and that of the under-signed secretary, and sealed by our seal, and that it was done in the city of Zaragoza on the twelfth day of the month of January of the year of the birth of Our Lord, 1469, and of our Kingdom of Navarra, 44 , and of our other Kingdoms, 12.

[Signatures.]

Translated by Eladio Cortesano Albert Foreste. From: Alfonso Garcia-Gall, Antologia de fuentes del Antiguo Derecho. Manuel de Historio del Derecho Español (Madrid, 1967), Vol. II.

Republic of Sri Lanka

Sri Lanka, formerly Ceylon, is an island
nation southeast of India in the Indian Ocean.
Occupied by the Portuguese in the 16th century and
by the Dutch in the seventeenth and eighteenth
centuries, Ceylon (Sri Lanka) was surrendered to
Great Britain in 1796. It became a British colony
in 1798. Independence was granted by Great
Britain in the Ceylon Independence Act of 1947.
Sri Lanka adopted a constitution on May 22nd,
1972 that provided for the establishment of a
republic which derived its authority from the
people of Sri Lanka.

An Act to make provision for, and in connection with, the attainment by Ceylon of fully responsible status within the British Commonwealth of Nations.

[10th December 1947.]

BE it enacted by the King's most Excellent Majesty, by and with the advice and consent of the Lords Spiritual and Temporal, and Commons, in this present Parliament assembled, and by the authority of the same, as follows :—

1.—(1) No Act of the Parliament of the United Kingdom passed on or after the appointed day shall extend, or be deemed to extend, to Ceylon as part of the law of Ceylon, unless it is expressly declared in that Act that Ceylon has requested, and consented to, the enactment thereof.

(2) As from the appointed day His Majesty's Government in the United Kingdom shall have no responsibility for the government of Ceylon.

(3) As from the appointed day the provisions of the First Schedule to this Act shall have effect with respect to the legislative powers of Ceylon.

Ceylon Independence Act, 11 & 12 George 6, c.7 (1947)

Democratic Republic of the Sudan

Located in northeastern Africa, Sudan had
been historically a number of small independent
kingdoms. In 1820 much of Sudan came under Egyptian
rule. Egyptian rule lasted until 1880 when Muhammed Ahmad al-Mahdi led revolts against the foreign
rule. A brief period of independence was ended
in 1899 when British and Egyptian troops regained
control. The next year the country was proclaimed
a joint British-Egyptian condominium. In 1953,
Great Britain and Egypt concluded an agreement
providing for Sudanese self-determination. On
December 19th, 1955, the House of Representatives
declared Sudan to be an independent sovereign.
Sudan became independent on January 1, 1956.

No. 2127. AGREEMENT BETWEEN THE EGYPTIAN GOVERNMENT AND THE GOVERNMENT OF THE UNITED KINGDOM OF GREAT BRITAIN AND NORTHERN IRELAND CONCERNING SELF-GOVERNMENT AND SELF-DETERMINATION FOR THE SUDAN. SIGNED AT CAIRO, ON 12 FEBRUARY 1953

The Egyptian Government and the Government of the United Kingdom of Great Britain and Northern Ireland (hereinafter called the " United Kingdom Government "), firmly believing in the right of the Sudanese people to Self-Determination and the effective exercise thereof at the proper time and with the necessary safeguards, have agreed as follows :—

Article 1

In order to enable the Sudanese people to exercise Self-Determination in a free and neutral atmosphere, a transitional period providing full Self-Government for the Sudanese shall begin on the day specified in Article 9 below.

Article 2

The transitional period, being a preparation for the effective termination of the dual Administration, shall be considered as a liquidation of that Administration. During the transitional period the sovereignty of the Sudan shall be kept in reserve for the Sudanese until Self-Determination is achieved.

Article 3

The Governor-General shall, during the transitional period, be the supreme constitutional authority within the Sudan. He shall exercise his powers as set out in the Self-Government Statute with the aid of a five-member Commission, to be called the Governor-General's Commission, whose powers are laid down in the terms of reference in Annex I to the present Agreement.

Article 4

This Commission shall consist of two Sudanese proposed by the two Contracting Governments in agreement, one Egyptian citizen, one citizen of the United Kingdom and one Pakistani citizen, each to be proposed by his respective Government. The appointment of the two Sudanese members shall be subject to the subsequent approval of the Sudanese Parliament when it is elected, and the Parliament shall be entitled to nominate alternative candidates in case of disapproval. The Commission hereby set up will be formally appointed by Egyptian Government decree.

Article 5

The two Contracting Governments agree that, it being a fundamental principle of their common policy to maintain the unity of the Sudan as a single territory, the special powers which are vested in the Governor-General by Article 100 of the Self-Government Statute shall not be exercised in any manner which is in conflict with that policy.

Article 6

The Governor-General shall remain directly responsible to the two Contracting Governments as regards :—

(a) external affairs;

(b) any change requested by the Sudanese Parliament under Article 101 (1) of the Statute for Self-Government as regards any part of that Statute;

(c) any resolution passed by the Commission which he regards as inconsistent with his responsibilities. In this case he will inform the two Contracting Governments, each of which must give an answer within one month of the date of formal notice. The Commission's resolution shall stand unless the two Governments agree to the contrary.

Article 7

There shall be constituted a Mixed Electoral Commission of seven members. These shall be three Sudanese appointed by the Governor-General with the approval of his Commission, one Egyptian citizen, one citizen of the United Kingdom, one citizen of the United States of America, and one Indian citizen. The non-Sudanese members shall be nominated by their respective Governments. The Indian member shall be Chairman of the Commission. The Commission shall be appointed by the Governor-General on the instructions of the two Contracting Governments. The terms of reference of this Commission are contained in Annex II to this Agreement.

Article 8

To provide the free and neutral atmosphere requisite for Self-Determination there shall be established a Sudanisation Committee consisting of :—

(a) an Egyptian citizen and a citizen of the United Kingdom to be nominated by their respective Governments and subsequently appointed by the Governor-General, together with three Sudanese members to be selected from a list of five names submitted to him by the Prime Minister of the Sudan. The selection and appointment of these Sudanese members shall have the prior approval of the Governor-General's Commission;

(b) one or more members of the Sudan Public Service Commission who will act in a purely advisory capacity without the right to vote.

653

The function and terms of reference of this Committee are contained in Annex III to this Agreement.

Article 9

The transitional period shall begin on the day designated as " the appointed day " in Article 2 of the Self-Government Statute. Subject to the completion of Sudanisation as outlined in Annex III to this Agreement, the two Contracting Governments undertake to bring the transitional period to an end as soon as possible. In any case this period shall not exceed three years. It shall be brought to an end in the following manner. The Sudanese Parliament shall pass a resolution expressing their desire that arrangements for Self-Determination shall be put in motion and the Governor-General shall notify the two Contracting Governments of this resolution.

Article 10

When the two Contracting Governments have been formally notified of this resolution the Sudanese Government, then existing, shall draw up a draft law for the election of the Constituent Assembly which it shall submit to Parliament for approval. The Governor-General shall give his consent to the law with the agreement of his Commission. Detailed preparations for the process of Self-Determination, including safeguards assuring the impartiality of the elections and any other arrangements designed to secure a free and neutral atmosphere shall be subject to international supervision. The two Contracting Governments will accept the recommendations of any international body which may be set up to this end.

Article 11

Egyptian and British Military Forces shall withdraw from the Sudan immediately upon the Sudanese Parliament adopting a resolution expressing its desire that arrangements for Self-Determination be put in motion. The two Contracting Governments undertake to complete the withdrawal of their forces from the Sudan within a period not exceeding three months.

Article 12

The Constituent Assembly shall have two duties to discharge. The first will be to decide the future of the Sudan as one integral whole. The second will be to draw up a constitution for the Sudan compatible with the decision which shall have been taken in this respect, as well as an electoral law for a permanent Sudanese Parliament. The future of the Sudan shall be decided either :

(a) by the Constituent Assembly choosing to link the Sudan with Egypt in any form, or

(b) by the Constituent Assembly choosing complete independence.

Article 13

The two Contracting Governments undertake to respect the decision of the Constituent Assembly concerning the future status of the Sudan and each Government will take all the measures which may be necessary to give effect to its decision.

Article 14

The two Contracting Governments agree that the Self-Government Statute shall be amended in accordance with Annex IV to this Agreement.

Article 15

This Agreement together with its attachments shall come into force upon signature.

IN WITNESS WHEREOF the undersigned duly authorised thereto have signed the present Agreement and have affixed thereto their Seals.

DONE at Cairo this twelfth day of February, 1953.

For the Egyptian Government :
(*Signed*) Mohamed NAGUIB
Major General
[SEAL]
For the Government of the United Kingdom
of Great Britain and Northern Ireland :
(*Signed*) Ralph Skrine STEVENSON
[SEAL]

In two copies one of which shall remain deposited in the archives of the Egyptian Government, and one of which shall remain deposited in the archives of the Government of the United Kingdom of Great Britain and Northern Ireland.

161 United Nations Treaty Series, pp. 158-165, (1953)

Republic of Surinam

Formerly Dutch Guiana, Surinam's colonial status officially ended in 1922 when it became an integral part of the Kingdom of the Netherlands. Its status was advanced to that of an autonomous unit of the Kingdom with the promulgation of the amended Netherlands constitution of 1954--the other units being the Netherlands Antilles in the West Indies and the "mother country" of The Netherlands. Meeting in The Hague from March 17 to 27, 1975, Dutch and Surinamese representatives discussed the terms of Surinam's separation/independence from the other two units of the Kingdom. Birth of the new nation was set for November 25, 1975.

Since Surinam was already an autonomous entity, it was not "granted" its "independence" from or by the Kingdom of the Netherlands. November 25, 1975 was the date of self-proclaimed nationhood. This is indicated by the words of the Preamble to the Surinam constitution promulgated on that date.

REPUBLIC OF SURINAM

PREAMBLE

WE, THE PEOPLE OF SURINAM, IN PARLIAMENT ASSEMBLED THROUGH THE INTERMEDIARY OF OUR REPRESENTATIVES,

— Considering the equality before the law of all citizens without distinction as to race, sex, religion, view of life or political persuasion,

— Convinced of the duty to respect and safeguard fundamental human rights and freedoms,

— Inspired by the ideals of freedom, forbearance, democracy and progress of our nation,

— Determined to live and work together in peace and friendship with one another and with all peoples in the world on the basis of freedom, equality, brotherhood and human solidarity,

SOLEMNLY DECLARE THAT WE GIVE OURSELVES THE FOLLOWING CONSTITUTION:

Kingdom of Swaziland

Located in southeastern Africa, the Kingdom of Swaziland, originally consisted of groups of clans. During the 19th century the clans merged into a distinct tribal unit. A conflict with the Zulu in the 1840's led the Swazi ruler to seek help from the British. From this point European influence was established. Although being guaranteed independence by the British in 1881 and 1884, the Kingdom of Swaziland remained under British or South African control until the 1960's. In 1964, the Imbokodvos, a moderate political party, won all seats in the legislature and adopted immediate independence as one of its goals. Parlimentary elections were held in 1967 and independence was granted by the British on September 5, 1968, pursuant to the Swaziland Independence Act of July 26, 1968.

Swaziland Independence Act 1968

1968 CHAPTER 56

An Act to make provision for, and in connection with, the attainment by Swaziland of fully responsible status within the Commonwealth. [26th July 1968]

BE IT ENACTED by the Queen's most Excellent Majesty, by and with the advice and consent of the Lords Spiritual and Temporal, and Commons, in this present Parliament assembled, and by the authority of the same, as follows:—

1. On 6th September 1968 (in this Act referred to as " the appointed day ") Swaziland shall cease to be a protected state ; and on and after that day Her Majesty shall have no jurisdiction over Swaziland.

Swaziland Independence Act 1968, c.56

Kingdom of Sweden

While Sweden was known as a separate nation as early as 1000, it lost this identity in 1397 when it joined with Norway and Denmark to form the Union of Kalmar. Gustav Eriksson Vasa, who succeeded in taking Sweden out of the Union in 1523, is popularly regarded as the consolidator of the present Swedish Kingdom.

Sweden's national existence is proclaimed in its Instrument of Government adopted in 1809 which serves as the nation's constitution.

THE INSTRUMENT OF GOVERNMENT

Chapter 1. The Basic Principles of the Constitution

Art. 1. All public power in Sweden emanates from the people.

The Swedish democracy is founded on freedom of opinion and on universal and equal suffrage and shall be realized through a representative and parliamentary polity and through local self-government.

Public power shall be exercised under the laws.

Art. 2. The Instrument of Government, the Act of Succession and the Freedom of the Press Act are the fundamental laws of the Realm of Sweden.

Art. 3. The Riksdag is the principal representative of the people.

The Riksdag enacts the laws, decides on taxes and determines how public funds shall be used. The Riksdag shall examine the government and administration of the country.

Art. 4. The King is the Head of State.

Art. 5. The Government rules the country. It is responsible to the Riksdag.

Translation provided by the Swedish Information Service.

Swiss Confederation

Switzerland is located in central Europe
and is bounded to the north by the Federal Republic
of Germany, to the east by Austria and Liechtenstein, to the south by Italy, and to the west by
France. The early history of the Swiss Confederation is marked by continuing revolt against neighboring ruling states. Switzerland became a member
of the Holy Roman Empire in the 11th century and
was ruled by feudal families. In 1231 and 1240,
charters of independence were granted to Uri and
Schwyz (cantons in Switzerland) by the Roman
Emperor. The Hapsburgs, the ruling family, refused
to recognize the charters of independence. On
August 1, 1291, Uri and Schwyz were joined by another
forest canton, Unterwalden, in signing a pact
forming an alliance against the Habsburgs. The
original three cantons were joined by others during
the 14th and 15th centuries. Today Switzerland
consists of twenty-two cantons, three of which
are subdivided. The joinder of Uri, Schwyz, and
Unterwalden is regarded as the beginning of the
independent Swiss nation.

SWISS CONFEDERATION

ALLIANCE OF THE COMMUNITIES

OF URI, SCHWYTZ AND UNTERWALD

AUGUST 1, 1291

In the name of the Lord, amen. It is an honorable action, beneficial to the public good, to confirm, according to consecrated forms, conventions having as an object security and peace.

Let it be known then that, taking into serious consideration the gravity of the time and in order to be better able to defend and to maintain in their integrity persons and property, the men of the valley of Uri, the community of Schwytz and the community of the men of Nidwald have pledged, by an oath taken in all good faith, to sustain each other against anyone and everyone who would commit toward them or any one of them, with the intention of harming persons or property, an act of violence or an injustice; and to this end they will aid each other, advise each other and give mutual assistance of every kind, in their valleys and elsewhere, with persons and property, with all their power and all their efforts. Each of the communities promises to the other that it will come to its aid on any occasion if need be and, to the extent that circumstances require, it will oppose, at its own expense, the attacks of ill-intentioned people and will avenge the wrong suffered.

This is what, by the consecrated form, they have sworn to observe in all loyalty, renewing by these pledges the former pact of alliance also made under oath. However, each one remains no less bound to his Lord in obedience and obligations that his personal condition imposes upon him.

After deliberation in common and approval given unanimously, we have also sworn, ruled and decided not to accept or recognize in any way in the said valleys any judge who has bought his post with money or any other way, or who is not a resident of our valleys or a member of our communities.

If a disagreement arises between members of the confederation, those members whose counsel has the most weight must intervene as mediators to pacify the difference by the means which they find effective; other members of the confederation must oppose any party who might reject their judgment. Each member owes obedience to his judge. In the event that someone refuses to submit to a judgment and a member of the confederation suffers harm from the fact of this refusal, all members of the confederation are bound to constrain the recalcitrant member to give satisfaction.

Should a war or conflict arise between members of the confederation, and should one of the parties refuse to put his case in the hands of justice or to enter into a settlement, the members of the confederation are bound to find for the other party.

The above decisions recorded, made in the interest and to the benefit of all, must last, God willing, forever.

Translation by Edward Kreaser, American Counsul, Bern, Switzerland

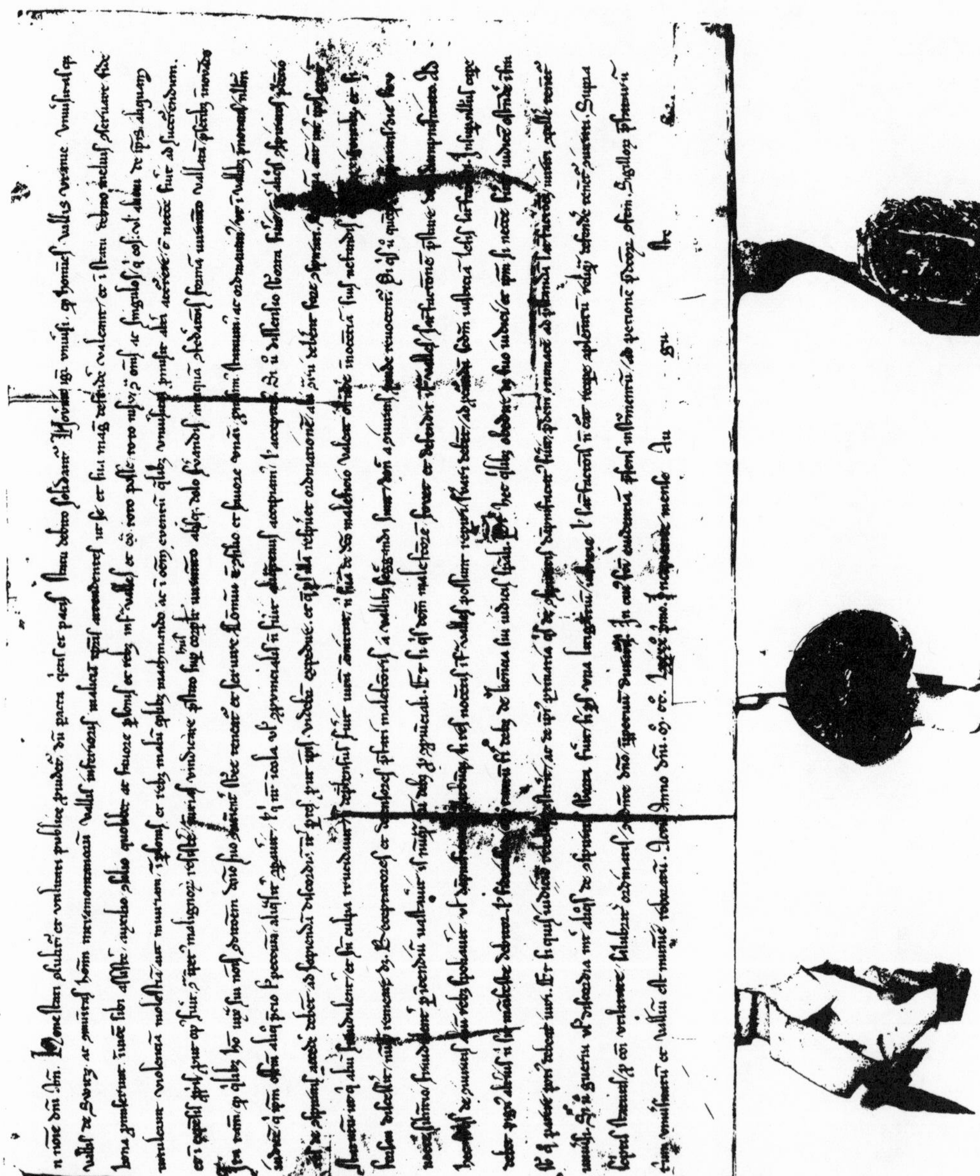

Der Bundesbrief der Landleute von Uri, Schwyz und Unterwalden vom 1. August 1291

Alliance entre les Waldstetten Uri, Schwytz et Unterwald premier Août 1291

Patto del Primo Agosto 1291 conchiuso fra le comunità di Uri, di Svitto e di Untervaldo

Ligia perpetna dils vischins dellas vals de Uri, Sviz ed Unterwalden digl Uost 1291

Lia Eterna dels vaschins dels Comüns dad Uri, Sviz e Suot-il-God dels prüms Avuost 1291

Der Bundesbrief der Landleute von Uri, Schwyz und Unterwalden vom 1. August 1291

Im Namen des Herrn, Amen. Es ist ein ehrbar Werk und dient gemeinem Nußen, die Bünde, so die Ruhe und den Frieden fördern, zu erhalten und zu festigen, wie es sich ziemt. So sei denn allen kund und zu wissen:

Angesichts der bösen Zeit haben die Männer des Tals von Uri, die Landsgemeinde des Tals von Schwyz und die Gemeinde des niedern Tals von Unterwalden, um sich und ihre Habe besser zu schirmen und sicherer in gesiemendem Stande zu erhalten, in guten Treuen versprochen: sich gegenseitig mit Hilfe, allem Rat und jeder Gunst, mit Leib und Gut beizustehen, und zwar innerhalb und außerhalb der Täler, mit aller Macht und Kraft, wider alle und jeden, der ihnen oder einem der Ihren irgend Gewalt antun, sie beläftigen, schädigen oder gegen ihr Leib und Gut Böses im Schilde führen wollte. Und es hat jede Gemeinde versprochen, auf jeden Fall der andern zu Hilfe zu eilen, sobald diese ihrer bedürfe, auch auf eigne Kosten, soweit das nötig sei, dem Angriff Böswilliger zu widerstehen und geschehenes Unrecht zu rächen.

Darauf haben sie einen körperlichen Eid geschworen, ohn' alle Gefährde das Versprechen zu halten, und haben so die alte eidlich bekräftigte Gestalt der Eidgenossenschaft durch gegenwärtige Urkunde erneuert. Doch so, daß jedermann nach dem Stande seines Namens gehalten sein soll, seinem Herrn untertan zu sein und zu dienen, wie es sich gebührt.

Auch haben wir in gemeinem Rat einhellig und einstimmig gelobt, beschlossen und verordnet, daß wir in obgenannten Tälern keinen Richter annehmen oder irgend anerkennen wollen, der solches Amt um einen Preis oder etwa um Geld erworben hätte, oder der nicht unser Landsmann oder Miteinwohner wäre.

Sollte aber ein Streit unter Eidgenossen entstehen, so sollen die Verständigern unter ihnen herzutreten und die Zwietracht unter den Parteien schlichten, wie es ihnen förderlich scheinen mag. Welcher Teil aber diesen Schiedsspruch sich nicht fügen wollte, gegen den müßten sich die andern Bundesgenossen wenden.

Jeder soll seinem Richter gehorchen. Wiberfeßt sich aber einer dem Urteil und kommt durch seine Hartnäckigkeit einer der Eidgenossen zu Schaden, so sind alle Verbündeten gehalten, den Wiberspenstigen zu zwingen, daß er Genugtuung leiste.

Wenn aber Krieg oder Zwietracht unter einigen der Verbündeten entstanden und ein Teil der Streitenden nicht gesinnt ist, den Richterspruch anzunehmen oder Genugtuung zu leisten, so verpflichten sich die Verbündeten, den andern Teil zu schützen.

Was wir hier beschlossen und geschrieben, ist zu gemeinem Nuß und Frommen so verordnet und soll, so Gott will, ewig dauern.

668

Alliance entre les Waldstetten Uri, Schwytz et Unterwald premier Août 1291

Au nom du SEIGNEUR, amen. C'est accomplir une action honorable et profitable au bien public que de confirmer, selon les formes consacrées, les conventions ayant pour objet la sécurité et la paix.

Que chacun sache donc que, prenant en sérieuse considération la gravité des temps et pour être mieux à même de défendre et maintenir dans leur intégrité leurs personnes et leurs biens, les hommes de la vallée d'Uri, la communauté de Schwytz et celle des hommes de Nidwald se sont engagés, sous serment pris en toute bonne foi, à se soutenir les uns les autres contre tous ceux et contre chacun de ceux qui commettraient envers eux ou l'un quelconque d'entre eux, dans l'intention de nuire à leurs personnes et à leurs biens, un acte de violence ou une injustice; et, à cet effet ils se secourront, se conseilleront et s'entraideront de toute façon, dans leurs vallées et au dehors, de leurs personnes et de leurs biens, de tout leur pouvoir, de tous leurs efforts. Chacune des communautés promet à l'autre d'accourir à son aide en toute occasion s'il en est besoin, et, dans la mesure où l'exigeront les circonstances, de s'opposer, à ses propres frais, aux attaques de gens mal intentionnés et de tirer vengeance du tort subi.

C'est ce que, par le geste consacré, ils ont juré d'observer en toute loyauté, renouvelant par les présents engagements l'ancien pacte d'alliance fait aussi sous serment. Toutefois chacun n'en reste pas moins tenu envers son seigneur à l'obéissance et aux prestations que sa condition personnelle lui impose.

Après délibération en commun et approbation donnée à l'unanimité, nous avons aussi juré, statué et décidé de n'accueillir et ne reconnaître en aucune façon dans les dites vallées un juge qui aurait acheté sa charge, à prix d'argent ou par quelque autre moyen, ou qui ne serait pas habitant de nos vallées ou membre de nos communautés.

Si une dissension surgit entre quelques-uns des confédérés, ceux dont le conseil a le plus de poids doivent intervenir comme médiateurs pour apaiser le différend selon le mode qui leur paraîtra efficace; et les autres confédérés devront se tourner contre la partie qui rejetterait leur sentence. Chacun doit obéissance à son juge. Au cas où quelqu'un refuserait de se soumettre à un jugement et où l'un des confédérés subirait quelque dommage du fait de ce refus, tous les confédérés sont tenus de contraindre le récalcitrant à donner satisfaction.

Et surgisse une guerre ou un conflit entre quelques-uns des confédérés, si l'une des parties se refuse à remettre sa cause entre les mains de la justice ou à entrer en composition, les confédérés sont tenus de prendre fait et cause pour l'autre partie.

Les décisions ci-dessus consignées, prises dans l'intérêt et au profit de tous, devront, si Dieu le permet, durer à perpétuité.

Patto del Primo Agosto 1291
conchiuso fra le comunità di Uri, di Svitto e di Untervaldo

Nel nome del SIGNORE, così sia. E opera onorevole ed utile confermare, nelle debite forme, i patti della sicurezza e della pace. Sia noto dunque a tutti, che gli uomini della valle di Uri, la comunità della valle di Svitto e quella degli uomini di Untervaldo, considerando la malizia dei tempi ed allo scopo di meglio difendere e integralmente conservare sè ed i loro beni, hanno fatta leale promessa di prestarsi riciproco aiuto, consiglio e appoggio, a salvaguardia così delle persone come delle cose, dentro le loro valli e fuori, con tutti i mezzi in loro potere, con tutte le loro forze, contro tutti coloro e contro ciascuno di coloro che ad essi o ad uno d'essi facesse violenza, molestia od ingiuria con il proposito di nuocere alle persone od alle cose. Ciascuna delle comunità promette di accorrere in aiuto dell'altra, ogni volta che sia necessario, e di respingere, a proprie spese, secondo le circostanze, le aggressioni ostili e di vendicare le ingiurie sofferte. A conferma che tali promesse saranno lealmente osservate, prestano giuramento, rinnovando con il presente accordo l'antico patto pure conchiuso sotto giuramento; con l'avvertenza tuttavia che ognuno di loro, sarà tenuto, secondo la sua personale condizione, a prestare al proprio signore l'obbedienza ed i servigi dovutigli.

Abbiamo pure, per comune consenso e deliberazione unanime, promesso, statuito ed ordinato di non accogliere nè riconoscere in qualsiasi modo, nelle suddette valli, alcun giudice il quale abbia acquistato il proprio ufficio mediante denaro od altra prestazione, ovvero non sia abitante delle nostre valli o membro delle nostre comunità.

Se sorgesse dissenso fra i confederati, i più prudenti di loro hanno l'obbligo d'intervenire a sedar la discordia, nel modo che loro sembrerà migliore; e se una parte respinge il giudizio proferito, gli altri confederati le si mettano contro.

Ognuno deve pure obbedire al suo giudice. E se alcuno si rifiutasse d'assoggettarsi al giudizio e da questa ribellione venisse danno ad alcuno dei confederati, tutti sono in obbligo di costringere il contumace a dar soddisfazione.

Se poi insorgesse guerra o discordia fra alcuni dei confederati, e una parte non volesse rimettersi al giudice o accettare soddisfazione, i confederati difenderanno l'altra parte.

Tutte le decisioni qui sopra esposte sono state prese nell'interesse ed a vantaggio comune, e dureranno, se il Signore lo consente, in perpetuo.

Ligia perpetna dils vischins dellas vals de Uri, Sviz ed Unterwalden digl Uost 1291

El num dil SEGNER, Amen. Igl ei ina caussa che descha e survescha al cumin etel de confirmar en dueivla fuorma ils patgs che segireschan pasch e ruaus. Perquei duei in e scadin saver, che ils umens della val d'Uri, la cuminonza della val de Sviz ed il cumin dils umens della val sut d'Unterwalden, considerond la malezia dil temps, sinaquei che els possien pli tgunsch defender e mantener en stan dueivel sesez ed il lur, han empermess en buna fei d'assister in l'auter cun agid, cussegl e sustegn, cun veta e beins, enteifer las vals ed ordeifer, tenor tut puder e saver, encunter tuts ed encunter scadin, che commettess enviers els ne in d'els in act de violenza, mulestia ne ingiuria, culla mira de far donn a persunas ne caussas. E per scadin cass ha mintgin dils cumins empermess de prestar siu succuors, sco che ei fagess basegns de gidar, e quei sin agen splendi, ton sco ei sedrovi, per resister ad attaccas de glieud malvuglida e prender vendetga per malgiustias caschunadas da lur vard. Cun detta stendida han els prestau serament de salvar tut quei senza negina malart, renovond cul patg present la brev della ligia gia engirada pli da vegl. Quei denton taluisa, che in e scadin resti obligaus tenor la condiziun de siu num de star sut e survir convegnentamein a siu signur. Suenter cussegl communabel havein nus empermess, stabiliu ed ordinau cun consentiment unanim, che nus vegnien en nossas vals sura numnadas maina vertir ne acceptar in derschader, che havess cumprau siu uffeci per prezi de daner ne autruisa ne fussi buca nies convischin ne habitont della tiara. Mo sche ei dess carplina denter entgins confederai, lu duein ils pli sabis denter els intervegnir e lugar la dispeta denter las parts taluisa, sco ei para ad els convegnent, ed alla part che sbittass il truament, duein tuts ils auters confederai semetter encunter.

Scadin duei obedir a siu derschader. E sche enzatgi serebellass encunter il truament ed in dils confederai pitess donn per sia stinadadad, ein tuts confederai obligai de sfurzar il renitent de dar satisfacziun. Mo sche ei sesalzass uiara ne discordia denter entgins dils confederai e che ina part senuspess de seremetter al dretg ne de dar satisfacziun, ein ils confederai obligai de sustener l'autra vart. Ils tschentaments sura screts, stabili per il cumin etel e salid, duein, sche Dieus vul, cuzzar en perpeten.

Lia Eterna dels vaschins dels Comüns dad Uri, Sviz e Suot-il-God dels prüms Avuost 1291

In nom del SEGNER, Amen. Que ais üna chosa onorabla e chi serva all'ütilità publica, da consolidar in debita fuorma ils pats da sgürezza e pasch.

Perquai saja fat contschaint a minchün, cha'ls homens della val d'Uri, la comunità complettà della val da Sviz e la comunità dels homens della val inferiura da Suot-il-God, considerand attentamaing la malizia del temp, per ch'els possan plü bain defender e mantgnair in debit stadi a sai stess e'l lur, impromettettan in buna fai, da's assister vicendevolmaing con agüd, con mincha cussagl e favur, con vita e roba, nellas vals e dadour quellas, con tuot lur podair e tuot lur sforz, cunter tuots e cunter singuls, chi volessan far alchüna violenza, molestia o ingiuria ad els o a qualchün dad els, tscherchand con astuzia da far del mal a persunas o roba.

E minchüna dellas comunitats impromettet allas otras, d'accuorrer in mincha occasiun, chi füss dabsögn da succuors, e quai a propria spaisa, suainter chi füss necessari, da resister als attachs d'inimis maligns e da vindichar las ingiurias, prestand lasupra ün güramaint corporal e renovand sainza frod con quaist documaint l'antica fuorma della confederaziun, fingià consecrada tras güramaint.

Quaist però in möd, cha mincha hom, suainter la condizium da seis nom, dess restar sudet conveniaintamaing a seis patrun ed al servir.

Eir impromettettan, statuittan ed ordinettan nus da comün consens e favur unanimamaing, cha nellas valladas prenotadas nus non recognuoschan ne acceptan in ingüna maniera ingün güdesch, chi avess cumprà seis offizi per qualsia predsch o per monaida in qualche möd, o chi non füss abitant da nos pajais o nos convaschin.

Scha però füss nada üna dissensiun tanter qualchüns dels confederats, dessan intervgnir oters confederats plü prudaints a balchar la discordia tanter las parts nel möd, sco ad els parerà conveniaint, ed a quella part, chi repudiess lur ordinaziun, as dessan lura opponer ils oters confederats.

Minchün dess obedir a seis güdesch. Ma scha qualchün as revoltes cunter üna sentenza e scha tras quaista obstinaziun qualchün dels confederats füss dannegià, sun tuots ils confederats in dovair, da sforzar il renitent a prestar satisfacziun.

Scha però füss insorta guerra o discordia tanter qualchüns dels confederats, e scha üna part dels litigants refüsess da's suottametter al güdesch o da retschaiver satisfacziun, dessan ils confederats defender l'otra part. Quaists soprascrits statuts, ordinats per l'ütilità comüna salüdaivelmaing, han da dürar, scha Dieu conceda, in eternità.

672

Syrian Arab Republic

Located in south west Asia, Syria is bordered
by Turkey on the north, Iraq on the west, Jordon on
the south, and the Mediterannean Sea on the west.
Once a Roman province, Syria was ruled by the Omay-
yads and Mamluks before becoming part of the
Ottoman Empire in the early 16th century . During
World War II, the Turks were evicted from Syria
and Syrian nationalists declared independence in
1918. In 1920, French troops, acting on a mandate
from the League of Nations, occupied the country
and established French power. Mounting nationalistic
pressure over the next 20 years led to a French
declaration proclaiming the independence of Syria
on September 27, 1941. However, independence was
not immediately granted. A February 1946 United
Nations resolution asked France to abandon the
country. April 17, 1946, is recognized by the
Syrians as Evacuation Day, symbolizing the end
of French rule.

SYRIA

TEXT OF THE FRENCH DECLARATION

PROCLAIMING THE INDEPENDENCE OF SYRIA

Syrians,

Last June 8th, at the time of the entry in
the Levant of the Allied Armies, in a manifesto
that I addressed to you in the name of Free France
and its leader, General de Gaulle, I recognized
Syria as a sovereign and independent State, under
the guarantee of a treaty defining our reciprocal
relations.

The British Government, an Ally of Free France,
acting in accord with it, has associated itself
with that important political act.

On the 16th of this month, I put into effect
my declaration of June 8th, transferring it from
the level of theory to the level of institutions
and realities.

The era is thus opened in which an independent
and sovereign Syria will control its own destiny.

His Excellency Sheikh Tageddine el Hassani
has agreed to organize the new government of independence. His business experience and his profound perception of public needs have designated
him for this high mission. I assure him, as well
as the whole Syrian Nation, of my support and my
loyal collaboration.

I will exercise this collaboration relaying
on the following principles:

The Syrian State enjoys from this time forward the rights and prerogatives connected with
the status of a sovereign and independent State.
These rights and prerogatives will be subject only
to the restrictions imposed by the present state
of war and the security of the territory and of
the occupying armies.

In addition, its position as a de facto Ally of Free France and Great Britain requires a strict conformity of its policies with those of the Allies.

In acceding to international life, Syria accedes naturally to the rights and obligations subscribed to up to now in its name.

It has the power to designate diplomatic representatives to countries where it judges that its interests require the installation of such representation. Everywhere else, the authorities of Free France will lend their good offices in order to assure the defense of Syria's general rights and interests, as well as the protection of Syrian nationals.

The Syrian State has the power to establish national military forces. To this end, Free France will cooperate fully.

Since Great Britain has already pledged on several occasions to recognize the independence of Syria, Free France will intercede without delay among other allied or friendly powers in order that they also recognize the independence of the Syrian State.

Free France considers that the Syrian State constitutes politically and territorially an indivisible unit, the integrity of which must be preserved from all dismemberment. Free France will therefore encourage the strengthening of the political, cultural and economic ties which unite the different parts of Syria. To this end, the Delegate General and Plenipotentiary of Free France will revise the texts setting up the special statutes previously granted to certain regions, so that, while conserving the financial and administrative autonomy to which they are firmly attached, they are politically subordinate to the Syrian central authority. In this way the principle of Syrian unity and the special aspirations of these regions are reconciled.

In addition, it is still agreed that the guarantees of public law registered in the organic statutes to the benefit of individuals and communities will be maintained and will have full force.

Free France undertakes to mediate between Syria and Lebanon in order that the bases of an economic collaboration between the two countries be sought and instituted and that the difficulties which this collaboration is encountering in the present be eliminated.

This accord, which is necessary between neighboring brother countries, must guarantee the legitimate and respective rights of the two parties and will establish their relations on the basis of mutual confidence.

With a view to safeguarding the independence and sovereignty of Syria and to succeeding in the common struggle, the Allies will assume, during the period of war, the defense of the country. To this end, the Syrian Government will place at the disposal of the Allied Command the Syrian national forces in order to cooperate in the defense of the territory. Also, the Allied Command will use henceforth, to the extent that military necessity requires, the equipment and public services of Syria, especially the means of communication, the airfields and the coastal facilities. The defense of the territory requires also that a strict collaboration exist at all times among the Commander in Chief and the Delegate General, and the services of the gendarmerie, the police and the internal security of the Syrian State. Syria must in effect be defended in time of war not only against its enemies from without, but also those from within.

Because of the inclusion of Syria in the war zone and in the economic and financial system of the Allies, the strictest collaboration between the Syrian Government and the Allies is also necessary to assure, for the duration of hostilities and in the common interest, the recognition and respect of all measures taken with the view toward leading the economic war to a successful end.

Toward this goal, during the hostilities the greatest flexibility will be granted to assure the greatest freedom of exchange between Syria and the countries of the sterling bloc. Syria, having now entered into the sterling bloc, will adopt in the economic and financial field, and especially in the area of exchange, the measures necessary to remain in harmony with the general policy of the sterling bloc.

The preceding stipulations reconcile respect for the independence and sovereignty of Syria with the necessities of a state of war. They are inspired by one thought, which is to win the war and, by this means, to assure to Syria a future as a free people. They bring to the Franco-Syrian problem a solution stemming from the desire of the French people not to delay, in spite of the war, the accomplishment of Syrian national aspirations and the execution of the commitments of the Allies. But it is necessary that definitive regulations be substituted for them as soon as possible, in the form of a Franco-Syrian treaty which will consecrate definitively the independence of the country.

LONG LIVE INDEPENDENT SYRIA.

LONG LIVE FRANCE.

Damas, September 27, 1941

Journal Officiel de la Republique Syrienne, Damascus, No. 40 bis, October 14, 1941, pp. 8,9.

Translation by Yorguy Hamkim

Texte de la déclaration française portant proclamation
de l'indépendance de la Syrie

Syriens.

Le 8 Juin dernier, lors de l'entrée au Levant des Armées Alliées, dans un manifeste que je vous ai adressé au nom de la France Libre et de son chef, le Général de Gaulle, j'ai reconnu à la Syrie la qualité d'Etat souverain et indépendant, sous la garantie d'un traité définissant nos rapports réciproques.

Le Gouvernement britannique. Allié de la France Libre, agissant en accord avec elle, s'est, par une déclaration simultanée, associé à cet acte politique important.

Le 16 de ce mois, jai rendu effective ma déclaration du 8 Juin, en la faisant passer du plan du principe acquis à celui des institutions et des réalités

L'ère est donc ouverte où la Syrie indépendante et souveraine régira elle-même ses destinées.

Son Excellence le Cheikh Tageddine el Hassani a accepté d'organiser le nouveau régime d'indépendance. Son expérience des affaires et son sentiment profond des nécessités publiques le désignaient pour cette haute mission. Je l'assure, ainsi que toute la Nation Syrienne, de mon appui et de ma loyale collaboration.

J'exercerai cette collaboration en m'inspirant des principes ci après :

L'Etat de Syrien jouit dès maintenant des droits et prérogatives attachés à la qualité d'Etat indépendant et souverain. Ces droits et ces prérogatives subiront les seules restrictions qu'imposent l'état actuel de guerre et la sécurité du territoire et des armées occupantes

Par ailleurs, sa position d'Allié de fait de la France Libre et de la Grande Bretagne requiert une étroite conformité de sa politique avec celle des Alliés.

En accédant à la vie internationale la Syrie accède naturellement aux droits et obligations souscrits jusqu'ici en son nom.

Elle a la faculté de désigner des représentants diplomatiques auprès des pays où elle jugera que ses intérêts exigent l'installation d'une pareille représentation. Partout ailleurs, les autorités de la France Libre lui prêteront leurs offices pour assurer la défense des droits et intérêts généraux de la Syrie, ainsi que la protection des ressortissants syriens.

L'Etat Syrien a la faculté de constituer ses forces militaires nationales. La France Libre lui prêtera, à cette fin, tout son concours.

La Grande Bretagne s'étant déjà engagée à plusieurs reprises à reconnaitre l'indépendance de la Syrie, la France Libre interviendra, sans délai, auprès des autres puissances alliées ou amies, pour que celles-ci reconnaissent également l'indépendance de l'Etat Syrien.

La France Libre considère que l'Etat de Syrie constitue politiquement et territorialement une unité indivisible, dont l'intégrité doit être préservée de tout démembrement. Elle favorisera, en conséquence, le resserrement des liens politiques, culturels et économiques qui unissent les différentes fractions de la Syrie. A cette fin, le Délégué Général et Plénipotentiaire de la France Libre révisera les textes fixant les statuts particuliers accordés antérieurement à certaines régions, de manière que, tout en conservant l'autonomie financière et administrative à laquelle elles se montrent fermement attachées, elles soient politiquement subordonnées au pouvoir central syrien. Ainsi se trouvent conciliés le principe de l'unité syrienne et les aspirations particulières de ces régions.

Il demeure en outre entendu que les garanties de droit public inscrites dans les statuts organiques en faveur des individus et des communautés sont maintenues et recevront leur plein effet.

La France Libre s'engage à s'entremettre auprès de la Syrie et du Liban afin que soient recherchées et instituées les bases d'une collaboration économique entre les deux pays, et que soient éliminées les difficultés que cette collaboration rencontre dans le présent.

Cette entente, nécessaire entre deux pays frères et voisins, doit garantir les droits légitimes et respectifs des deux parties, et établir leurs rapports sur la base de la confiance réciproque.

En vue de sauvegarder l'indépendance et la souveraineté de la Syrie et pour mener à bien la lutte commune, les Alliés assumeront, pendant la période de guerre, la défense du pays. A cette fin, le Gouvernement Syrien mettra à la disposition du Commandement Allié pour coopérer à la défense du territoire, les forces nationales syriennes. De même, le commandement allié disposera dès maintenant dans la mesure où les nécessités militaires l'exigeront, de l'équipement et des services publics de la Syrie notamment des voies de communication, des aérodromes et des aménagements côtiers. La défense du territoire exige également qu'une étroite collaboration existe en tous temps entre le Général Commandant en Chef et Délégué Général, et les services de gendarmerie, de police et de sûreté de l'Etat syrien. La Syrie doit être en effet, défendue en temps de guerre, non seulement contre ses ennemis du dehors, mais aussi contre ceux du dedans.

En raison de l'inclusion de la Syrie dans la zone de guerre et dans le système économique et financier des Alliés, la plus étroite collaboration entre le Gouvernement syrien et les Alliés est également nécessaire pour assurer, pendant la durée des hostilités et dans l'intérêt commun, l'obligation et le respect de toutes mesures prises en vue de conduire à bonne fin la guerre économique.

Dans ce but, pendant la durée des hostilités, les plus grandes facilités seront accordées pour assurer dans la plus large mesure, la liberté des échanges entre la Syrie et les pays du bloc sterling. La Syrie, entrée maintenant dans le bloc sterling, adoptera, dans l'ordre économique et financier, et notamment dans le domaine du change, les mesures nécessaires pour rester en harmonie avec la politique générale du bloc sterling.

Les stipulations qui précèdent concilient le respect de l'indépendance et de la souveraineté syriennes avec les nécessités de l'état de guerre. Elles sont inspirées par une pensée unique, qui est celle de gagner la guerre et d'assurer par ce moyen à la Syrie, un avenir de peuple libre. Elles apportent au problème franco-syrien une solution qui procède de la volonté de la France Libre de ne pas retarder, malgré la guerre l'accomplissement des aspirations nationales syriennes et l'exécution des engagements des Alliés. Mais il est nécessaire qu'un règlement définitif y soit substitué au plus tôt, sous la forme du traité franco-syrien qui consacrera définitivement l'indépendance du pays.

VIVE LA SYRIE INDEPENDANTE.

VIVE LA FRANCE.

Damas, le 27 Septembre 1941

النص الرسمي للبروتوكول
التونسي ـ الفرنسي

في الثالث من شهر جوان ١٩٥٥ التقت الحكومتان الفرنسية والتونسية اثر مفاوضات حرة دارت بين وفديهما على الاعتراف لتونس بالتصرف الكامل في سيادتها الداخلية .

وقد اكدا بذلك ارادتهما في تمكين الشعب التونسي من ادراك ازدهاره الكامل والتحكم في مصيره على مراحل .

وتعترف الحكومتان بان التوسع المنسجم والسلمي للعلاقات التونسية الفرنسية يستجيب بمقتضيات العالم العصري كما تلاحظان بارتياح ان هذا التطور يسمح بالارتقاء الى السيادة الكاملة بدون حصول ويلات للشعب او صدمات للدولة .

وتؤكد ان وثوقهما من ان تونس وفرنسا اذ تقيمان علاقاتهما على قاعدة الاحترام المتبادل والكامل لسيادتهما في نطاق استقلال وتساوي الدولتين انما تدعمان التضامن الذي يربط بينهما لصالح البلادين .

واشر خطاب التولية الذي فاه به رئيس الحكومة الفرنسية ورد جلالة الباي المؤكدين لعزمهما المشترك على توطيد علاقاتهما بنفس روح السلام والسؤدد نتجت الحكومتان مفاوضات بباريس في السابع والعشرين من شهر فيفري سنة ١٩٥٦ .

وعليه .

فان فرنسا تعترف رسميا وعلى رؤوس الاشهاد باستقلال تونس .

ويترتب عن ذلك .

أ ـ ان المعاهدة التي ابرمت في ١٢ ماية ١٨٨١ بين فرنسا وتونس لم يعد في امكانها ضبط العلاقات الفرنسية التونسية .

ب ـ ان كل ما يتنافى من تدابير الاتفاقيات المبرمة في ٣ جوان ١٩٥٥ مع النظام الجديد لتونس بوصفها دولة مستقلة وذات سيادة فانه سيقع تحويره او الغاؤه .

ﻫ ــ ويترتب عن ذلك ايضا •

مباشرة تونس لمسؤولياتها في ميادين الشؤون الخارجية والامن والدفاع وكذلك تأليف جيش وطني تونسي وتتفق فرنسا وتونس على أن تحدد او تتمم في دائرة احترام سيادتيهما تدابير التكافل الذي يتحقق بحرية

(٢)

وذلك بتنايم تعاونهما في الميادين التي تشترك فيها مصالحهما وخاصة في مادتي الدفاع والعلاقات الخارجية •

وستضبط الاتفاقات بين فرنسا وتونس شروط الاعانة التي تقدمها فرنسا لتونس قصد تأليف الجيش الوطني التونسي •

وستستأنف المفاوضات في ١٦ أفريل ١٠٥٦ والغاية منها الوصول في اقصر الآجال الممكنة وطبقا للمبادئ المقرر لها في هذا البروتوكول الى ابرام العقود اللازمة لاجراء العمل بها •

وحرر بباريس في نسختين في ٢٠ مارس ١٠٥٦ •

عن تونس   عن فرنسا

الطاهر بن عمار   كريستيان بينو

United Republic of Tanzania

      Tanzania, in east central Africa, is made
up of two formerly independent states, Tanganyika
and Zanzibar. Tanganyika was ruled first by the
Arabs and then the Germans until 1919 when Great
Britain took over administration. A nationalist
movement, begun in 1954, resulted in the Tanganyika
Independence Act of November 22, 1961, which granted
independence effective December 8, 1961. In Zanzibar, also governed by Great Britain, the nationalist
movement resulted in independence on December 10,
1963. One month later a revolt occured which
Tanganyika helped stop. On April 22, 1964, the
two Republics were united into the United Republic
of Tanzania.

An Act to make provision for, and in connection with, the attainment by Tanganyika of fully responsible status within the Commonwealth.   [22nd November, 1961]

BE it enacted by the Queen's most Excellent Majesty, by and with. the advice and consent of the Lords Spiritual and Temporal, and Commons, in this present Parliament assembled, and by the authority of the same, as follows:—

1.—(1) On the ninth day of December, nineteen hundred and sixty-one (in this Act referred to as the appointed day) Tanganyika (the limits of which are defined in Article 1 of the Tanganyika Order in Council, 1920) shall become part of Her Majesty's dominions under the name of Tanganyika and as from that day Her Majesty's Government in the United Kingdom shall have no responsibility for the government of Tanganyika.

(2) No Act of the Parliament of the United Kingdom passed on or after the appointed day shall extend, or be deemed to extend, to Tanganyika as part of the law thereof, and the provisions of the First Schedule to this Act shall have effect as from that day with respect to the legislative powers of Tanganyika.

(3) Subsection (1) of this section shall not affect the operation in Tanganyika of any enactment, or any other instrument having the effect of law, passed or made before the appointed day, or be taken to extend any such enactment or instrument to Tanganyika as part of the law thereof.

Independence Message to TANU

On the 9th December the green, black, and gold flag of independent Tanganyika will be flying over us. This is the moment we have all been working for, and it has come sooner than any of us dreamed possible in 1954.

This flag is flying because thousands upon thousands of people have determined that it shall fly and have worked together selflessly for that end. In the press of the world the names of various Tanganyika leaders will be repeated over and over again as the Celebrations are reported; yet really the names, even of the founders of TANU, are unimportant. This day has dawned because the people of Tanganyika have worked together in unity, and yet with great individual enterprise and initiative, for this one purpose, the attainment of *Uhuru*. The TANU Committee men in villages too small to be marked on any school map, the men, women, and children who took around news of meetings and reports of speeches and events, the people who collected money and honestly sent it forward for use in the struggle, the people who built offices and the people who kept them clean; every one of these people is responsible for the flying of Tanganyika's flag this month. Every person who has done a job, however small, to build up and strengthen TANU can feel pride and satisfaction in what he has achieved.

I am sure that every one of us will celebrate Independence Day with great joy. We are celebrating a victory. Yet it is essential that we remember even on that day that what we have won is the right to work for ourselves, the right to design and build our own future. It is like obtaining the land on which to build a house. To obtain that land against opposition is a great thing and it deserves celebrating, but the house does not appear during the Celebrations; the house calls for more work, and even harder work, for the exercise of skill, sweat and patience, if it is to be a source of pride to us, its owners.

We have been talking for a long time about what sort of house we want to build on this land. Now we have the chance to do it. We have already agreed on certain basic principles; now is the time to put these principles into operation. All the time that TANU has been campaigning for *Uhuru* we have based our struggle on our belief in the equality and dignity of all mankind and on the Declaration of Human Rights. We have agreed that our nation shall be a nation of free and equal citizens, each person having an equal right and opportunity to develop himself, and contribute to the maximum of his capabilities to the development of our society. We have said that neither race nor tribe nor religion nor cleverness, nor anything else, could take away from a man his own rights as an equal member of society. This is what we have now to put into practice.

Yet we know that on the 9th December we shall not have achieved these objects. Poverty, ignorance, and disease must be overcome before we can really establish in this country the sort of society we have been dreaming of. These obstacles are not small ones, they are more difficult to overcome than any alien government. From now on we are fighting not man but nature, and we are seeking to wrest from nature a better and fuller life for ourselves. In this struggle the only weapon is our own determination and our own effort. We will be able to get help from outside Tanganyika; we will be able to draw on the experience of other countries and upon the knowledge of other people, but the work, the effort and the sacrifice is ours. It will be a long and hard struggle, and although we can learn lessons from others there is no blueprint, there is no ideal state we can look at and say, 'That is what we must do,' or 'That is what we must become.' We have to build Tanganyika ourselves, primarily with our own resources and by our own efforts.

I believe that the people of Tanganyika can build a good society, in every meaning of the word. We have been told before that we are dreaming, that we are not capable of doing certain things, but we, the people of Tanganyika, have now shown our strength, to ourselves most of all. Through TANU, we have flexed our muscles, and in so doing we have broken the bonds which have prevented us from going forward. If we can do this—and that we have done it the Flag shows—then we can move into this struggle to overcome our material disabilities.

We can do it by working, and by working together. In other words, we do it in the same way as we carried on the first phase of our struggle, by united effort. We can use the same instrument— our National Movement, TANU. The tasks themselves will be different in the coming years—more complex in some ways. It is the job of the Government to work out an overall plan and to chart the direction in which we move, just as the TANU National Executive in the past worked out the tactics of the struggle. But in the same way as TANU National Executive would have been helpless without the activity in every village of the country, so the Government can achieve nothing by itself. What really matters in the coming years, what really will determine our progress, is the attitude and the participation of the people.

In all this TANU has a vital role to play. It is an organization of the people. Through it the people can and must express their desires and their worries to the Government. Through it the Government can and must explain to the people what it is doing and why. TANU must be a broad channel along which ideas flow back and forth. In the past, despite colonial government opposition, we have started educational campaigns, we have organized voluntary effort, we have even started our own adult college. Now we must intensify these activities, co-operating with the new Government and co-ordinating our activities so that the direct initiative of the people supplements the work which Government can do and is supplemented by it. Now, because we have achieved our first objective—a TANU government—we can proceed ourselves with work to further our other objectives. It is not necessary for us to sit and wait to see what the Government we have elected will do; indeed this would be disastrous, and would make all our past efforts a waste of time and energy. We must use the grounds we have won by our past work as a base from which to advance.

To do all this new work the TANU organization must become even stronger. It must husband even more carefully the money of the people, and it must make even further efforts to ensure that its officers can get the education and understanding which they need in this next phase of our struggle. The task before TANU is a great one, a worthy challenge to a world-famed organization; but it is not just a challenge to an organization, it is a challenge to every one of us, old and young, men and women, educated and and uneducated. Each of us has a part to play.

TANU has done much in the past because every one of us has looked first to what he himself could do. In this same spirit we can achieve even more in the future. *Uhuruna kazi*!

Receiving the Instruments of
Independence

I have listened to Your Royal Highness's expressions of goodwill and to those which you have brought to us from Her Majesty; and I have received these Instruments which are the embodiment of my country's freedom with the deepest emotion. This is the day for which we have looked so long, the day when every Tanganyikan can say, 'I am a citizen of a sovereign independent state.'

Joyful though this moment is, you, sir, have rightly reminded us that it is a moment heavy with responsibility. This our people well appreciate. Our responsibilities towards our own people will, in all conscience, be difficult enough to discharge. In a country such as ours the struggle to raise the standards of our people and to lift up our economy will be severe; but however severe it may be it will be waged with all the confidence and resolve that inspire this new nation.

In addition we have wider duties than those we bear towards ourselves alone. We have our responsibilities towards all those other African states with which our links are bound to be so close;

687

and further, even the newest of nations has, in these days, duties towards all the nations upon earth and opportunities to influence by example the policies even of the most powerful.

Nevertheless today is our day of rejoicing. And so I will say no more of the many problems that face us, both in Tanganyika and in the larger world outside, than to remind our people that they exist, and that together we must grapple with them.

Let me now pay tribute to all who have helped us forward to this happy day of the culmination of our hopes. First, to the people of Tanganyika on whose faithful support and steady good sense Tanganyika's political advance has rested. And then to those many true friends of Tanganyika, at home and overseas, the British officers in the service of the Government, the men of religion working for the missions, the planters and men of commerce who founded our economy, private individuals, all that great host of people who by faith and toil and steadfast devotion to their duty have nobly helped to bring this day about. Some I would like to mark by name, but this is no time to pick out individuals. Those who are no longer with us, those who still remain, I salute them all.

To Your Royal Highness I must express our grateful thanks for your presence here amongst us; and to Her Majesty for sending her husband to be with us on this great occasion.

May God guide us all, so that our country goes forward in happiness and prosperity, and in fellowship with the nations of the world.

From UHURU

An Act to make provision in connection with Zanzibar becoming an independent State within the Commonwealth. [3rd December 1963]

BE IT ENACTED by the Queen's most Excellent Majesty, by and with the advice and consent of the Lords Spiritual and Temporal, and Commons, in this present Parliament assembled, and by the authority of the same, as follows:—

1.—(1) Subject to this Act, on and after 10th December 1963 (the date on which Zanzibar ceases to be a protectorate and becomes an independent State within the Commonwealth and which is referred to in this Act as "the appointed day") all law which, whether being a rule of law or a provision of an Act of Parliament or of any other enactment or instrument whatsoever, is in force on that day or has been passed or made before that day and comes into force thereafter, shall, unless and until provision to the contrary is made by Parliament or some other authority having power in that behalf, have the same operation in relation to Zanzibar, and persons and things belonging to or connected with Zanzibar, as it would have apart from this subsection if there had been no change in the status of Zanzibar on the appointed day.

(2) Schedule 1 to this Act shall apply to the enactments there mentioned (of which those in Part I are enactments applicable to Commonwealth countries having fully responsible status, and those in Part II are thereby excepted from the operation of section 1(1) of this Act), but that Schedule shall not extend to Zanzibar as part of the law of Zanzibar.

(3) Subsection (1) of this section applies to law of or of any part of the United Kingdom, the Channel Islands and the Isle of Man and, in relation only to any enactment of the Parliament of the United Kingdom or any Order in Council made by virtue of any such enactment whereby any such enactment applies in relation to Zanzibar, to law of any other country or territory to which that enactment or Order extends.

Kingdom of Thailand

Located in southeastern Asia, Thailand is
bounded to the north and west by Burma, to the
east by Laos, and to the southeast by Cambodia.
Although several kingdoms were formed in the
sixth century, Thailand was not established until
the 14th century. British and French influence
became important in the late 19th century.
The rivalry between the two European countries and
the desire for a buffer zone between the French
Lao state and the British Shan states contributed
to Thailands continued existence. The Anglo-French
Agreement of 1896 established a boundary between
the two empires and guaranteed the independence of
the Menam Chao Phaya valley. Later treaties in
1907 and 1909 resulted in Thailand granting
concessions of land to England and France but also
recognized Thailand's independent existence.

ANGLO-FRENCH AGREEMENT AS TO SIAM.

Mr. Eustis to Mr. Olney.

No. 450.] EMBASSY OF THE UNITED STATES,
Paris, January 22, 1895. (Received Feb. 3.)

SIR: I send herewith a copy of the Yellow Book just issued by the French Government, containing the official text, in English and in French, of the arrangement concluded between Great Britain and France with reference to the boundary of Siam. The arrangement signed by Lord Salisbury and the French ambassador at London, M. de Courcel, is made in the shape of a joint declaration and does not need the approval of the Chambers.

I have, etc.,

J. B. EUSTIS.

DECLARATION.

The undersigned, duly authorized by their respective Governments, have signed the following declaration:

I. The Governments of France and Great Britain engage to one another that neither of them will, without the consent of the other, in any case or under any pretext, advance their armed forces into the region which is comprised in the basins of the Petcha Bouri, Meiklong, Menam, and Bang Pa Kong (Petriou) rivers and their respective tributaries, together with the extent of coast from Muong Bang Tapan to Muong Pase, the basins of the rivers on which those two places are situated and the basins of the other rivers, the estuaries of which are included in that coast; and including also the territory lying to the north of the basin of the Menam and situated between the Anglo-Siamese frontier, the Mekong River, and the eastern watershed of the Me Ing. They further engage not to acquire within this region any special privilege or advantage which shall not be enjoyed in common by or equally open to France and Great Britain and their nationals and dependents.

These stipulations, however, shall not be interpreted as derogating from the special clauses which, in virtue of the treaty concluded on the 3d October, 1893, between France and Siam, apply to a zone of 25 kilom. on the right bank of the Mekong and to the navigation of that river.

II. Nothing in the foregoing clause shall hinder any action on which the two powers may agree and which they shall think necessary in order to uphold the independence of the Kingdom of Siam. But they engage not to enter into any separate agreement permitting a third power to take any action from which they are bound by the present declaration themselves to abstain.

III. From the mouth of the Nam Houk northwards as far as the Chinese frontier the thalweg of the Mekong shall form the limit of the possessions or spheres of influence of France and Great Britain. It is agreed that the nationals and dependents of each of the two countries shall not exercise any jurisdiction or authority within the possessions or sphere of influence of the other.

The police of the islands in this part of the river which are separated from the British shore by a branch of the river shall, so long as they are thus separated, be intrusted to the French authorities. The fishery shall be open to the inhabitants of both banks.

IV. The two Governments agree that all commercial and other privileges and advantages conceded in the two Chinese provinces of Yünnan and Szechuan either to France or Great Britain in virtue of their respective conventions with China of the 1st March, 1894, and the 20th June, 1895, and all privileges and advantages of any nature which may in the future be conceded in these two Chinese provinces, either to France or Great Britain, shall, as far as rests with them, be extended and rendered common to both powers and to their nationals and dependents, and they engage to use their influence and good offices with the Chinese Government for this purpose.

V. The two Governments agree to name commissioners delegated by each of them, who shall be charged to fix by mutual agreement, after examination of the titles produced on either side, the most equitable delimitation between the French and British possessions in the region situated to the west of the lower Niger.

VI. In conformity with the stipulations of Article XL of the general convention concluded between Great Britain and the Regency of Tunis on the 19th July, 1875, which provides for a revision of that treaty "in order that the two contracting parties may have the opportunity of hereafter treating and agreeing upon such other arrangements as may tend still further to the improvement of their mutual intercourse, and to the advancement of the interests of their respective people," the two Governments agree at once to commence negotiations for replacing the said general convention by a new convention, which shall correspond with the intentions proposed in the article above referred to.

Done at London, the 15th January, 1896.

[L. S.]   ALPH. DE COURCEL.

[L. S.]   SALISBURY.

Foreign Relations of the United States 1896, pp. 139-40.

SIAM.

TREATY WITH GREAT BRITAIN.

File No. 10883/32–38.

Minister King to the Secretary of State.

[Extract.]

No. 484.]

AMERICAN LEGATION,
Bangkok, May 13, 1909.

S:R: I have the honor to transmit a copy of the Anglo-Siamese treaty with associated papers.

I have, etc.,

HAMILTON KING.

[Enclosure 2.]

His Majesty the King of Siam and His Majesty the King of the United Kingdom of Great Britain and Ireland and of the British Dominions beyond the Seas, Emperor of India, being desirous of settling various questions which have arisen affecting their respective dominions, have decided to conclude a Treaty, and have appointed for this purpose as their Plenipotentiaries:—

His Majesty the King of Siam, His Royal Highness Prince Devawongse Varoprakar, Minister for Foreign Affairs, etc.

His Majesty the King of Great Britain, Ralph Paget, Esq., his Envoy Extraordinary and Minister Plenipotentiary, etc., who, after having communicated to each other their respective full powers, and found them to be in good and due form, have agreed upon and concluded the following Articles:—

ARTICLE 1.

The Siamese Government transfers to the British Government all rights of suzerainty, protection, administration, and control whatsoever which they possess over the States of Kelantan, Tringganu, Kedah, Perlis, and adjacent islands. The frontiers of these territories are defined by the Boundary Protocol annexed hereto.

ARTICLE 2.

The transfer provided for in the preceding article shall take place within thirty (30) days after the ratification of this treaty.

ARTICLE 3.

A mixed commission, composed of Siamese and British officials and officers, shall be appointed within six months after the date of ratification of this Treaty, and shall be charged with the delimitation of the new frontier. The work of Commission shall be commenced as soon as the season permits, and shall be carried out in accordance with the Boundary Protocol annexed hereto.

Subjects of His Majesty the King of Siam residing within the territory described in Article 1 who desire to preserve their Siamese nationality will, during the period of six months after the ratification of the present Treaty, be allowed to do so if they become domiciled in the Siamese dominions. His Britannic Majesty's Government undertake that they shall be at liberty to retain their immovable property within the territory described in Article 1.

It is understood that in accordance with the usual custom where a change of suzerainty takes place, any concessions within the territories described in Article 1 hereof to individuals or Companies, granted by or with the approval of the Siamese Government, and recognized by them as still in force on the date of the signature of the Treaty, will be recognized by the Government of His Britannic Majesty.

ARTICLE 4.

His Britannic Majesty's Government undertake that the Government of the Federated Malay States shall assume the indebtedness to the Siamese Government of the territories described in Article 1.

The jurisdiction of the Siamese International Courts, established by Article 8 of the Treaty of 3rd September, 1883, shall under the conditions defined in the jurisdiction Protocol annexed hereto, be extended to all British subjects in Siam registered at the British Consulates before the date of the present Treaty.

This system shall come to an end, and the jurisdiction of the International Courts shall be transferred to the ordinary Siamese Courts after the promulgation and the coming into force of the Siamese codes, namely, the Penal Code, the Civil and Commercial Codes, the Codes of Procedure, and the Law for Organization of Courts.

All other subjects in Siam shall be subject to the jurisdicti.n of the ordinary Siamese Courts under the conditions defined in the Jurisdiction Protocol.

ARTICLE 6.

British subjects shall enjoy throughout the whole extent of Siam the rights and privileges enjoyed by the natives of the country, notably the right of property, the right of residence and travel.

They and their property shall be subject to all taxes and services, but these shall not be other or higher than the taxes and services which are or may be imposed by law on Siamese subjects. It is particularly understood that the limitation in the Agreement of 20th September, 1900, by which the taxation of land shall not exceed that on similar land in Lower Burmah, is hereby removed.

British subjects in Siam shall be exempt from all military service, either in the army or navy, and from all forced loans or military exactions or contributions.

ARTICLE 7.

The provisions of all Treaties, Agreements, and Conventions between Great Britain and Siam, not modified by the present Treaty, remain in full force.

ARTICLE 9.

The present Treaty shall be ratified within four months from its date.

In witness whereof the respective Plenipotentiaries have signed the present Treaty and affixed their seals.

Done at Bangkok in duplicate the tenth day of March in the year one thousand nine hundred and nine.

(Signed)	DEVAWONGSE VAROPRAKAR [SEAL]
(Signed)	RALPH PAGET [SEAL]

Foreign Relations of the United States 1909, pp. 535-6.

Republic of Togo

Togo is a West African country bounded to the west by Ghana and to the south by the Gulf of Guinea. Until the late 19th century the coast of West Africa including all of Togo was ruled by different kingdoms. In 1884 Togo became a German protectorate. After World War I it was divided into British and French Protectorates. The French Protectorate, what is now the Republic of Togo, began its drive toward self government on July 4, 1955, when a territorial assembly adopted a motion asking the French to draft a new statute ending the trusteeship system. On August 24, 1956, an amended decree was taken by the French Council of Ministers. On October 28, 1956, the population overwhelmingly voted in favor of independence. The United Nations on November 29, 1957, passed a resolution approving the new form. A joint decree with France dated December 30 ,1958, stated that Togo was a democratic state which on its own demand would be proclaimed an independent and sovereign republic. On April 23, 1960, the Togolese Chamber of Deputies exercised its option and declared Togo to be an independent republic effective April 27, 1960. A speech given that date by the Prime Minister of Togo also marks the independence.

Togo Ordinance No. 58-1376 of December 30, 1958, concerning the status of the Togolese Republic.

The President of the Council of Ministers,

With the agreement of the Overseas Minister of France;

In view of the trusteeship accord of December 13, 1946;

In view of the Constitution of October 5, 1958, especially Article 92;

In view of the motion of the Togolese Chamber of Deputies dated October 27, 1958;

The State Council is in accord;

The Council of Ministers is in accord;

IT SHALL BE ORDERED:

TITLE I

The Republic of Togo

FIRST ARTICLE: Togo is a democratic state, which shall be proclaimed an independent and sovereign Republic at the decision of the Togolese people under the provisions of the international trusteeship system.

Relations with the French Republic shall be defined by both this statute and convention.

Consequences resulting from the temporary continuance of the international trusteeship, shall be specified in Articles 32 and 33. . . .

PARIS, December 30, 1958

Translated by Sarah J. Campbell and Matthew Jodziewicz

JOINT ACTS OF THE GOVERNMENT OF THE
REPUBLIC OF TOGO AND THE HIGH COMMISSION
OF THE FRENCH REPUBLIC FOR TOGO

Decree No. 39-58/HC/PM of December 31, 1958, putting
into effect Togo Ordinance No. 58-1376 of December
30, 1958, concerning the status of the Togolese Republic.

The High Commissioner of the French Republic
for Togo

The Prime Minister of the Republic of Togo

In view of the Trusteeship accord of December
13, 1946;

In view of the Constitution of October 5, 1958,
especially Article 92;

In view of the Decree of February 22, 1958,
modifying the Decree of August 24, 1956, concerning
the status of Togo, especially Article 34;

DECREE:

FIRST ARTICLE: Ordinance No. 58-1376 of December 30, 1958, concerning the status of Togo,
shall be promulgated for Togo.

SECOND ARTICLE: This decree shall be recorded,
published and communicated wherever it shall be
needed.

Lomé, December 31, 1958.

Translated by Sarah J. Campbell and Matthew
Jodziewicz

ACTS OF THE GOVERNMENT OF THE REPUBLIC OF TOGO

Law No. 60-10 of April 23, 1960, modifying the organization of the Institutions of the Togolese Republic.

The Chamber of Deputies has deliberated and adopted,

The Prime Minister promulgates the following:

TITLE I

The Togolese Republic

FIRST ARTICLE: Togo shall be an independent, sovereign and democratic Republic.

ARTICLE 33: This law shall enter into force on April 27, 1960.

Lomé, April 23, 1960.

S. E. OLYMPIO

Translated by Sarah J. Campbell and Matthew Jodziewicz

TOGO

Speech of the Prime Minister

(delivered on Wednesday, April 27, 1960 at midnight in the Governmental Palace)

"Sentry, what do you think about night?"

"Night is long, but day comes," answered the sentry.

Excellencies, Ladies and Gentlemen.

The great day so often dreamed of has finally arrived. Our country Togo, which since 1884 has been a German protectorate, under Franco-British rule, and a French trusteeship, has today, April 27, 1960, finally reattained its lost liberty of yesteryear.

From this moment and forever after, freed from all subjugation, from all shackles, master of its own destiny, Togo, my country, you are finally free.

Free to be yourself, to follow your own ideas and inclinations, to choose according to your own reasoning and feelings, to decide following your own will, finally free in refound dignity to prove and reaffirm your own identity.

Our joy is both profound and great. It is so profound that it cannot help being also grand. Day has come, but the night has been long. So many years have passed before this independence was achieved. So many hopes for remaining firm to this goal fell along a route sown with deception. So many wishes to know finally the hour when we would know how to live with joy.

But young Togo is here; proud of its power, impatient to enter the arena. It bears on its forehead the pride of a free people and its zealous heart is filled with enthusiasm for the task before it, most certainly a formidable one, but also an elating one. How its joy blazes out! How in all the country no other feeling fills the hearts so that this instant, unique in the life of

a nation, remains pure in the memory of those who
actually have participated.

This is also an historic moment.

In this place, on this day, at this hour, in
the name of Togolese people, I solemnly proclaim
the independence of Togo, our Fatherland.

And now, citizens of Togo, let us move forward as the national anthem urges us. Let us go
forth together to build the city.

Translated by Sarah J. Campbell and Matthew
Jodziewicz

DISCOURS du 1er. MINISTRE

(MERCREDI 27 AVRIL 1960 A 19 HEURES, AU COURS DE L'INAUGURATION
DE LA PLACE ET DU MONUMENT DE L'INDEPENDANCE.)

-:-:-:-:-:-:-:

En ce jour merveilleux où les mots nous manquent pour exprimer toute notre joie et toute notre fierté, c'est pour moi un agréable devoir d'inaugurer cette place et ce monument érigés pour perpétuer l'accession de notre cher pays à l'Indépendance.

Ainsi le souvenir de cet instant que nous vivons sera-t-il transmis de génération en génération.

La signification de l'ensemble architectural qui va être dévoilé est profonde. Mes félicitations les plus chaleureuses vont à l'auteur de cette oeuvre M. GeorgesCoustère qui a ajouté à ses remarquables talents bien connus le meilleur de son coeur.

L'idée qui a présidé à l'élaboration de l'oeuvre est la suivante : lutte pour l'Indépendance, conquête de cette Indépendance.

L'obstacle occasionnant la lutte est représenté par la menace d'écrasement par le bloc de granit. Il a fallu le supporter, ledisloquer, le franchir enfin.

L'effort c'est la brèche, cette trouée héroïque qui porte l'empreinte humaine et dessine une silhouette d'hercule.

Le seuil franchi enfin, c'est la liberté et la lumière représentée par une figure hiératique, située en avant du passage triomphale ; elle porte les flammes sacrées tandis que de part et d'autre du roc se déploient les ailes de l'espérance.

Il convient également de remercier M. François Coustère frère de notre architecte dont les talents de sculpteur ont permis la parfaite exécution de l'ouvrage.

Nos remerciements vont également au personnel de l'entreprise Travaux Afrique, aux ouvriers et agents de maîtrise, en particulier M. Bossa dont l'enthousiasme et le labeur acharné ont permis que le travail soit aujourd'-hui achevé avec tout le soin désirable.

Beau et émouvant, ce monument est érigé sur une place dite de l'Indépendance que nous avons délibérément choisie vaste pour montrer la grande valeur que nous attachons à cet événement.

........11

DISCOURS DU PREMIER MINISTRE DEVANT LE MONUMENT DE

L'INDEPEDANCE (Suite)

-:-:-:-:-:-:-:-:-

L'ensemble qui aura pour nous un sens historique incarne à la fois, le courage et le sacrifice du peuple togolais pour la naissance de notre nation. Il constitue un symbole de pérennité que nous rappellera notre devoir de sauvegarder à jamais notre Indépendance.

En cette circonstance, ma pensée fraternelle va à tout l'immense continent noir trop longtemps livré à la domination étrangère mais qui a marqué ces dix dernières années de l'éveil de sa conscience politique.

J'ai le ferme espoir que très bientôt de nombreux monuments de l'Indépendance s'élèveront partout et porteront la même signification pour tous nos frères d'Afrique.

Peuple togolais, cet événement historique que nous célébrons aujourd'hui, c'est toi qui l'as voulu et l'as obtenu au prix de nombreux sacrifices. Sans te lasser tu as soutenu ceux que tu as chargés d'exprimer ton aspiration profonde. Par ta compréhension et ta collaboration étroite de tous les instants, tu leur as permis d'atteindre le but fixé. Sois en remercié non seulement par la pierre et le bronze mais par notre très profond et très respectueux hommage.

Demain, dans tes heures de joie et aussi dans tes heures d'épreuve, regroupe-toi sur cette place, devant ce monument, et souviens-toi que par ta foi, ta volonté, ton courage, tu as forgé la nation togolaise.

```
        ^o^
    oo  ^ ^  oo
        ^o^
```

TIRAGE 2000 exemplaires.

DEPOT LEGAL N° 174 du 6 MAI 1960.

Boîte Postale N°263

L O M E

Kingdom of Tonga

The Kingdom of Tonga is made up of three
groups of islands loacted east of Fiji and south
of Samoa in the South Pacific Ocean. First explored
by the Dutch in the 17th century, Tonga remained
an independent state until it became a British
protectorate in 1900. Following World War II the
Tongans assumed greater control over their own
affairs. Tonga became independent on June 4, 1970
as a member of the British Commonwealth.

Tonga Act 1970

1970   CHAPTER 22

An Act to make provision in connection with the attainment by Tonga of fully responsible status within the Commonwealth.   [15th May 1970]

B E IT ENACTED by the Queen's most Excellent Majesty, by and with the advice and consent of the Lords Spiritual and Temporal, and Commons, in this present Parliament assembled, and by the authority of the same, as follows:—

1.—(1) The following provisions of this section shall have effect on and after 4th June 1970 (the date on which Tonga ceases to be a protected state and becomes an independent State within the Commonwealth); and that day is in the following provisions of this Act referred to as the appointed day.

(2) Subject to the following provisions of this Act, all law which, whether being a rule of law or a provision of an Act of Parliament or of any other enactment or instrument whatsoever, is in force on the appointed day or has been passed or made before that day and comes into force thereafter, shall, unless and until provision to the contrary is made by Parliament or some other authority having power in that behalf, have the same operation in relation to Tonga, and persons and things belonging to or connected with Tonga, as it would have apart from this subsection if there had been no change in the status of Tonga on the appointed day.

(3) Part I of the Schedule to this Act (which relates to enactments applicable to Commonwealth countries having fully responsible status) and Part II of that Schedule (which relates to enactments excepted from the operation of the preceding subsection) shall have effect in relation to the enactments therein mentioned; but that Schedule shall not extend to Tonga as part of its law.

(4) Subsection (2) of this section applies to law of, or of any part of, the United Kingdom, the Channel Islands and the Isle of Man and, in relation only to any enactment of the Parliament of the United Kingdom or any Order in Council made by virtue of any such enactment whereby any such enactment applies in relation to Tonga, to the law of any other country or territory to which that enactment or Order extends.

Tonga Independence Act 1970, c.22

Trinidad and Tobago

Trinidad and Tobago is made up of the two
southernmost islands of the West Indies. Trinidad
discovered by Christopher Columbus, was under
French control until 1797 when it was captured by
the British. British sovereignty was confirmed
by the Treaty of Amiens in 1802. Tobago was
under Dutch, English, and French rule. The Treaty
of Amiens established French control in 1802.
In 1814 Tobago was ceded to Great Britain. In
1888 Trinidad and Tobago were merged into one crown
colony. It entered the Federation of the West
Indies in 1958. With disintegration of the
Federation , Dr. Eric Williams, at a Special
Convention of the People's National Movement on
January 27-28, 1962, gave a speech on the desire
to leave the Federation and form an independent
state. On May 31, 1962, the Federation disolved
and on August 31, 1962, Trinidad and Tobago became
independent, pursuant to the Trinidad and Tobago
Independence Act of 1962.

AN ACT to make provision for, and in connection with, the attainment by Trinidad and Tobago of fully responsible status within the Commonwealth.

1. (1) As from the thirty-first day of August, nineteen hundred and sixty-two (in this Act referred to as "the appointed day"), Her Majesty's Government in the United Kingdom shall have no responsibility for the government of Trinidad and Tobago.

(2) No Act of the Parliament of the United Kingdom passed on or after the appointed day shall extend, or be deemed to extend, to Trinidad and Tobago as part of the law thereof; and as from that day the provisions of the First Schedule to this Act shall have effect with respect to the legislative powers of Trinidad and Tobago.

Trinidad and Tobago Independence Act 1962, c.54

Republic of Tunisia

The Republic of Tunisia, a North African
country on the Mediterranean Sea, was the home of
the Carthaginians. After centuries under the
Roman, Vandals, and by Byzantium, the area came
under Arab rule. This was followed by Turkish
rule under which Tunisia achieved a high degree
of autonomy. Financial difficulties led to
European intervention and on May 12, 1881, Tunisia
became a French protectorate. Following a brief
period of independence during World War II a
rising nationalist movement led to several administrative reforms. On July 31, 1954, internal
autonomy was granted by France. A Declaration of
Independence was signed by Tunisia and France on
March 20, 1956. On July 25, 1957, the "Resolution
of the National Constituent Assembly Proclaiming
the Republic" abolished the existing Monarchy
and established a democratic system.

REPUBLIC OF TUNISIA

FRENCH-TUNISIAN PROTOCOL OF ACCORD

MARCH 20, 1956

On June 3, 1955, following free negotiations
that had taken place between their delegations,
the French Government and the Tunisian Government
agreed to recognize for Tunisia a full exercise
of internal sovereignty. Thus they showed their
intention to allow the Tunisian people to reach
full development and to assume, by stages, control
of their destiny.

The two Governments recognize that harmonious
and peaceful development of French-Tunisian relations meets the imperatives of the modern world.
They note with satisfaction that this evolution
allows accession to complete sovereignty without
suffering for the people and without disturbance
for the State. They affirm their conviction that,
by founding their relations on mutual and complete
respect of their sovereignties, in the independence and equality of the two States, France and
Tunisia reinforce the solidarity that unites them
for the greatest benefit of the two countries.

Following the declaration of investiture of
the French President of the Council and the answer
of His Highness the Bey, reaffirming their common
intention to promote their relations in the same
spirit of peace and friendship, the two Governments began negotiations on February 27 in Paris.

Therefore:

France solemnly recognizes the independence
of Tunisia.

As a result:

a) the treaty concluded between France and
Tunisia on May 12, 1881, may no longer govern
French-Tunisian relations;

b) those provisions of the June 3, 1955, Conventions which would be in contradiction with the new status of Tunisia, a sovereign and independent State, will be modified or abrogated.

Also as a result:

c) Tunisia may exercise its responsibilities in the areas of foreign affairs, security, and defense, as well as constituting a Tunisian national army.

Respecting their sovereignties, France and Tunisia agree to define and complete the terms of an interdependence freely achieved between the two countries, by organizing their cooperation in areas of common interest, especially in matters concerning defense and foreign relations.

Agreements between France and Tunisia will establish the terms of the assistance that France will provide to Tunisia in the building of the Tunisian national army.

Negotiations will resume on April 16, 1956, with a view of concluding, in as short a time as possible and in conformity with the principles laid down in this Protocol, the acts necessary to their implementation.

Established in Paris, in double original copies, on March 20, 1956.

For France: For Tunisia:

/signed/   /signed/

Christian Pineau   Tahar Ben Ammar

Ambassade de France, Service de Presse et d'Information, Foreign Affairs #12, March 1956.

RESOLUTION OF THE

NATIONAL CONSTITUENT ASSEMBLY

PROCLAIMING THE REPUBLIC

We the deputies of the Tunisian State, members of the National Constituent Assembly,
-- deriving all the power we hold from the people,
-- in order to strengthen the basis of independence and the sovereignty of the people, and
-- in order to establish a democratic system, which has been the purpose of the Assembly in drawing up this constitution,
-- take, in the name of the people, the following decisions, which become law and are executed immediately:

1) We abolish the Monarchy completely.

2) We proclaim that Tunisia is a republic.

3) We entrust to Mr. Habib Bourguiba, President of the Council, the duties of Head of State in its present form, until the constitution is applied and we give him the title "President of the Republic."

4) We charge the government with the execution of this decision and of all measures necessary to safeguard the republican regime. We further charge the President of the Assembly, the Secretary General of the Working Committee of the Assembly and the Government to inform the public of this decision.

Proclaimed at the Chambers of the Assembly, at the Bardo, on Thursday, 26th doul hidja 1376 - 25th July, 1957 - at 6 p.m.

President of the National Constituent Assembly,
Jellouli Faris.

Translation from Secretary of Information, Tunisia.

Protocole d'accord franco-tunisien
(20 Mars 1956)

L E 3 juin 1955, à la suite de libres négociations qui étaient intervenues entre leurs délégations, le Gouvernement français et le Gouvernement tunisien convenaient de reconnaître à la Tunisie le plein exercice de la souveraineté interne. Ils manifestaient ainsi leur volonté de permettre au peuple tunisien d'atteindre son plein épanouissement et d'assumer par étapes le contrôle de son destin.

Les deux Gouvernements reconnaissent que le développement harmonieux et pacifique des rapports franco-tunisiens répond aux impératifs du monde moderne. Ils constatent avec satisfaction que cette évolution permet l'accession à la complète souveraineté sans souffrances pour le peuple et sans heurts pour l'Etat. Ils affirment leur conviction qu'en fondant leurs rapports sur le respect mutuel et entier de leurs souverainetés, dans l'indépendance et l'égalité des deux Etats, la France et la Tunisie renforcent la solidarité qui les unit, pour le plus grand bien des deux pays.

A la suite de la déclaration d'investiture du Président du Conseil français, et de la réponse de Son Altesse le Bey, réaffirmant leur commune volonté de promouvoir leurs relations dans le même esprit de paix et d'amitié, les deux Gouvernements ont ouvert des négociations à Paris, le 27 février.

En conséquence :

La France reconnait solennellement l'indépendance de la Tunisie.

Il en découle :

a) que le Traité conclu entre la France et la Tunisie le 12 mai 1881, ne peut plus régir les rapports franco-tunisiens ;

b) que celle des dispositions des Conventions du 3 juin 1955 qui seraient en contradiction avec le nouveau statut de la Tunisie, Etat indépendant et souverain, seront modifiées ou abrogées.

Il en découle également :

c) l'exercice par la Tunisie de ses responsabilités en matière d'affaires extérieures, de sécurité et de défense ainsi que la constitution d'une armée nationale tunisienne.

Dans le respect de leurs souverainetés, la France et la Tunisie conviennent de définir ou compléter les modalités d'une interdépendance librement réalisée entre les deux pays, en organisant leur coopération dans les domaines où leurs intérêts sont communs, notamment en matière de défense et de relations extérieures.

Les accords entre la France et la Tunisie établiront les modalités du concours que la France apportera à la Tunisie dans l'édification de l'armée nationale tunisienne.

Les négociations reprendront le 16 avril 1956 en vue de conclure, dans des délais aussi brefs que possible et conformément aux principes posés dans le présent Protocole, les actes nécessaires à leur mise en œuvre.

Fait à Paris, en double original, le 20 mars 1956.

Pour la France :
Signé : Christian PINEAU

Pour la Tunisie :
Signé : TAHAR BEN AMMAR

Republic of Turkey

Turkey was at one time the center of the Ottoman Empire, but was in a state of gradual decline until World War I. Having been a member of the Central Powers, the Ottoman Empire was in an advanced state of collapse following the war. With many portions of Turkey being occupied by the Allied Powers, Turkish Parliament issued the National Pact on January 28, 1920, declaring that Turkey was an independent state and that freedom must continue. A three year period of resistance to the allies resulted in the Treaty of Lausanne of 1923 recognizing Turkish sovereignity.

REPUBLIC OF TURKEY

THE TURKISH NATIONAL PACT

28 January 1920

The Members of the Ottoman Chamber of Deputies recognise and affirm that the independence of the State and the future of the Nation can be assured by complete respect for the following principles, which represent the maximum of sacrifice which can be undertaken in order to achieve a just and lasting peace, and that the continued existence of a stable Ottoman Sultanate and society is impossible outside of the said principles:

Art. 1.   Inasmuch as it is necessary that the destinies of the portions of the Turkish Empire which are populated exclusively by an Arab majority, and which on the conclusion of the armistice of the 30th October 1918 were in the occupation of enemy forces, should be determined in accordance with the votes which shall be freely given by the inhabitants, the whole of those parts whether within or outside the said armistice line which are inhabited by an Ottoman Moslem majority, united in religion, in race and in aim, imbued with sentiments of mutual respect for each other and of sacrifice, and wholly respectful of each other's racial and social rights and surrounding conditions, form a whole which does not admit of division for any reason in truth or in ordinance.

Art. 2.   We accept that, in the case of the three [Kurdish] Sandjaks which united themselves by a general vote to the mother country when they first were free, recourse should again be had, if necessary, to a free popular vote.

Art. 3.   The determination of the juridical status of Western Thrace also, which has been made dependent on the Turkish peace, must be effected in accordance with the votes which shall be given by the inhabitants in complete freedom.

Art. 4. The security of the city of Constantinople, which is the seat of the Caliphate of Islam, the capital of the Sultanate, and the headquarters of the Ottoman Government, and of the Sea of Marmora must be protected from every danger. Provided this principle is maintained, whatever decision may be arrived at jointly by us and all other Governments concerned, regarding the opening of the Bosphorus to the commerce and traffic of the world, is valid.

Art. 5. The rights of minorities as defined in the treaties concluded between the Entente Powers and their enemies and certain of their associates shall be confirmed and assured by us-- in reliance on the belief that the Moslem minorities in neighbouring countries also will have the benefit of the same rights.

Art. 6. It is a fundamental condition of our life and continued existence that we, like every country, should enjoy complete independence and liberty in the matter of assuring the means of our development, in order that our national and economic development should be rendered possible and that it should be possible to conduct affairs in the form of a more up-to-date regular administration.

For this reason we are opposed to restrictions inimical to our development in political, judicial, financial, and other matters.

The conditions of settlement of our proved debts shall likewise not be contrary to these principles.

Official Translation

Republic of Uganda

A land locked country in East Central Africa,
the Republic of Uganda was made a British protectorate in 1894. In 1900 the Buganda Agreement
provided for internal autonomy in return for
support of the British. A futile attempt by Great
Britain to unify the country led to the creation
of nationalist organizations. Independence was
achieved on October 9, 1962 by an act of
British Parliament.

Uganda Act 1964

1964 CHAPTER 20

An Act to make provision as to the operation of the law in relation to Uganda as a Commonwealth Country not within Her Majesty's dominions.   [25th March 1964]

BE IT ENACTED by the Queen's most Excellent Majesty, by and with the advice and consent of the Lords Spiritual and Temporal, and Commons, in this present Parliament assembled, and by the authority of the same, as follows:—

1.—(1) Subject to this Act, all law which whether being a rule of law or a provision of an Act of Parliament or of any other enactment or instrument whatsoever, was in force on 9th October 1963 (being the date on which Uganda ceased to be part of Her Majesty's dominions), or, having been passed or made before that day, comes or has come into force thereafter, shall, unless and until provision to the contrary is made by Parliament or some other authority having power in that behalf, have the same operation in relation to Uganda, and persons and things belonging to or connected with Uganda, as it would have apart from this subsection if Uganda had not ceased to be part of Her Majesty's dominions.

(2) This section applies to law of or of any part of the United Kingdom, the Channel Islands and the Isle of Man and, in relation only to any enactment of the Parliament of the United Kingdom or any Order in Council made by virtue of any such enactment whereby any such enactment applies in relation to Uganda, to law of any other country or territory to which that enactment or Order extends.

(3) This section shall be deemed to have had effect from 9th October 1963.

Uganda Independence Act, 10&11 Eliz.2, c.57 (1962)

United Arab Emirates

Located on the eastern Arabian Peninsula, the
United Arab Emirates is bounded to the north by
the Persian Gulf. Pirate activity during the
19th century led Great Britain to sign a treaty
with coastal shaikhs in 1853. An 1892 treaty
established the area as a British protectorate.
In the 1960's Great Britain announced its decision
to terminate the treaty relationship. On December 1, 1971 seven of the nine shaikh-doms became
independent, Bahrain and Qater becoming independent
earlier. On December 2, 1971 the United Arab Emirates was formed.

UNITED ARAB EMIRATES

We, the Rulers of the Emirates of Abu Dhabi, Dubai, Sharjah, Ajman, Umm al Qaiwain, Ras al Khaimah and Fujairah;

Whereas it is our desire and the desire of the people of our Emirates to establish a Union between these Emirates to promote a better life, more enduring stability and a higher international status for the Emirates and their people;

Desiring to create closer links between the Arab Emirates in the form of an independent, sovereign, federal state, capable of protecting its existence and the existence of its members, in cooperation with the sister Arab states and with all other friendly states which are members of the United Nations Organisation and members of the family of nations in general, on a basis of mutual respect and reciprocal interests and advantage;

Desiring also to lay the foundations of Union Law in the coming years on a sound basis, corresponding with the realities and the capacities of the Emirates at the present time, enabling the Union, so far as possible, freely to achieve its goals, sustaining the identity of its members where this is not inconsistent with those goals and preparing the people of the Union at the same time for a noble and free constitutional life, progressing by steps towards a comprehensive, representative, democratic regime in an Islamic and Arab society free from fear and anxiety;

And whereas the realisation of the foregoing was our greatest desire, towards which we have bent our strongest resolution, being desirous of advancing our country and our people to the position which befits them and which will restore to them their appropriate place among civilised states and nations;

For all these reasons and in order that the preparation of the permanent constitution for the Union may be completed, we proclaim before the Supreme and Omnipotent Creator, and before all people

our agreement to this provisional Constitution, to
which our signatures were appended, which shall be
implemented during the transitional period indicated in it;

May Allah, our best Protector and Defender,
grant us success.

1971

Official translation

COMMUNIQUE OF STATE

UNITED ARAB EMIRATES

December 2, 1971

On this day, Thursday the 15th of Shawwal
1391, corresponding to 2 December 1971, the Rulers
of the emirates of Abu Dhabi, Dubai, Sharjah,
Ajman, Umm al-Quwain and Fujairah, signatories of
the provisional constitution of the State of
United Arab Emirates, held a meeting in Dubai in
an atmosphere characterized by fraternal sentiments, mutual confidence and a deep concern for
fulfilling the wishes of the people of these
amirates, and issued a proclamation of the coming
into force of the provisions of the said constitution with effect from today.

The Rulers then resumed their meeting as the
Supreme Council of the Federation and elected his
Highness Shaikh Zayid ibn Sultan Al Nuhayyan, the
Ruler of the Emirate of Abu Dhabi, as President
of the State of the United Arab Emirates for a
five-year term, and his Highness Shaikh Rashid
ibn Sa'id al-maktum, the Ruler of the Emirate of
Dubai, as Vice President for the same term. Each
of them took the oath of office according to the
provisions of the constitution. His Highness
Shaikh Maktum ibn Rashid al-Maktum, the Crown
Prince of the Emirate of Dubai, was appointed
President of the Federal Council of Ministers.
The Council will hold its second meeting in Abu
Dhabi on Tuesday 7 December 1971.

The Supreme Council announces this auspi-
cious happening to the people of the State of
United Arab Emirates, all the sister Arab states,
the friendly states and the world as a whole, and
declares the establishment of the State of United
Arab Emirates as an independent and soverign
state forming part of the Arab homeland. Its aim
is to preserve its independence, sovereignty,
security and stability, to ward off any aggression
against itself or any of its member emirates, to
safeguard the rights and freedoms of its people,

and to establish close cooperation between its
member emirates for their common benefit. For
these objectives and in order to promote its prosperity and advancement in all fields, to ensure a
better life for all its citizens, to support Arab
and Islamic causes and interests, and to cement
ties of friendship and cooperation with all states
and peoples on the basis of the principles of the
Arab League Charter, the UN Charter and international morality, the State of the United Arab
Emirates was created.

The Federation denounces the principle of
the use of force and regrets the action taken by
Iran recently in occupying a cherished part of
the Arab homeland; it stresses the importance of
respecting the legitimate rights of all countries
and of discussing any disputes which may arise
between states in accordance with internationally
recognized practice.

The Supreme Council of the Federation,
while expressing thanks to the Almighty on this
historic occasion for His support and aid, and
while addressing congratulations to the people of
the Federation on the fulfillment of their aspirations, believes that any unity or federation in
any part of the Arab homeland represents a step
in the direction of the legitimate ofjective of
complete Arab unity.

The Federation welcomes the adherence of
other sister emirates who signed the agreement
for the Federation of Arab Emirates of 27 February
1968 in Dubai* to the State of United Arab
Emirates.

*Bahrain, Qatar and Ras al-khaimah

United Kingdom of Great Britain
and Northern Ireland

The United Kingdom of Great Britain and
Northern Ireland consists of England, Wales, Scotland, Northern Ireland and a number of minor islands such as the Orkneys, the Shetland Islands,
the Hebrides, Anglesey, and the Isle of Wight.

Each of the major parts of the United Kingdom was at one time a separate nation. Wales
was incorporated with England by virtue of the
1536 Act for the Government of Wales. Scottish
Union was obtained in 1706 with the Act for the
Union with Scotland. Ireland was formally joined
with England in 1719 by the Dependency of Ireland
Act.

The effect of these three statutes was to
end the independent status of Wales, Scotland
and Ireland absorbing them into the entity now
known as the United Kingdom of Great Britain and
Northern Ireland. While parliamentary representation is provided each of the regions of the United
Kingdom, Northern Ireland has a separate government
and a parliament with legislative powers. The
Irish Free State (now the Republic of Ireland)
obtained its independence from Great Britain in
1922, leaving the six counties of Northern Ireland
still joined to the United Kingdom.

ACT FOR THE GOVERNMENT OF WALES (1536)

An act for laws and justice to be ministered in Wales in like form as it is in this realm. Albeit the dominion, principality, and country of Wales justly and righteously is and ever hath been incorporated, annexed, united, and subject to and under the imperial crown of this realm as a very member and joint of the same, wherefore the king's most royal majesty of . . . very right is very head, king, lord, and ruler; yet, notwithstanding, because that in the same country, principality, and dominion divers rights, usages, laws, and customs be far discrepant from the laws and customs of this realm, and also because that the people of the same dominion have and do daily use a speech nothing like nor consonant to the natural mother tongue used within this realm, some rude and ignorant people have made distinction and diversity between the king's subjects of this realm and his subjects of the said dominion . . . of Wales, whereby great discord . . . and sedition hath grown between his said subjects: his highness, therefore, of a singular zeal, love, and favour that he beareth towards his subjects of his said dominion of Wales, minding and intending to reduce them to the perfect order, notice, and knowledge of his laws of this his realm, and utterly to extirp all and singular the sinister uses and customs differing from the same, and to bring his said subjects of this his realm and of his said dominion of Wales to an amicable concord and unity, hath by the deliberate advice, consent, and agreement of the lords spiritual and temporal and the commons in this present parliament assembled, and by the authority of the same . . . , established that his said country or dominion of Wales shall be, stand, and continue forever from henceforth incorporated, united, and annexed to and with this his realm of England; and that all and singular person and persons born and to be born in the said . . . dominion of Wales shall have, enjoy, and inherit all and singular freedoms, liberties, rights, privileges, and laws within this realm and other the king's dominions, as other the king's subjects naturally born within the same have, enjoy, and inherit; and that all and singular person and persons inheritable to any manors, lands, tenements, rents, reversions, services, or other hereditaments which shall descend after the feast of All Saints next coming within the said . . . dominion of Wales, or within any particular lordship part or parcel of the said . . . dominion of Wales, shall forever from and after the said feast of All Saints inherit and be inheritable to the same manors [etc.] . . . after the English tenure, without division or partition, and after the form of the laws of this realm of England, and not after any tenure nor after the form of any Welsh laws or customs; and that the laws, ordinances, and statutes of this realm of England forever, and none other laws . . . , from and after the said feast of All Saints . . . , shall be had, used, practised, and executed in the said . . . dominion of Wales and every part thereof in like manner, form, and order as they are and shall be . . . executed in this realm and in such like manner and form as hereafter by this act shall be further established and ordained. . . .

Also be it enacted . . . that all justices, commissioners, sheriffs, coroners . . . , and their lieutenants, and all other officers and ministers of the laws, shall proclaim and keep the sessions, courts, hundreds, leets, sheriff's courts, and all other courts in the English tongue, and all oaths of officers, juries, and inquests, and all other affidavits, verdicts, and wagers of law to be given and done in the English tongue; and also that from henceforth no person or persons that use the Welsh speech or language shall have or enjoy any manner office or fees within the realm of England, Wales, or other the king's dominions, upon pain of forfeiting the same offices or fees, unless he or they use and exercise the speech or language of English. . . .

ACT FOR THE UNION WITH SCOTLAND,
1706

6 Anne, c. 11.

Most gracious Sovereign

Whereas Articles of Union were agreed on the Twenty second Day of July in the Fifth Year of Your Majesties Reign by the Commissioners nominated on Behalf of the Kingdom of England under Your Majesties Great Seal of England . . . in pursuance of an Act of Parliament made in England . . . and the Commissioners nominated on the Behalf of the Kingdom of Scotland under Your Majesties Great Seal of Scotland . . . in pursuance of the Fourth Act of the Third Session of the present Parliament of Scotland to treat of and concerning an Union of the said Kingdoms And whereas an Act hath passed in the Parliament of Scotland at Edinburgh . . . wherein 'tis mentioned that the Estates of Parliament . . . had agreed to and approved of the said Articles of Union with some Additions and Explanations and that Your Majesty with Advice and Consent of the Estates of Parliament for establishing the Protestant Religion and Presbyterian Church Government within the Kingdom of Scotland had passed in the same Session of Parliament an Act intituled Act for securing of the Protestant Religion and Presbyterian Church Government which by the Tenor thereof was appointed to be inserted in any Act ratifying the Treaty and expresly declared to be a fundamental and essential Condition of the said Treaty or Union in all Times coming the Tenor of which Articles as ratified and approved of with Additions and Explanations by the said Act of Parliament of Scotland follows

ARTICLE I. That the Two Kingdoms of England and Scotland shall upon the First Day of May which shall be in the Year One thousand seven hundred and seven and for ever after be united into One Kingdom by the Name of Great Britain and that the Ensigns Armorial of the said United Kingdom be such as Her Majesty shall appoint and the Crosses of St. George and St. Andrew be conjoyned in such Manner as Her Majesty shall think fit and used in all Flags Banners Standards and Ensigns both at Sea and Land.

ARTICLE II. That the Succession to the Monarchy of the United Kingdom of Great Britain and of the Dominions thereto belonging after Her most Sacred Majesty and in Default of Issue of Her Majesty be remain and continue to the most Excellent Princess Sophia Electoress and Dutchess Dowager of Hanover and the Heirs of Her Body being Protestants upon whom the Crown of England is settled . . . And that all Papists and Persons marrying Papists shall be excluded from and for ever incapable to inherit possess or enjoy the Imperial Crown of Great Britain and the Dominions thereunto belonging or any Part thereof and in every such Case the Crown and Government shall from time to time descend to and be enjoyed by such Person being a Protestant as should have inherited and enjoyed the same in case such Papist or Person marrying a Papist was naturally dead

ARTICLE III. That the United Kingdom of Great Britain be represented by One and the same Parliament to be stiled The Parliament of Great Britain.

ARTICLE IIII. That all the Subjects of the United Kingdom of Great Britain shall from and after the Union have full Freedom and Intercourse of Trade and Navigation to and from any Port or Place within the said United Kingdom and the Dominions and Plantations thereunto belonging and that there be a Communication of all other Rights Privileges and Advantages which do or may belong to the Subjects of either Kingdom except where it is otherwise expresly agreed in these Articles.

THE DEPENDENCY OF IRELAND ACT,
1719
6 Geo. I, c. 5.

' I. Whereas the House of Lords of *Ireland* have of late, against Law, assumed to themselves a Power and Jurisdiction to examine, correct and amend the Judgments and Decrees of the Courts of Justice in the Kingdom of *Ireland*:' Therefore for the better securing of the Dependency of *Ireland* upon the Crown of *Great Britain*, May it please your most Excellent Majesty that it may be declared, and be it declared . . . That the same Kingdom of *Ireland* hath been, is, and of Right ought to be subordinate unto and dependent upon the Imperial Crown of *Great Britain*, as being inseparably united and annexed thereunto; and that the King's Majesty, by and with the Advice and Consent of the Lords Spiritual and Temporal, and Commons of *Great Britain* in Parliament assembled, had, hath, and of Right ought to have full Power and Authority to make Laws and Statutes of sufficient Force and Validity, to bind the Kingdom and People of *Ireland*.

II. And be it further declared . . . That the House of Lords of *Ireland* have not, nor of Right ought to have any Jurisdiction to judge of, affirm or reverse any Judgment, Sentence or Decree, given or made in any Court within the said Kingdom, and that all Proceedings before the said House of Lords upon any such Judgment, Sentence or Decree, are, and are hereby declared to be utterly null and void to all Intents and Purposes whatsoever.

United States of America

The Declaration of Independence of the Thirteen Colonies of North America is the first national independence document in world history. Adopted by the Second Continental Congress on July 4, 1776, the Declaration announced the separation of those colonies from Great Britain, at the same time establishing the United States.

The first draft was prepared by Thomas Jefferson, revised by Jefferson, John Adams and Benjamin Franklin and then sent to Congress where it was changed again into its present language.

The Declaration of Independence, perhaps the most important of all American historical documents, has long provided a source of inspiration for other peoples seeking freedom and independence. The actual date of American independence was July 2, 1776, because of the passage of the Lee-Adams resolution of independence on that date. However, because of the stirring, powerful message of the Declaration its adoption became a national holiday and July 4th became the date popularly accepted as the occasion of celebration of the event of independence.

The principles that "all men are created equal" and that they possess the inalienable rights to "life, liberty, and the pursuit of happiness" have provided both a philosophy of government and a justification for rebellion ever since.

the united states of america

declaration of independence *

The unanimous Declaration of the thirteen United States of America.

When, in the Course of human events, it becomes necessary for one people to dissolve the political bands which have connected them with another, and to assume, among the Powers of the earth, the separate and equal station to which the Laws of Nature and of Nature's God entitle them, a decent respect to the opinions of mankind requires that they should declare the causes which impel them to the separation.

We hold these truths to be self-evident, that all men are created equal, that they are endowed by their Creator with certain unalienable Rights, that among these, are Life, Liberty, and the pursuit of Happiness. That, to secure these rights, Governments are instituted among Men, deriving their just Powers from the consent of the governed. That, whenever any form of Government becomes destructive of these ends, it is the Right of the People to alter or to abolish it, and to institute new Government, laying its foundation on such Principles, and organizing its Powers in such form, as to them shall seem most likely to effect their Safety and Happiness. Prudence, indeed, will dictate that Governments long established should not be changed for light and transient causes; and, accordingly, all experience hath shewn, that mankind are more disposed to suffer, while evils are sufferable, than to right them-

* *The original spelling, capitalization, and punctuation have been retained.*

selves by abolishing the forms to which they are accustomed. But, when a long train of abuses and usurpations, pursuing invariably the same Object, evinces a design to reduce them under absolute Despotism, it is their right, it is their duty, to throw off such Government, and to provide new Guards for their future Security. Such has been the patient sufferance of these Colonies; and such is now the necessity which constrains them to alter their former Systems of Government. The history of the present King of Great Britain is a history of repeated injuries and usurpations, all having in direct object the establishment of an absolute Tyranny over these States. To prove this, let Facts be submitted to a candid world.

He has refused his Assent to Laws the most wholesome and necessary for the public good.

He has forbidden his Governors to pass Laws of immediate and pressing importance, unless suspended in their operation till his Assent should be obtained; and when so suspended, he has utterly neglected to attend to them.

He has refused to pass other Laws for the accommodation of large districts of People, unless those People would relinquish the right of Representation in the legislature; a right inestimable to them and formidable to tyrants only.

He has called together legislative bodies at places unusual, uncomfortable, and distant from the depository of their Public Records, for the sole Purpose of fatiguing them into compliance with his measures.

He has dissolved Representative Houses repeatedly, for opposing, with manly firmness, his invasions on the rights of the People.

He has refused for a long time, after such dissolutions, to cause others to be elected; whereby the Legislative Powers, incapable of Annihilation, have returned to the People at large for their exercise; the State remaining in the mean time exposed to all the dangers of invasion from without, and convulsions within.

He has endeavoured to prevent the Population of these States; for that purpose obstructing the Laws for Naturalization of Foreigners; refusing to pass others to encourage their migrations hither, and raising the conditions of new Appropriations of Lands.

He has obstructed the Administration of Justice, by refusing his Assent to Laws for establishing Judiciary Powers.

He has made Judges, dependent on his Will alone, for the tenure of their offices, and the amount and payment of their salaries.

He has erected a multitude of New Offices and sent hither swarms of Officers to harrass our People, and eat out their substance.

He has kept among us, in times of Peace, Standing Armies, without the Consent of our legislatures.

He has affected to render the Military independent of and superior to the Civil Power.

He has combined with others to subject us to a jurisdiction foreign to our constitution, and unacknowledged by our laws; giving his Assent to their Acts of pretended Legislation:

For quartering large bodies of armed troops among us:

For protecting them, by a mock Trial, from Punishment for any Murders which they should commit on the Inhabitants of these States:

For cutting off our Trade with all parts of the world:

For imposing Taxes on us without our Consent:

For depriving us, in many cases, of the benefits of Trial by Jury:

For transporting us beyond Seas to be tried for pretended offences:

For abolishing the free System of English Laws in a neighbouring province, establishing therein an Arbitrary government, and enlarging its Boundaries, so as to render it at once an example and fit instrument for introducing the same absolute rule into these Colonies:

For taking away our Charters, abolishing our most valuable Laws, and altering fundamentally the Forms of our Governments:

For suspending our own Legislatures, and declaring themselves invested with Power to legislate for us in all cases whatsoever.

He has abdicated Government here, by declaring us out of his protection, and waging War against us.

He has plundered our seas, ravaged our Coasts, burnt our towns, and destroyed the Lives of our People.

He is at this time transporting large Armies of foreign Mercenaries to compleat the works of death, desolation and tyranny, already begun with circumstances of Cruelty and perfidy scarcely paralleled in the most barbarous ages, and totally unworthy the Head of a civilized nation.

He has constrained our fellow Citizens, taken Captive on the high Seas, to bear Arms against their Country, to become the executioners of their friends and Brethren, or to fall themselves by their Hands.

He has excited domestic insurrections amongst us, and has endeavoured to bring on the inhabitants of our frontiers, the merciless Indian Savages, whose known rule of warfare, is an undistinguished destruction of all ages, sexes and conditions.

In every stage of these Oppressions, We have Petitioned for Redress, in the most humble terms: Our repeated Petitions, have been answered only by repeated injury. A

Prince, whose character is thus marked by every act which may define a Tyrant, is unfit to be the ruler of a free People.

Nor have We been wanting in attentions to our British brethren. We have warned them from time to time of attempts by their legislature to extend an unwarrantable jurisdiction over us. We have reminded them of the circumstances of our emigration and settlement here. We have appealed to their native justice and magnanimity, and we have conjured them by the ties of our common kindred, to disavow these usurpations, which, would inevitably interrupt our connexions and correspondence. They too have been deaf to the voice of justice and consanguinity. We must, therefore, acquiesce in the necessity, which denounces our Separation, and hold them, as we hold the rest of mankind, Enemies in war, in Peace Friends.

WE, THEREFORE, the Representatives of the UNITED STATES OF AMERICA, in GENERAL CONGRESS assembled, appealing to the Supreme Judge of the World for the rectitude of our intentions, DO, in the Name, and by Authority of the good People of these Colonies, solemnly PUBLISH and DECLARE, That these United Colonies are, and of Right, ought to be FREE AND INDEPENDENT STATES; that they are Absolved from all Allegiance to the British Crown, and that all political connexion between them and the State of Great Britain, is and ought to be totally dissolved; and that, as FREE and INDEPENDENT STATES, they have full Power to levy War, conclude Peace, contract Alliances, establish Commerce, and to do all other Acts and Things which INDEPENDENT STATES may of right do. AND for the support of this Declaration, with a firm reliance on the protection of divine Providence, we mutually pledge to each other our Lives, our Fortunes, and our sacred Honour.

Official Text

IN CONGRESS, JULY 4, 1776.

The unanimous Declaration of the thirteen united States of America,

When in the Course of human events it becomes necessary for one people to dissolve the political bands which have connected them with another, and to -sume among the powers of the earth, the separate and equal station to which the Laws of Nature and of Nature's God entitle them, a decent respect to the opinions of mankind requires that they -hould declare the causes which impel them to the separation. — We hold these truths to be self-evident, that all men are created equal, that they are endowed by their Creator -ith certain unalienable Rights, that among these are Life, Liberty and the pursuit of Happiness. — That to secure these rights, Governments are instituted among Men, deriving their just -owers from the consent of the governed, — That whenever any Form of Government becomes destructive of these ends, it is the Right of the People to alter or to abolish it, and to institute new -overnment, laying its foundation on such principles and organizing its powers in such form, as to them shall seem most likely to effect their Safety and Happiness. Prudence, indeed, -ill dictate that Governments long established should not be changed for light and transient causes; and accordingly all experience hath shewn, that mankind are more disposed to suffer, while -ils are sufferable, than to right themselves by abolishing the forms to which they are accustomed. But when a long train of abuses and usurpations, pursuing invariably the same Object -inces a design to reduce them under absolute Despotism, it is their right, it is their duty, to throw off such Government, and to provide new Guards for their future security. — Such has -en the patient sufferance of these Colonies; and such is now the necessity which constrains them to alter their former Systems of Government. The history of the present King of Great -ritain is a history of repeated injuries and usurpations, all having in direct object the establishment of an absolute Tyranny over these States. To prove this, let Facts be submitted to a candid -orld. — He has refused his Assent to Laws, the most wholesome and necessary for the public good. — He has forbidden his Governors to pass Laws of immediate -nd pressing importance, unless suspended in their operation till his Assent should be obtained; and when so suspended, he has utterly neglected to attend to them. — He has refused to -ss other Laws for the accommodation of large districts of people, unless those people would relinquish the right of Representation in the Legislature, a right inestimable to them and formidable -tyrants only. — He has called together legislative bodies at places unusual, uncomfortable, and distant from the depository of their public Records, for the sole purpose of fatiguing them into -mpliance with his measures. — He has dissolved Representative Houses repeatedly, for opposing with manly firmness his invasions on the rights of the people. — He has refused for -long time, after such dissolutions, to cause others to be elected; whereby the Legislative powers, incapable of Annihilation, have returned to the People at large for their exercise; the State remain-g in the mean time exposed to all the dangers of invasion from without, and convulsions within. — He has endeavoured to prevent the population of these States; for that purpose obstruc-ng the Laws for Naturalization of Foreigners; refusing to pass others to encourage their migrations hither, and raising the conditions of new Appropriations of Lands. — He has obstructed the -dministration of Justice, by refusing his Assent to Laws for establishing Judiciary powers. — He has made Judges dependent on his Will alone, for the tenure of their offices, and the amount -d payment of their salaries. — He has erected a multitude of New Offices, and sent hither swarms of Officers to harrass our people and eat out their substance. — He has kept among -, in times of peace, Standing Armies without the Consent of our legislatures. — He has affected to render the Military independent of and superior to the Civil power. — He has combined -ith others to subject us to a jurisdiction foreign to our constitution, and unacknowledged by our laws; giving his Assent to their Acts of pretended Legislation: — For Quartering large bodies of -med troops among us: — For protecting them, by a mock Trial, from punishment for any Murders which they should commit on the Inhabitants of these States: — For cutting off -r Trade with all parts of the world: — For imposing Taxes on us without our Consent: — For depriving us in many cases, of the benefits of Trial by Jury: — For transporting us beyond -as to be tried for pretended offences — For abolishing the free System of English Laws in a neighbouring Province, establishing therein an Arbitrary government, and enlarging its Boundaries -o as to render it at once an example and fit instrument for introducing the same absolute rule into these Colonies: — For taking away our Charters, abolishing our most valuable Laws and -tering fundamentally the Forms of our Governments: — For suspending our own Legislatures, and declaring themselves invested with power to legislate for us in all cases whatsoever. — He has abdicated Government here, by declaring us out of his Protection and waging War against us. — He has plundered our seas, ravaged our Coasts, burnt our towns, and destroyed the lives -ur people. — He is at this time transporting large Armies of foreign Mercenaries to compleat the works of death, desolation and tyranny, already begun with circumstances of Cruelty & perfidy -rcely paralleled in the most barbarous ages, and totally unworthy the Head of a civilized nation. — He has constrained our fellow Citizens taken Captive on the high Seas to bear Arms against -ir Country, to become the executioners of their friends and Brethren, or to fall themselves by their Hands. — He has excited domestic insurrections amongst us, and has endeavoured to bring on the -habitants of our frontiers, the merciless Indian Savages, whose known rule of warfare, is an undistinguished destruction of all ages, sexes and conditions. In every stage of these Oppressions We -ve Petitioned for Redress in the most humble terms: Our repeated Petitions have been answered only by repeated injury. A Prince, whose character is thus marked by every act which may define a Tyrant, -unfit to be the ruler of a free people. Nor have We been wanting in attentions to our Brittish brethren. We have warned them from time to time of attempts by their legislature to extend an unwarrant-e jurisdiction over us. We have reminded them of the circumstances of our emigration and settlement here. We have appealed to their native justice and magnanimity, and we have conjured them -the ties of our common kindred to disavow these usurpations, which, would inevitably interrupt our connections and correspondence. They too have been deaf to the voice of justice and of -sanguinity. We must, therefore, acquiesce in the necessity, which denounces our Separation, and hold them, as we hold the rest of mankind, Enemies in War, in Peace Friends. —

We, therefore, the Representatives of the united States of America, in General Congress, Assembled, appealing to the Supreme Judge of the world for the rectitude of our in-tions, do, in the Name, and by Authority of the good People of these Colonies, solemnly publish and declare, That these United Colonies are, and of Right ought to be Free and Independent -ates; that they are Absolved from all Allegiance to the British Crown, and that all political connection between them and the State of Great Britain, is and ought to be totally dissolved; and -t as Free and Independent States, they have full Power to levy War, conclude Peace, contract Alliances, establish Commerce, and to do all other Acts and Things which Independent -ates may of right do. — And for the support of this Declaration, with a firm reliance on the protection of divine Providence, we mutually pledge to each other our Lives, our Fortunes -d our sacred Honor.

Button Gwinnett
Lyman Hall
Geo Walton.

Wm Hooper
Joseph Hewes,
John Penn

Edward Rutledge 1.

Thos Heyward Junr.
Thomas Lynch Junr.
Arthur Middleton

John Hancock

Samuel Chase
Wm. Paca
Thos. Stone
Charles Carroll of Carrollton

George Wythe
Richard Henry Lee
Th Jefferson
Benja Harrison
Thos Nelson jr.
Francis Lightfoot Lee
Carter Braxton

Robt Morris
Benjamin Rush
Benja. Franklin
John Morton
Geo Clymer
Jas. Smith
Geo. Taylor
James Wilson
Geo. Ross
Caesar Rodney
Geo Read
Tho M:Kean

Wm Floyd
Phil. Livingston
Frans. Lewis
Lewis Morris
Richd Stockton
Jno Witherspoon
Fras. Hopkinson
John Hart
Abra Clark

Josiah Bartlett
Wm Whipple
Saml Adams
John Adams
Robt Treat Paine
Elbridge Gerry
Step Hopkins
William Ellery
Roger Sherman
Samel Huntington
Wm Williams
Oliver Wolcott
Matthew Thornton

THE DECLARATION OF INDEPENDENCE

Republic of Upper Volta

The Republic of Upper Volta is bounded on
the northwest by the Sudanese Republic, on the
northeast by Niger, and on the south by Ivory
Coast, Ghana, and Togo. After exploration in the
early part of the century, the French made Upper
Volta a protectorate in 1897. It became a
separate colony in 1919. Though divided among
neighboring colonies in 1932, Upper Volta was
again made a separate entity as an overseas territory
of the French Union following World War II. It
became an autonomous republic on December 11, 1958.
A July 11, 1960, agreement between France and
Upper Volta provided for independence. On August
5, 1960, the President of the Republic of Upper
Volta, Maurice Yameogo, announced to the people
its new status as an independent republic.

AGREEMENT

TRANSFERRING THE POWERS OF THE "COMMUNAUTE"

The parties, consisting of,

The governments of the Republic of Upper Volta, and the French Republic, agree as follows:

Article I. With the full support and friendship of the French Republic, the powers of the Communaute are terminated and the Republic of Upper Volta assumes international sovereignty and independence.

Article II. All of the powers given by Article 78 of the Constitution of October 4, 1958, are, where applicable, transferred to the Republic of Upper Volta, effective upon the completion by the contracting parties of the procedures contained in Article 87 of the said Constitution.

Done at Paris, July 11, 1960

For the Government of the   For the Government of
Republic of Upper Volta   the French Republic

Maurice Yaméogo   Michel Debré

Translated by Matthew Jodziewicz

UPPER VOLTA

Article 1. The Republic of Upper Volta receives with the full agreement and friendship of the French Republic both international sovereignty and independence through the transfer of legal powers from the French Communaute.

Article 2. All the legal powers granted by article 78 of the Constitution of October 4, 1958, are, as far as they are applicable, transferred to the Republic of Upper Volta, after the contracting parties have complied with the procedure outlined in article 87 of the said Constitution.

Article 87 requires each Parliament to ratify this agreement before it can come into effect.

Translated by Matthew Jodziewicz

UPPER VOLTA

PROCLAMATION OF INDEPENDENCE

Today, at midnight, August 5, 1960, I will
solemnly proclaim the independence of the Republic
of Upper Volta in the name of the natural right of
man for justice, for equality, for brotherhood.
Nine centuries of history have revealed to the
world the moral valor of the Voltan man. In the
name of this philosophy upon which we desire to
build our nation, I express my profound gratitude
to all the artisans of our National Independence.
To France, to General de Gaulle whose courage and
magnificent astuteness gain immortality for him in
the eyes of history, to all the nations who assist
us, to the clergy who supply this country its first
elite giving favorable support, to the French pro-
fessors, who have patiently formed the spirit of
the decision makers of this country, to our traditional leaders who have been able to safeguard the
integrity of our state against outside attacks, to
the servicemen and old soldiers, always faithful
to honor, to all our members of Parliament, to political supporters at all echelons, to valiant
servicemen who died for the triumph of our liberty,
I address, in the name of the Government, the homage
of my profound gratitude.

Long live independent Upper Volta, long live
France, long live the brotherhood of the peoples
of the earth.

Translated by Matthew Jodziewicz

Oriental Republic of Uruguay

Uruguay is bounded by Brazil to the north, the
Atlantic Ocean to the east, and Argentina to the
south and west. Originally settled by the Portuguese
in 1680, by the 1770's Spain had settled most of
the country. In 1777 Spain drove the last Portuguese
out of Uruguay. Independence from Spain was declared
on May 25, 1810, by Gose Gervasis Artigas.
Fighting continued until 1820 when Portugal invaded
and seized the country. Uruguay was annexed to
Brazil and Artiges was exiled. Followers of
Artiges on August 25, 1825, declared their
independence from Portugal and Brazil. In 1828
Brazil and Argentina recognized Uruguay as an
independent republic. A constitution was adopted
in 1829.

URUGUAY

August 25, 1825

The vested sovereignty, ordinary and extraordinary, which constitutes the political existence of the peoples comprising it --

1) Declares null and void, dissolved and forevermore of no value all acts of incorporation, all acclamations and oaths wrested from the peoples of the Eastern Province by violence and force, along with the treachery of the intruding powers of Portugal and Brazil, who have tyrannized, trampled and usurped their inalienable rights, subjecting them to the yoke of an absolute despotism from the year 1817 to the present year, 1825.

2) As a consequence of the preceding declaration, the Eastern Province, assuming once again the full rights, liberties and prerogatives inherent with other peoples of the earth, declares itself, in fact and in law, free and independent of the King of Portugal, the Emperor of Brazil, and any other individual in the Universe, with full power to take on the forms which, in the use and exercise of its sovereignty, it deems appropriate.

Translated by Sarah J. Campbell

Republic of Venezuela

Discovered for Spain by Christopher Columbus
in 1498, Venezuela remained a Spanish colony
through the 18th century. After several unsuccessful
revolts in the early 19th century, Venezuela refused
to support the new Spanish government of Joseph
Bonaparte who had deposed Ferdinand VII. A junta
was established in 1810 supporting Ferdinand. A
coastal blockade and strong demands made by the
new Spanish Government led to a declaration of
independence on July 5, 1811. Independence lasted
until July 26, 1812 when the country was surrendered
to Spain. A struggle led by Simon Bolivar resulted
in the elimination of all Spanish strongholds and
the establishment of Venezuelan independence.

VENEZUELA

In the name of the Most High, We, the Representatives of the Federal Provinces of Caracas, Cumana, Barinas, Margarita, Barcelona, Merida, and Truxillo, constituting the Confederation of Venezuela, on the Southern continent of America, in Congress assembled:

Considering that we have been in full and entire possession of our natural rights since the 19th of April, 1810: which we re-assumed in consequence of the transactions at Bayonne, the abdication of the Spanish Throne, the conquest of Spain, and the accession of a new Dynasty, established without our consent: and that we avail ourselves of the rights of men, withheld from us by force for more than three centuries, to which we are restored by the political revolutions of human affairs: We think it becoming to state to the world the reasons by which we are called to the free exercise of the sovereign authority.

We deem it unnecessary to insist upon the unquestionable right which every conquered country possesses, to restore itself to liberty and independence. We pass over in general silence the long series of afflictions, oppressions, and privations, in which the fatal law of conquest has indiscriminately involved the discoverers, conquerors, and settlers of these countries whose condition has been made wretched by the very means which would have promoted their felicity. Throwing a veil over three centuries of Spanish dominion in America, we shall confine ourselves to the narration of recent and well-known facts, which prove how much we have been afflicted, and that we ought not to be involved in the commotions, disorders, and conflicts, which have divided Spain.

The disorders of Europe have increased the evils under which we before suffered, by obstructing complaints and frustrating the means of redress; and by enabling the Governors placed over us by Spain, to insult and oppress us with impunity, leaving us without the protection or support of the laws.

It is contrary to the order of Nature, impracticable in relation to the Government of Spain, and most afflicting to America, that territories so much more extensive and a population incomparably more numerous, should be subject to and dependent upon a peninsular corner of the European continent.

The cession and abdication made at Bayonne, the transactions at the Escorial and Aranjuez, and the orders issued by the Imperial Lieutenant, the Marshall Duke of Berg, to America, authorized the exercise of those rights, which, until that period, the Americans had sacrificed for the preservation and integrity of the Spanish nation.

The people of Venezuela were the first who generally acknowledged and preferred that integrity, and who would never have forsaken the interests of their European brethren, while there remained the least prospect of security.

America has acquired a new existence; she was able and was bound to take charge of her own security and prosperity; she was at liberty to acknowledge or to reject the authority of the King, who was so little mindful of that authority as to regard his personal safety above that of the nation over which he had been placed.

All the Bourbons who concurred in the futile stipulations of Bayonne, having withdrawn from the Spanish territory, contrary to the will of the people, have thereby abrogated, dishonored, and violated all the sacred obligations which they had contracted with the Spaniards of both worlds, who by their blood and treasure had placed them on the Throne, in opposition to the efforts of the House of Austria. Such conduct has rendered them unfit to reign over a free people whom they have disposed of like a gang of slaves.

The intrusive governments which have arrogated to themselves the authority which belongs only to the national representation, have treacherously availed themselves of the known good faith of the Americas, the distance, and the effect which ignorance and oppression had produced among them, to direct their passions against the new Dynasty which

had been imposed upon Spain, in opposition to their
own principles; they have kept up the illusion among
us in favor of Ferdinand, only to baffle our national hopes; and in order to make us with greater
impunity their prey, they hold forth to us promises
of liberty, equality and fraternity, in pompous
discourses, the more effectually to conceal the
snare which they are insidiously laying for us by
an inefficient and degrading offer of representation.

As soon as the various forms of the Spanish
Government had been overthrown, and others had
been successfully substituted, an imperious necessity taught Venezuela to look to her own safety,
in order to support the King, and to afford an a-
sylum to their European brethren, against the calamities with which they were menaced. All our
former services were disregarded, new measures
were adopted against us, and the very steps we had
taken for the preservation of the Spanish government were branded with the names of insurrection,
perfidy, and ingratitude, only because the door
was closed against the monopoly of power which
they had expected to perpetuate, in the name of a
King whose dominion was imaginary.

Notwithstanding our moderation, our generosity,
and the purity of our intentions, and in opposition
to the wishes of our brethren in Europe, we were
declared to the world in a state of blockade; hostilities were commenced against us; agents were
sent among us to excite to revolt and to arm us
against each other: while our national character
was traduced, and foreign nations were excited to
make war upon us.

Deaf to our remonstrances, without submitting
our reasons to the impartial judgment of mankind,
and deprived of every other arbitration but that
of our enemies, we were prohibited from all intercourse with our brethren; and, adding contempt to
calumny, they undertook without our consent to
appoint Delegates for us, who were to assist in
their Cortes, the more effectually to dispose of
our persons and property, and to subject us to the
power of our enemies.

In order to defeat the wholesome measure of our national representation, when obliged to recognize it, they contrived to reduce the ratio of our population; and to submit the form of election to special committees acting at the disposal of arbitrary rulers; thus insulting our inexperience and good faith, and showing themselves to be utterly regardless of our political importance and welfare.

The Spanish Government, ever deaf to the demands of justice, undertook to frustrate all our legitimate rights, by condemning as criminals and devoting to the infamy of the gibbet, or to confiscation and banishment, those Americans who at different periods had employed their talents and services for the benefit of their country.

Such have been the causes which have at length impelled us to look to our own security, and to avert those disorders and horrible calamities which we could perceive were otherwise inevitable, and from which we shall ever keep aloof. By their fell policy, they have rendered our brethren indifferent to our misfortunes, and have armed them against us; they have effaced from their hearts the tender impressions of affection and consanguinity, and have converted into enemies many members of our great family.

When, faithful to our promises, we were sacrificing our peace and dignity to support the cause of Ferdinand of Bourbon, we saw that to the bonds of power by which he united his fate to that of the Emperor of the French, he had added the sacrifice of kindred and friends, and that on this account the existing Spanish rulers themselves had already resolved to acknowledge him only conditionally. In this painful state of perplexity, three years have elapsed in political irresolution, so dangerous, so fraught with evil, that this alone would have authorized the determination which the faith we had pledged and other fraternal attachments had caused us to defer, until imperious necessity compels us to proceed further than we had at first contemplated. But, pressed by the hostile and unnatural conduct of the Spanish rulers, we are at length absolved from the conditional oath which we had taken, and we now take upon ourselves the august sovereignty which we are here called upon to exercise.

But as our glory consists in establishing principles consistent with human happiness, and not in securing a partial felicity on the misfortunes of our fellow men, we hereby proclaim and declare, that we shall regard as friends and companions in our destiny, and participators in our happiness, all those who, united by the relations of blood, language, and religion, have suffered oppression under the ancient establishments, and who shall assert their independence thereof, and of every Foreign Power whatsoever; engaging that all who shall cooperate with us shall be united with us in life, fortune, and intention; declaring and recognizing not only them, but those of every Nation,---in war, Enemies;---in Peace, Friends, Brethren, and Fellow-Citizens.

In consideration, therefore, of the solid, public, and incontestible motives, which force upon us the necessity of reassuming our natural rights, thus restored to us by the revolution of human affairs; and in virtue of the imprescriptible right of every people, to dissolve every agreement, convention, or social compact, which does not establish the purpose for which alone all Governments are instituted; we are convinced that we cannot and ought not any longer to endure the chains by which we were connected with the Government of Spain: and we do declare, therefore, like every other independent people, that we are free and are determined to hold no dependence on any potentate, power, or government, excepting that which we ourselves establish; and that we now assume among the sovereign nations of the earth the rank which the Supreme Being and Nature have assigned to us, and to which we have been called by the succession of human events and by a due regard for our own happiness.

Although we are aware of the difficulties which may attend our new situation, and of the obligations which we contract by the rank which we are about to occupy in the political order of the world; and above all, of the powerful influence of ancient forms and habits, by which to our regret we have been hitherto affected;--yet we also know that a shameful submission to them, when it is in our power to shake them off, would prove more ignominous to ourselves, and more fatal to posterity, than a continued and painful servitude. It therefore becomes our indispensable duty to provide for our security, liberty and happiness, by an essential and entire reform and subversion of our ancient Establishments.

Wherefore, believing, for all these reasons, that we have complied with the respect which we owe to the opinions of mankind, and to the dignity of other nations, among whom we are about to take our rank, and of whose friendly intercourse we assure ourselves:

We, the Representatives of the Confederated Provinces of Venezuela, invoking the Most High to witness the justice of our cause, and the rectitude of our intentions: imploring His Divine assistance to ratify, at the epoch of our political birth, the dignity to which His Providence has restored us, and our ardent desire to live and die free; and in the belief and defense of the Holy Catholic and Apostolic Religion of Jesus Christ, as the first of our duties;

Therefore, in the name, by the will, and under the authority which we hold from the virtuous inhabitants of Venezuela, we do solemnly declare to the world, that these United Provinces are and ought to be, from this day forth, in fact, and of right, Free, Sovereign and Independent States;--- that they are absolved from all allegiance to the Crown of Spain, and to those who now call, or may hereafter call themselves their Representatives or Agents; and that as free, sovereign, and independent States, we possess full power to adopt whatever form of Government may be deemed suitable to the general will of its inhabitants; to declare war, make peace, form alliances, contract commercial alliances, conclude commercial treaties, define boundaries, and regulate navigation: and to propose and execute all other acts, usually made and executed by free and independent nations; and for the due fulfillment, validity and stability of this our solemn declaration, we mutually and reciprocally pledge, and bind the Provinces to each other, our lives, fortunes, and the honor of the Nation.

Done at the Federal Palace of Caracas, signed with our hands, and sealed with the Great Seal of the Provincial Confederation, and countersigned by the Secretary to the Congress assembled, on the 5th day of July, in the year 1811, and in the first of our Independence.

[Signatures]

Official Venezuelan translation

ACTA SOLEMNE DE INDEPENDENCIA

EN EL NOMBRE DE DIOS TODOPODEROSO

Nosotros, los representantes de las provincias unidas de Caracas, Cumaná, Barinas, Margarita, Barcelona, Mérida y Truxillo, que forman la confederación americana de Venezuela en el continente meridional, reunidos en Congreso, y considerando la plena y absoluta posesión de nuestros derechos, que recobramos justa y legítimamente desde el 19 de abril de 1810, en consecuencia de la jornada de Bayona y la ocupación del Trono español, por la conquista y sucesión de otra nueva dinastía, constituída sin nuestro consentimiento; queremos, antes de usar de los derechos de que nos tuvo privados la fuerza por más de tres siglos, y nos ha restituído el orden político de los acontecimientos humanos, patentizar al universo las razones que han emanado de estos mismos acontecimientos, y autorizar el libre uso que vamos a hacer de nuestra soberanía.

No queremos, sin embargo, empezar alegando los derechos que tiene todo país conquistado para recuperar su estado de propiedad e independencia; olvidamos generosamente la larga serie de males, agravios y privaciones que el derecho funesto de conquista ha causado indistintamente a todos los descendientes de los descubridores, conquistadores y pobladores de estos países, hechos de peor condición por la misma razón que debía favorecerlos; y corriendo un velo sobre los trescientos años de dominación española en América, sólo presentaremos los hechos auténticos y notorios que han debido desprender y han desprendido de derecho a un mundo de otro, en el trastorno, desorden y conquista que tiene ya disuelta la nación española.

Este desorden ha aumentado los males de la América, inutilizándole los recursos y reclamaciones y autorizando la impunidad de los gobernantes de España, para insultar y oprimir esta parte de la nación, dejándola sin el amparo y garantía de las leyes.

Es contrario al orden, imposible al gobierno de España y funesto a la América, el que teniendo ésta un territorio infinitamente más extenso y una población incomparablemente más numerosa, dependa y esté sujeta a un ángulo peninsular del continente europeo.

Las sesiones y abdicaciones de Bayona, las jornadas del Escorial y de Aranjuez y las órdenes del Lugar Teniente Duque de Berg a la América, debieron poner en uso los derechos que, hasta entonces, habían sacrificado los americanos a la unidad e integridad de la nación española.

Venezuela, antes que nadie, reconoció y conservó generosamente esta integridad, por no abandonar la causa de sus hermanos, mientras tuvo la menor apariencia de salvación.

La América volvió a existir de nuevo, desde que pudo y debió tomar a su cargo su suerte y conservación; como la España pudo reconocer o no los derechos de un rei que había apreciado más sus existencia que la dignidad de la nación que gobernaba.

Cuantos Borbones concurrieron a las inválidas estipulaciones de Bayona, abandonando el territorio español contra la voluntad de los pueblos, faltaron, despreciaron y hollaron el deber sagrado que contrajeron con los españoles de ambos mundos, cuando con su sangre y sus tesoros los colocaron en el Trono, a despecho de la casa de Austria: por esta conducta quedaron inhábiles e incapaces de gobernar a un pueblo libre, a quien entregaron como un rebaño de esclavos.

Los intrusos gobiernos que se arrogaron la representación nacional, aprovecharon pérfidamente las disposiciones que la buena fe, la distancia, la opresión y la ignorancia daban a los americanos contra la nueva dinastía que se introdujo en España por la fuerza, y contra sus mismos principios sostuvieron entre nosotros la ilusión a favor de Fernando, para devorarnos y vejarnos impunemente cuando más nos prometían la libertad, la igualdad y la fraternidad, en discursos pomposos y frases estudiadas, para encubrir el lazo de una representación amañada, inútil y degradante.

Luego que se disolvieron, sustituyeron y destruyeron entre sí las varias formas de gobierno de España, y que la lei imperiosa de la necesidad dictó a Venezuela el conservarse a sí misma, para ventilar y conservar los derechos de su rei y ofrecer un auxilio a sus hermanos de Europa contra los males que les amenazaban, se desconoció toda su anterior conducta, se variaron los principios y se llamó insurrección, perfidia e ingratitud a lo mismo que sirvió de norma a los gobiernos de España, porque ya se les cerraba la puerta al monopolio de administración que querían perpetuar a nombre de un rei imaginario.

A pesar de nuestras protestas, de nuestra moderación, de nuestra generosidad y de la inviolabilidad de nuestros principios, contra la voluntad de nuestros hermanos de Europa, se nos bloquea, se nos hostiliza, se nos declara en estado de rebelión, se nos envían agentes a amotinarnos unos contra otros y se procura desacreditarnos entre todas las naciones del mundo, implorando sus auxilios para deprimirnos.

Sin hacer el menor aprecio de nuestras razones, sin presentarlas al imparcial juicio del mundo y sin otros jueces que nuestros enemigos, se nos condena a una dolorosa incomunicación con nuestros hermanos; y para añadir el desprecio a la calumnia, se nos nombran apoderados contra nuestra expresa voluntad, para que en sus cortes dispongan arbitrariamente de nuestros intereses, bajo el influjo y la fuerza de nuestros enemigos.

Para sofocar y anonadar los efectos de nuestra representación, cuando se vieron obligados a concedérnosla, nos sometieron a una tarifa mezquina y diminuta, y sujetaron a la voz pasiva de los ayuntamientos, degradados por el despotismo de los Gobernadores, las formas de la elección; lo que era un insulto a nuestra sencillez y buena fe, más bien que una consideración a nuestra incontestable importancia política.

Sordos siempre a los gritos de nuestra justicia, han procurado los gobiernos de España desacreditar todos nuestros esfuerzos, declarando criminales y sellando con la infamia, el cadalso y la confiscación todas las tentativas que, en diversas épocas, han hecho algunos americanos por la felicidad de su país, como lo fué la que últimamente nos dictó la propia seguridad, para no ser envueltos en el desorden que presentíamos y conducidos a la horrorosa suerte que vamos ya a apartar de nosotros para siempre; con esta atroz política han logrado hacer a nuestros hermanos insensibles a nuestras desgracias, armarlos contra nosotros, borrar de ellos las dulces impresiones de la amistad y de la consanguinidad y convertir en enemigos una parte de nuestra gran familia.

Cuando nosotros, fieles a nuestras promesas, sacrificábamos nuestra seguridad y dignidad civil por no abandonar los derechos que generosamente conservamos a Fernando de Borbón, hemos visto que a las relaciones de la fuerza que lo ligaban con el Emperador de los franceses ha añadido los vínculos de sangre y amistad, por lo que hasta los gobiernos de España han declarado ya su resolución de no reconocerle sino condicionalmente.

En esta dolorosa alternativa hemos permanecido tres años en una indecisión y ambigüedad política, tan funesta y peligrosa, que ella sola bastaría a autorizar la resolución que la fe de nuestras promesas y los vínculos de la fraternidad nos habían hecho diferir, hasta que la necesidad nos ha obligado a ir más allá de lo que nos propusimos, impelidos por la conducta hostil y desnaturalizada de los gobiernos de España, que nos ha relevado del juramento condicional con que hemos sido llamados a la augusta representación que ejercemos.

Mas nosotros, que nos gloriamos de fundar nuestro proceder en mejores principios y que no queremos establecer nuestra felicidad sobre la desgracia de nuestros semejantes, miramos y declaramos como amigos nuestros, compañeros de nuestra suerte y partícipes de nuestra felicidad a los que, unidos con nosotros por los vínculos de al sangre, la lengua y la religión, han sufrido los mismos males en el anterior orden; siempre que reconociendo nuestra *absoluta independencia* de él y de toda otra dominación extraña, nos ayuden a sostenerla con su vida, su fortuna y su opinión, declarándonos y reconociéndonos (como a todas las demás naciones) en guerra, enemigos, y en paz, amigos, hermanos y compatriotas.

En atención a todas estas sólidas, públicas e incontestables razones de política, que tanto persuaden la necesidad de recobrar la dignidad natural, que el orden de los sucesos nos ha restituído; en uso de los imprescriptibles derechos que tienen los pueblos para destruir todo pacto, convenio o asociación que no llena los fines para que fueron instituídos los gobiernos, creemos que no podemos ni debemos conservar los lazos que nos ligaban al gobierno de España, y que, como todos los pueblos del mundo, estamos libres y autorizados para no depender de otra autoridad que la nuestra, y tomar entre las potencias de la tierra el puesto igual que el Ser Supremo y la naturaleza nos asignan y a que nos llaman la sucesión de los acontecimientos humanos y nuestro propio bien y utilidad.

Sin embargo de que conocemos las dificultades que trae consigo y las obligaciones que nos impone el rango que vamos a ocupar en el orden político del mundo y la influencia poderosa de las formas y habitudes a que hemos estado, a nuestro pesar, acostumbrados; también conocemos que la vergonzosa sumisión a ellas, cuando podemos sacudirlas, sería más ignominioso para nosotros y más funesto para nuestra prosperidad que nuestra larga y penosa servidumbre, y que es ya de nuestro indispensable deber proveer a nuestra conservación, seguridad y felicidad, variando esencialmente todas las formas de nuestra anterior constitución.

Por tanto, creyendo con todas estas razones satisfecho el respeto que debemos a las opiniones del género humano y a la dignidad de las demás naciones, en cuyo número vamos a entrar, y con cuya comunicación y amistad contamos nosotros los representantes de las provincias unidas de Venezuela, poniendo por testigo al Ser Supremo de la justicia de nuestro proceder y de la rectitud de nuestras intenciones; implorando sus divinos y celestiales auxilios y ratificándole, en el momento que nacemos a la dignidad que su providencia nos restituye, el deseo de vivir y morir libres; creyendo y defendiendo la Santa, Católica y Apostólica Religión de Jesucristo como el primero de nuestros deberes. Nosotros, pues, a nombre y con la voluntad y autoridad que tenemos del virtuoso pueblo de Venezuela, declaramos solemnemente al mundo que sus provincias unidas son y deben ser desde hoy, de hecho y de derecho, Estados libres, soberanos e independientes, y que están absueltos de toda sumisión y dependencia de la Corona de España o de los que se dicen o dixeren sus apoderados o representantes, y que como tal Estado libre e independiente tiene un pleno poder para darse la forma de gobierno que sea conforme a la voluntad general de sus pueblos; declarar la guerra, hacer la paz, formar alianza, arreglar tratados de comercio, límites y navegación; hacer y executar todos los demás actos que hacen y executan las naciones libres e independientes. Y para hacer válida, firme y subsistente esta nuestra solemne declaración, damos y empeñamos mutuamente unas provincias a otras nuestras vidas, nuestras fortunas y el sagrado de nuestro honor nacional.

Dado en el Palacio Federal de Caracas, firmada de nuestras manos, sellada con el gran sello provisional de la Confederación y refrendada por el Secretario del Congreso, a cinco días del mes de julio del año de 1811, primero de nuestra Independencia.

Juan Ant.º Rodríguez Domínguez, **Presidente,**

Diputado de Nutrias.

Luis Ign.º Mendoza, **Vicepresidente,**

Diputado de la Villa de Obispos.

POR LA PROVINCIA DE CARACAS

Isidoro Antonio López Méndez,

Diputado de la Capital.

Martín Tovar Ponte,	Diputado por San Sebastián.
Juan Toro,	Diputado de Valencia.
Juan G. Roscio,	Diputado por la V.ᵃ de Calabozó.
Felipe F. Paúl,	Dipdo. de Sn. Sebn.
Jph. Ang. Alamo,	Dipdo. de Barqto.
Franc.º Xavier de Ustáriz,	Diputado de Sn. Sebastián.
N. de Castro,	Dipdo. de Cars.
Franc.º Hernández,	Dipdo. de Sn. Carlos.
Fernando de Peñalver,	Diputado de Valencia.
Gab. Pérez de Pagola,	Dipdo. de Ospino.
Lino de Clemente,	Dipdo. de Caracas.
Salvador Delgado,	Dipdo. de Nirgua.
El Marqués del Toro,	Dipdo. del Tocuyo.
J. A. Díaz Argote,	Dip. de la Villa de Cura.
Juan Joseph de Maya,	Diputdo. de Sn. Felipe.
Luis Jph. de Cazorla,	Dipdo. de Valencia.
José Vic. Unda,	Dp.º de Guanare.
Franc.º Xavier Yanes,	Dipdo. de Araure.

*Por haber quedado impedido de firmar, a causa de la herida que re-
cibió en la jornada de Valencia el S. Ponte, no pudo hacerlo al pasar al
libro la presente acta.*

(Aquí la rúbrica del Secretario Isnardy.)

(Aquí cuatro rayas en forma de cruz y más abajo la rúbrica del
Secretario Isnardy.)

POR LA PROVINCIA DE CUMANA

F. Xavier de Mayz.

Diputado de la Capital.

José Gabriel Alcalá,

Dipdo. de la Capital.

Mariano de la Cova,

Dipdo. del Norte.

Juan Bermúdez,

Dipdo. del Sur.

POR LA PROVINCIA DE BARINAS

Juan Nepom.º Quintana,

Diputado de Achaguas.

Ignacio Fernández,

Dipdo. de Barinas.

Josf de Sata y Bussy,

Diput.º de Sn. Fernando.

Jph. Luis Cabrera,

Dip. de Guanarito.

Manuel Palacio,

Dipdo. de Mijagual.

POR LA PROVINCIA DE BARCELONA

Fr: de Miranda,

Dip. del Pao.

Franc.º P. Ortiz,

Dip. de Sn. Diego.

José M.ª Ramírez,

Dipdo. de Aragua.

POR LA PROVINCIA DE MARGARITA

Manl. Plácido Maneyro,

Diputado de Margarita.

POR LA PROVINCIA DÉ MERIDA

A. Nicolás Briceño,

Dipdo. de Mérida.

Manl. Vte. de Maya,

Dipdo. de la Grita.

Franc.º Isnardy, Secretario.

Socialist Republic of Vietnam

The Socialist Republic of Vietnam is bounded
to the east by the China Sea, to the north by
China and to the west by the Kingdom of Laos.
Vietnam came under French control in 1883 and
later became part of the Indochinese Union. During World War II, with Japanese permission, the
Democratic Republic of Vietnam was established.
On September 2, 1945, the Democratic Republic of
Vietnam declared its independence of France, but
a protracted struggle took place which resulted
in full recognition of independence in a treaty
signed on June 4, 1954. Actual authority was
transferred by a treaty signed in Geneva on July
20, 1954. However, the Geneva Accord of 1954
gave rise to a long struggle between rival governments of North and South Vietnam, ending in the
eventual defeat of South Vietnamese forces in
1975. On July 2, 1976, after 22 years of separation of North and South Vietnam a "new country,"
called the Socialist Republic of Vietnam, was
formed. The former North Vietnamese flag, anthem
and emblem were adopted by the so-called new nation.

DECLARATION OF INDEPENDENCE

OF THE REPUBLIC OF VIETNAM

"All men are created equal . . . . They are endowed by their Creator with certain inalienable
rights. Among these are life, liberty, and the
pursuit of happiness."

These immortal words are from the Declaration
of Independence of the United States of America in
1776. Taken in a broader sense, these phrases
mean: "All peoples on earth are born equal; all
peoples have the right to live, to be free, to be
happy."

The Declaration of the Rights of the Man and
Citizen of the French Revolution of 1791 also proclaimed: "Men are born and remain free and with
equal rights."

These are undeniable truths.

Nevertheless for more than eighty years the
French imperialists, abusing their "liberty, equality, and fraternity," have violated the land of
our ancestors and oppressed our countrymen. Their
acts are contrary to the ideals of humanity and
justice.

In the political domain, they have deprived
us of all our liberties.

They have imposed upon us inhuman laws. They
have established three different political regimes
in the North, the Center and the South of Viet Nam
in order to destroy our historic and ethnic national unity.

They have built more prisons than schools.
They have acted without mercy toward our patriots.
They have drenched our revolutions in rivers of

blood.

They have subjugated public opinion and practiced obscurantism on the broadest scale. They
have imposed upon us the use of opium and alcohol
to weaken our race.

In the economic domain, they have exploited
us without respite, reduced our people to the
blackest misery and pitilessly looted our country.

They have despoiled our ricelands, our mines,
our forests, our raw materials. They have retained
the privilege of issuing banknotes and a monopoly
of foreign trade.

They have invented hundreds of unjustified
taxes, condemning our countrymen, especially the
peasants and small merchants, to extreme poverty.

They have prevented our capital from fructify-
ing; they have exploited our workers in the most
barbarous fashion.

In the autumn of 1940 when the Japanese
Fascists, with a view to fighting the Allies, invaded Indochina to organize new war bases, the
French imperialists, on their knees, surrendered
our country.

Since then, under the double Japanese and
French yokes, our people have literally bled. The
result has been terrifying. From Quangtri to the
North, two million of our countrymen died of fam-
ine in the first months of this year.

On March 9, 1945, the Japanese disarmed the
French troops. Once again, the French either fled
or unconditionally surrendered. Thus they have
been totally incapable of "protecting" us; on the
contrary, in the space of five years they have
twice sold our country to the Japanese.

Before March 9, the League of Viet-Minh several times invited the French to join it in struggle against the Japanese. Instead of responding
to this appeal, the French struck all the harder
at the partisans of the Viet-Minh. They went as

far as to murder a large number of the political
prisoners at Yen Bay and Caobang during their rout.

Despite all this, our countrymen have continued to maintain a tolerant and human attitude
toward the French. After the events of March 9,
the League of Viet-Minh helped many Frenchmen to
cross the frontier, saved others from Japanese
prisons, and besides protected the lives and property of all Frenchmen.

In fact, since the autumn of 1940, our country
has ceased to be a French colony and became a Japanese possession.

After the surrender of the Japanese, our entire people rose to regain their sovereignty and
founded the democratic Republic of Viet Nam.

The truth is that we seized our independence
from the hands of the Japanese and not from the
hands of the French.

The French fleeing, the Japanese surrendering,
Emperor Bao Dai abdicating, our people broke all
the chains which have weighed upon us for nearly
a hundred years and made our Viet Nam an independent country. Our people at the same time overthrew the monarchical regime established for tens
of centuries and founded the Republic.

For these reasons we, members of the Provisional Government, representing the entire population of Viet Nam, declare that we shall henceforth
have no relations with imperialist France, that we
cancel all treaties which France has signed on the
subject of Viet Nam, that we abolish all the privileges which the French have arrogated to themselves on our territory.

All the people of Viet Nam, inspired by the
same will, are determined to fight to the end
against any attempt at aggression by the French
imperialists.

We are convinced that the Allies who have
recognized the principles of equality of peoples
at the Conferences of Teheran and San Francisco

cannot but recognize the independence of Viet Nam.

A people which has obstinately opposed French domination for more than eighty years, a people who during these last years ranged themselves definitely on the side of the Allies to fight against Fascism, this people has the right to be free. This people must be independent.

For these reasons, we, members of the Provisional Government of the Democratic Republic of Viet Nam, solemnly proclaim to the entire world:

Viet Nam has the right to be free and independent and is, in fact, free and independent. All the people of Viet Nam are determined to mobilize all their spiritual and material strength, to sacrifice their lives and property, to safeguard their right to liberty and independence.

Hanoi, September 2, 1945

Signed: Ho Chi Minh, President.
Tran Huy Lieu, Vo Nguyen Giap, Chu Van Tan,
Duong Duc Hien, Nguyen Van To, Nguyen
Manh Ha, Cu Huy Can, Pham Ngoh Thach,
Nguyen Van Xuan, Vu Trong Khanh, Pham Van
Dong, Dao Trong Kim, Vu Din Hoc, Le Van
Hien.

Issued at Hanoi, September 2, 1945, following establishment of the new republican regime. Text is translated from La République, Issue No. 1, Hanoi, October 1, 1945. Official translation.

INDEPENDENCE TREATY OF VIETNAM

June 4, 1954

Article 1. France recognizes Vietnam as a fully independent and sovereign State, endowed with all authority recognized by International Law.

Article 2. Vietnam shall replace France in all rights and obligations resulting from international treaties or conventions contracted by France on the account and in the name of the State of Vietnam or from any other treaties and conventions concluded by France in the name of French Indochina to the extent that these acts concerned Vietnam.

Article 3. France is committed to transfer to the Vietnam government the authorities and public services which are still directed by France in the territory of Vietnam.

Article 4. This treaty, which will take effect from the date it is signed, shall repeal prior acts and provisions to the contrary. Ratification instruments of this treaty will be exchanged as soon as it is approved by the appropriate proceedings in France and Vietnam.

Paris, June 4, 1954.

Joseph LANIEL, BUU LOC.

Translated by Trans van Liem

RESOLUTIONS ON THE UNIFICATION OF VIETNAM

JULY 2, 1976

The Assembly on July 2 unanimously adopted the following resolutions:

(1) Vietnam was an independent, unified and socialist country, and was named the Socialist Republic of Vietnam.

(2) The national flag was a red flag with a five-pointed gold star in the middle, previously the flag of North Vietnam.

(3) The national emblem was a cogwheel, two ears of rice and a five-pointed gold star on a red ground, previously the emblem of North Vietnam.

(4) The capital was Hanoi.

(5) The national anthem was Tien Quan Ca ("Hymn of the Marching Army", composed in 1945 as the marching song of the Viet Minh, and subsequently the national anthem of North Vietnam).

(6) Saigon was officially renamed Ho Chi Minh City.

Report of Hanoi Radio broadcast, July 3, 1976.

The Independent State of
Western Samoa

Western Samoa is part of the Samoan islands
in the South Pacific Ocean southwest of Hawaii.
The Germans were the first to use Samoa as a
trading base in 1856. Plans to colonize by the
Germans conflicted with United States and British
plans. Under the Berlin Treaty of 1889 the three
powers agreed to create an independent state.
Native wars led the three to revoke the treaty
the same year and by the Convention of 1889,
Great Britain renounced all claims to the island.
Following World War I New Zealand received a
League of Nations mandate over the islands. It
became a United Nations trusteeship following
World War II. On January 1, 1962, Western
Samoa became an independent nation.

PART I

THE INDEPENDENT STATE OF WESTERN SAMOA AND ITS SUPREME LAW

Name and description
1. (1) The Independent State of Western Samoa (hereinafter referred to as Western Samoa) shall be free and sovereign.

(2) Western Samoa shall comprise the islands of Upolu, Savai'i, Manono and Apolima in the South Pacific Ocean, together with all other islands adjacent thereto and lying between the 13th and 15th degrees of south latitude and the 171st and 173rd degrees of longitude west of Greenwich.

The supreme law
2. (1) This Constitution shall be the supreme law of Western Samoa.

(2) Any existing law and any law passed after the date of coming into force of this Constitution which is inconsistent with this Constitution shall, to the extent of the inconsistency, be void.

PART II

FUNDAMENTAL RIGHTS

Definition of the State
3. In this Part, unless the context otherwise requires, "the State" includes the Head of State, Cabinet, Parliament and all local and other authorities established under any law.

Remedies for enforcement of rights
4. (1) Any person may apply to the Supreme Court by appropriate proceedings to enforce the rights conferred under the provisions of this Part.

(2) The Supreme Court shall have power to make all such orders as may be necessary and appropriate to secure to the applicant the enjoyment of any of the rights conferred under the provisions of this Part.

Right to life
    5. (1) No person shall be deprived of his life
intentionally, except in the execution of a sentence of a court following his conviction of an
offence for which this penalty is provided by Act.

From the constitution of the Independent State of
Western Samoa.

People's Democratic Republic
of Yemen

Democratic Yemen -- formerly known as
South Yemen and later as the People's Democratic
Republic of Yemen -- is located at the southwest
corner of the Arabian Peninsula. The country
consists of Aden and the former British Protectorate
of South Arabia. Invaded by Portugal, Turkey and
Great Britain between the 16th and 19th centuries,
Aden became a British protectorate in 1839. In
1959 Aden and several other states joined to form
the Federation of Arab Emirates. This later became the Federation of South Arabia. Independence
followed British evacuation on November 30, 1970.

DEMOCRATIC YEMEN

Believing in the unity of the Yemen and of the destiny of the Yemeni people in the territory and depending basically on the unity of the Yemeni people and land, our Yemeni people struggled bravely against imperialism and colonialism and against local re-actionary feudalism represented by the Imamic and Sultanic regimes.

Despite the exceptional and unusual conditions resulting from the division of the Yemeni territory into two parts, this division could not block the unity of the common national struggle of our Yemeni territory - northern and southern.

The Yemeni people in the South struggled side by side with the Yemeni people in the north to bring down the Imamic regime and set up a republican regime.

Similarly the Yemeni people in the north struggled side by side with the Yemeni people in the south in an armed struggle against British colonialist presence.

As a result of this struggle the revolution of 26th September 1962 came about to bring down the reactionary Imamic regime in Northern Yemen and to unite all the national democratic forces which established the republican regime.

Following the long struggle of our Yemeni people against the colonialist presence, the struggle was crowned with the armed revolution which started on 14th October 1963 against British occupation and the Sultanic regime, and united all sectors of the working people - the workers, the farmers, the educated, the small bourgeos and all honourable sections of the people, under the leadership of the National Front and so achieved national independence on 30th November 1967. Today, inspite of the parti-tion, the common struggle of the two parts of the Yemeni people continues to be linked and united not only against imperialist and reactionary conspiracies in the area, but also for final relief of the causes of partition and for the restoration of normal conditions for uniting the territory.

To make fruitful the steps taken by the National Front after the corrective operation of 22nd June, 1969, which are based on the political, economic, social and cultural achievements after independence in co-operation with other democratic sections desirous of following a course of freedom, social progress, democracy, peace and friendship with other nations so that the achievements of a national democratic revolution may lead to socialism by free will,

And while believing that all this is to ensure the common interest of the aims of the Yemeni people in the area and to make a revolutionary contribution towards the Arab revolutionary movement,

And to crown all these connected struggles to establish a democratic united Yemen as a preliminary step towards democratic Arab unity,

And to strengthen the results achieved through the struggle and work of our Yemeni people,

Our Yemeni people in the People's Democratic Republic of Yemen, give themselves this national democratic Constitution.

From the Preamble to the Constitution of Democratic Yemen.

Yemen Arab Republic

Bounded to the north by Saudi Arabia and
to the south by the People's Republic of Yemen, the
Yemen Arab Republic was the earliest seat of Arabian culture. After four centuries of Ottoman
domination, a revolt began in 1904. After
World War I the Mutawakkilite family established
a monarchy. A September 26, 1962, coup overthrew
the monarchy and established a republic. On
September 28th, 1962, independence was proclaimed.

YEMEN ARAB REPUBLIC

In the name of God the Merciful, the Compassionate...In the name of the Yemeni people who overcame despotism on the 26th of September 1962, we have sought to do the following:

1) To establish a peaceful society based on the principles of Islam.

2) To establish a peaceful and stable society on the basis of fraternity and equality, without discrimination by race or creed.

3) To mobilize a national army to defend Yemen and the Arab Nation.

4) To establish a representative system of government.

(Main text of constitution then follows)

Preamble translated by David W. McCintock

YEMEN ARAB REPUBLIC

CONSTITUTIONAL PROCLAMATION by the Revolution
    Command Council of the Yemen Arab Republic--
    Sana'a, 28th September, 1962

Out of a desire to consolidate the foundations of government during the transitional period, to regulate the rights and duties of all
citizens, to allow the country to enjoy comprehensive stability which will enable it to achieve
fruitful production, and to raise it to the level
to which the revolution aspires for the people,
the Revolution Command Council proclaims in the
name of the people that the government of the
country during the transitional period, which is
five years, shall be in accordance with the
following provisions:

I. GENERAL PRINCIPLES

Article 1--The revolution's objectives are
as follows:

(a) To return to the true law of Islam,
which former imams had violated during the past
1,100 years.

(b) To abolish racial discrimination and
consider all Yemenis alike before the law.

(c) To remove the rancour between Zaidites
and Shafitics.

(d) To issue a law defining the rights of
citizens. Crimes shall be specified, and penal-
ties shall be passed only after a fair trial
based on a law derived from the noble Islamic
law that shall regulate criminal proceedings and
insure freedom of defence.

(e) To set up the Yemen republic and pave
the way for holding a free election throughout
Yemen for a parliamentary chamber which will
choose the president of the republic.

(f) To achieve the aims of the Arab national-
ism so that the Arab nation will restore its
great glory and assume its appropriate position
among progressive nations.

(g) To achieve social justice.

(h) To set up a powerful national army that
will be a shield for Yemen and the Arab nation.

(i) To eliminate all the acts of injustice
of which the people complain.

(j) To raise the people's standard of living
by immediately initiating and implementing economic plans to exploit all resources of the state--
manpower and natural--and by creating economic
activity in inhabited and barren regions and
encouraging agriculture, industry, trade, and
other productive works.

Article 2--The noble Yemeni people are the
source of all powers.

Article 3--Personal freedom and freedom of
opinion are safeguarded within the limits of law,
and property and homes are inviolable under the
law.

Article 4--The extradition of political ref-
ugees is banned.

Article 5--All laws shall be drawn from the
Islamic law which is the official religion of the
state.

Article 6--Justice shall be independent and
shall not be subject to any mandate without law,
and its judgments shall be issued and executed in
the name of law and of the people.

II. THE SYSTEM OF GOVERNMENT

Article 7--The Revolution Command Council
shall assume the duties of supreme sovereignty
and in particular the measures it deems necessary
to safeguard this revolution and the system upon
which it is founded to achieve the people's ob-

jectives, and shall have the right to appoint and dismiss ministers.

Article 8--The cabinet and the ministers, each in his field of competence, shall carry out the duties of the executive authority.

Article 9--A national convention shall be formed from the Revolution Command Council and the cabinet to consider the general policy of the state and all matters relating to this, and debate whatever it seems necessary with regard to the work of each minister in his ministry.

Article 10--A higher defence council shall be formed from surety chieftains which will consider the state's security affairs. Every chieftain shall hold the rank of minister of state. During the period when the council is not in session each chieftain shall undertake the duty of protecting his region in his capacity as governor delegated by the Revolution Command Council.

Article 11--The Revolution Command Council decides to elect the revolution's leader, Brig.-Gen. Abdullah as-Sallal, as president of the republic, premier, and supreme commander of the armed forces during the transitional period. It also elects Dr. Abd ar-Rahman al-Baydani as vice-president with all his prerogatives. During the transitional period, a law for elections shall be formulated so that free elections may be held throughout the Yemen Arab Republic to vote on the final constitution which the government will submit and to elect the parliamentary chamber which will elect the president of the republic.

Citizens, while proclaiming these principles and provisions, the Revolution Command Council also wishes to proclaim its absolute belief in the necessity to set up a full constitutional democratic system during the transitional period. The council also proclaims its absolute belief in the necessity to provide a free and dignified life and bright future for all citizens.

God is the giver of success.

Issued by the Revolution Command Council.

ABDULLAH AS-SALLAL, Chairman.

Socialist Federal Republic of
Yugoslavia

Yugoslavia, a southeastern European country, is bounded to the north by Austria and Hungary, to the east by Rumania and Bulgaria, to the south by Greece, and to the west by the Adriatic Sea and Italy. Following Slavic migration in the 6th, 7th, and 8th centuries the Slavs divided into several major peoples who became increasingly differentiated. Croatia came under Hungarian rule in 1102 while Serbia and Montenegro came under Turkish rule. In 1804 the Serbs revolted. Though the revolt failed it set the stage for a successful 1815 revolt. The latter revolt resulted in Ottoman recognition of Serbian autonomy. Full independence for Serbia and Montenegro came with the Treaty of Berlin in 1878. The other present day Yugoslav states were under Hungarian rule until World War I. The entire country was occupied by the Central Powers in 1915 but was liberated by the Allies in 1918. On October 29, 1918, the National Council proclaimed independence. On November 24, 1918, the United Kingdom of the Serbs, Croats, and Slovenes was established. In 1921 it became a constitutional monarchy. On November 29, 1943, a group of loyalists resisting Nazi rule proclaimed the independence of all Yugoslavia.

YUGOSLAVIA

DECLARATION

of the

SECOND SESSION OF THE ANTI-FASCIST COUNCIL OF

THE PEOPLES' LIBERATION OF YUGOSLAVIA

(November 29, 1943)'

In the course of two and a half years of continuous peoples' liberation struggle against the
occupier and his collaborators, the peoples of Yugoslavia have achieved big and decisive successes,
both in internal and in foreign policy affairs.
After each attempt of the enemy to atomize our Peoples' Liberation Army, the military strength of our
Army has increased, consolidated its ranks and
raised them to a higher military and technical level. The more pressure the enemy put in an effort
to suppress the liberation movement of our peoples,
the closer became the ranks of the people in this
movement around the Supreme Headquarters and Com-
rade Tito, the celebrated leader of the people,
around the Anti-Fascist Council of the Peoples'
Liberation of Yugoslavia and around the national
political representatives of the individual nations
of Yugoslavia. Our liberated territory has steadily
increased, our material reserves and sources of
supply of our Peoples' Liberation Army and the population have increased also.

Simultaneously, organs of peoples' authority
and various economic and management organs in service of this authority have developed.

The recognition of the big successes of our
Peoples" Liberation War abroad on the one side and
the complete unmasking of the role and high treason
of the Yugoslavia "government"-in-exile on the other side have set entirely new tasks before the
leading organs of our peoples' liberation movement.
It was necessary systematically to consolidate all
these successes and to exploit them for a further
successful continuation of our Peoples' Liberation

War.

In view of these facts, the Anti-Fascist Council of the Peoples' Liberation of Yugoslavia at its Second Session, held on November 29, 1943,

ESTABLISHES:

I

1. The two and a half years of our Peoples' Liberation War have offered proof to the whole world that the peoples of Yugoslavia have set off, firmly and with determination, on a path of armed resistance to the occupier, on a path indicated to our peoples by the Communist Party of Yugoslavia, which all truly patriotic forces and political groups of our peoples have been pursuing with it. The enormous majority of the peoples of Yugoslavia have joined the ranks of the liberation movement, and extended active support to its Peoples' Liberation Army. Also all patriotic and honest functionaries from all political parties, groups and patriotic organizations, have, together with the people, actively participated in the peoples' liberation movement. All this is equally true of all the Yugoslav nations. By their activity in the peoples' liberation movement, the peoples of Yugoslavia have spoken up publicly in protest against the traitors, reactionaries and speculators in the country and abroad who stayed in power in old Yugoslavia by means of violence and deceit and are now once again trying - - by depending on the most reactionary circles - - to regain power with the help of treason, deceit and speculation. But all these endeavors cannot conceal the fact that an entirely new relation of political forces has been created in our country during the Peoples' Liberation War and that this new relation must be adequately expressed also in its management and state leadership.

2. One of the principal sources of power of our liberation struggle is the fact that the united peoples' liberation movement of the peoples of Yugoslavia and its Peoples' Liberation Army have grown from the liberation movement of all our nations. The Peoples of Yugoslavia did not need any previous agreements on equality, etc., in order to fight

against the occupier. They took up arms, began to
liberate their country and thus not only gained but
also secured the right to self-determination, including the right of secession from or unification
with other peoples. All forces which are partici-
pating in the peoples' liberation movement recognize all these rights to our nations from the very
first day. And, for this very reason, the peoples
of Yugoslavia have become even more closely united
in their common struggle. In the course of the
two years and a half of heroic struggle against the
occupier and his collaborators among the people of
Yugoslavia, vestiges of the great-Serbia hegemonist
policy have been crushed and so were attempts at
sowing mutual hatred and disunity among our nations.
Simultaneously, the vestiges of reactionary separa-
tism have been defeated too. In this way not only
material and general political but also all moral
conditions have been secured for creating the future
fraternal, democratic federative community of our
nations. Today, when they are about to expel the
occupier from their country for good, the peoples
of Yugoslavia justifiably demand that the country
be run by a leadership which will guarantee, both
by its composition and by its programme, that true
equality will be really secured to all nations of
Yugoslavia in Federative Yugoslavia.

3. The achievements in our Peoples' Liberation War have passed the flory of our people all
over the world, scattering the false ideas sown by
the enemies of our people, and have firmly consolidated the international political positions of Yugoslavia and her nations. The great contribution
of our peoples in the general struggle against the
fascist conquerors today is already recognized on
the part of all forces of the anti-Hitlerite bloc.
But this is not enough. The peoples of Yugoslavia
justifiably demand that the Allies and all their
friends recognize not only their struggle against
the occupier but also their free democratic will.
The peoples of Yugoslavia justifiably demand the
abolition of whatever support foreign countries
are still extending to the Yugoslav traitor "government" in exile and the clique around it. Simultaneously, the peoples of Yugoslavia justifiably
demand that the organs of their peoples' authority,
the fruit of this struggle, be recognized and

respected also abroad.

4.   While the peoples of Yugoslavia were soak-
ing the soil of their homeland in their own blood
in the effort to liberate it from the hateful conquerors, the reactionary clique in exile, which
calls itself the "Yugoslav government," did its
best in order to snatch the arms from our people.
With lies and slanders it was deceiving the world
abroad, trying to conceal the real will and wish
of the people of Yugoslavia, trying to prevent our
peoples from receiving any assistance of freedom-
loving countries. With lies and slanders it tried
to divert our peoples from their path of creating
a new, fraternal community of their own. With the
help of its agents, first of all Draza Mihajlovic,
this government systematically organized a fratricidal war in all lands of Yugoslavia, only to put
the blame for this, in its slanderous way, on the
peoples' liberation movement. This "government"
bears full responsibility for the bloodshed and
crimes which were, and are still being committed
by the Chetnik gangs, which formally bear the name
of "Yugoslav army in the Homeland." Simultaneously,
it was engaged in making ill blood between the nations of Yugoslavia, in egging them on against one
another. The so-called army of this "government"
- - Mihajlovic's Chetniks - - linked itself to the
occupier in life and death, and became the principal
stronghold of the fascist conquerors in the struggle
against our peoples. This "government" was in a
process of continuous disintegration. In its present composition, it includes the most fanatical
elements of great-Serbian hegemony, headed by Draza
Mihajlovic and Petar Zivkovic, although he is formally not a member of the Cabinet. This is a government of overt fratricidal war and chauvinist ter-
ror, a government in the service of the fascist oc-
cupiers, an outspokenly anti-democratic government
which works deliberately at undermining and split-
ting Yugoslavia. The peoples of Yugoslavia are
therefore justifiably coming forth with the demand
for this Yugoslav "government" in exile to be also
formally denied the right to represent them.

5.   Responsibility for the treacherous policy
aimed against the elementary interests of the peoples of Yugoslavia is borne, as well as the Govern-

ment, also by the reactionary monarchist clique. Acting on behalf of King Peter and the monarchy, the great-Serbia and other reactionary cliques organized and committed the most base crimes against their own people. Throughout this period of two and a half years King Peter backed the treacherous and criminal activity of the traitors with his whole authority. This is an unprecedented case of treason in history: the King is the Supreme Commander of the Chetnik gangs and traitors of Draza Mihajlovic, which are an integral part of the occupation army which our peoples are fighting in a war that is for them a matter of life or death. Now that all the antagonistic undertakings of the reactionary elements and traitors have proved a failure, the King and the monarchy have remained the last shelter, the center of all anti-national forces. Under the flag of the King and the monarchy the most abominable kind of high treason is taking place and the most cruel crimes being committed against the people. It is therefore necessary, as is demanded by the peoples of Yugoslavia, to undertake measures also with respect to the King and the monarchy which will be in accordance with their attitude towards the Peoples' Liberation War.

II

The Anti-Fascist Council of Peoples' Liberation of Yugoslavia expresses on behalf of all peoples of Yugoslavia whom it represents as their supreme legislative representative organ, warm feelings of friendship which the peoples of Yugoslavia foster for the peoples of the Union of Soviet Socialist Republics, Great Britain and the United States of America, along with feelings of admiration and recognition for the heroic struggle and glorious victories of the Red Army on the Eastern Front and of the Allied land, naval, and air forces over the fascist conquerors.

The peoples of Yugoslavia appreciate all signs which are showing that the struggle which our peoples have been pursuing for two years and a half and the role which belongs to it in the joint struggle of freedom-loving nations against the fascist plague are being more and more correctly evaluated in the Allied countries.

The peoples of Yugoslavia welcome and accept with pleasure the decisions of the Moscow Conference of the Representatives of the Governments of the USSR, Great Britain and the U.S. which secure to all nations the right to resolve the question of their respective internal state system freely, in accordance with their own freely declared wish. These decisions are of greatest importance also for the peoples of Yugoslavia, who have shown by their persistent liberation struggle their determination and readiness to build up their common homeland all by themselves, on new foundations of true democracy and equality among the nations.

The peoples of Yugoslavia will carry on and further intensify their struggle for final and complete victory over the fascist conquerors and will carry out their obligation which they feel towards the common cause for which all freedom-loving nations all over the world are fighting. They therefore expect that their efforts and the contribution they are making by their struggle and sacrifices to this common cause will be correctly evaluated in every respect, and that the Allied Governments will by their decisions and bearing in mind the interests of the common cause make it easier for the peoples of Yugoslavia to carry out their obligations which they voluntarily decided to fulfill, right to the end.

III

Bearing in mind all these facts, the Anti-Fascist Council of the Peoples' Liberation of Yugoslavia, which is the supreme and only true representation of the will and feelings of all the peoples of Yugoslavia,

DECIDES:

1. To constitute the Anti-Fascist Council of the Peoples' Liberation of Yugoslavia as the supreme legislative and executive representative organ of Yugoslavia, as the supreme representative of the sovereignty of the peoples and state of Yugoslavia as a whole, and to set up a National Committee of the Liberation of Yugoslavia as an organ with all the characteristics of a peoples' govern-

ment, through which the Anti-Fascist Council of the Peoples' Liberation of Yugoslavia will exercise its executive function.

2. To deprive the Yugoslav traitor "government" in exile of all the rights of a legal government of Yugoslavia and especially of the right to represent the peoples of Yugoslavia -- anywhere and before anyone.

Unofficial translation provided by Robert C. Mudd, U.S. Embassy, Belgrade, Yugoslavia

Republic of Zaire

Located in central Africa, the Republic of
Zaire first attracted European interest in 1878
when Belgium established the International
Congo Association. In 1884 it became the Congo
Free State with no institutional links to Belgium.
Financial difficulties and economic exploitation
led Belgium to take over the State as a colony
in 1908. Planned political change in the early
1950's was speeded up by a nationalist drive in
the late 50's. In December 1959 Belgium agreed
to allow independence that coming June. On May
19, 1960, the Loi Fondamentale, a Belgium Law,
established the governmental structure for
independence. Independence came on June 30, 1960
marked by a public eremony and a speech by Prime
Minister Patrice Lamombo. In 1971 the Democratic
Republic of the Congo became Zaire when the
Congo River was renamed.

REPUBLIC OF ZAIRE

JOINT DECLARATION OF THE CONGOLESE AND

BELGIAN GOVERNMENTS

The Congo this day has attained its independence and international sovereignty, in full accord and friendship with Belgium

Leopoldville, June 30, 1960

The Prime Minister of
   Belgium

   G. EYSKENS

The Prime Minister of
   the Congo

   P. LUMUMBA

The Minister of Foreign
   Affairs of Belgium

   P. WIGNY

The Minister of Foreign
   Affairs of the Congo

   J. BOMBOKO

ZAIRE

SPEECH AT PROCLAMATION OF INDEPENDENCE

Patrice Lumumba

June 30, 1960

Men and women of the Congo:

I salute you today in the name of the Congolese government as victorious combatants for independence.

I ask all my friends, all of you who have
fought unceasingly at our side, to make today, the
thirtieth of June, 1960, and illustrious date that
will be indelibly engraved upon your hearts, a date
whose meaning you will proudly teach your children,
so that they in turn will tell their children and
their children's children the glorious story of our
struggle for freedom.

For although today the independence of the
Congo is being proclaimed in a spirit of accord
with Belgium, a friendly country with which we are
dealing as equals, no Congolese worthy of the name
can ever forget that we fought to win it, a fight
waged each and every day, a passionate and ideal-
istic fight, a fight in which there was not one
effort, not one privation, not one suffering, not
one drop of blood that we ever spared ourselves.
We are proud of having struggled amid tears, fire,
and blood, down to our very heart of hearts, for it
was both a noble and just struggle, an indispensable struggle if we were to put an end to the
humiliating slavery that had been forced upon us.

The wounds that remain as evidence of the
fate we endured for eighty years under a colonialist regime are still too fresh and painful for us
to be able to erase them from our memory. Back-
breaking work has been exacted from us, in return
for wages that did not allow us to satisfy our

hunger, or to decently clothe or house ourselves, or to raise our children as creatures very dear to us.

We have been the victims of ironic taunts, of insults, of blows that we were forced to endure morning, noon, and night because we were blacks.

We have had our lands despoiled under the terms of what was supposedly the law of the land, but was in reality only a recognition of the right of the strongest.

We have known that the law was quite different in its treatment of whites and blacks; it was most accommodating for the former, while both cruel and inhuman for the latter.

We have known the atrocious sufferings of those banished to remote regions because of their political opinions or religious beliefs; exiles in their own country, a fate truly worse than death.

We have known that there were magnificent mansions for whites in the cities and ramshackle straw huts for blacks; that a black was never allowed into the so-called European movie theaters, restaurants, or stores; that a black travelled in the hold of boats, below the feet of the white in his special cabin.

Finally, who can forget the burst of rifle fire in which so many of our brothers died, the cells where the authorities brutally threw those who had escaped the bullets of the soldiers whom the colonialists had made the tool of their domination.

We have grievously suffered all this, my brothers.

But we who have been chosen to govern our beloved country by the vote of your elected representatives, we whose bodies and souls have suffered from colonialist oppression, loudly proclaim: all this is over and done with now.

The Republic of the Congo has been proclaimed and our country is now in the hands of its own children.

We are going to begin another struggle together, my brothers and sisters, a sublime struggle that will bring our country peace, prosperity and grandeur.

We are going to institute social justice and insure everyone a just remuneration for his labor.

We are going to show the world what the black man can do when he works in freedom. We are going to make the Congo the focal point for the development of all of Africa.

We are going to insure that the soil of our country really benefits its children. We are going to review all the old laws and make new ones that will be both just and noble.

We are going to put an end to the suppression of free thought and insure that all citizens enjoy to the fullest all of the fundamental freedoms laid down in the Declaration of the Rights of Man.

We are going to eliminate every form of discrimination and grant each one the rightful place that his human dignity, his labor, and his devotion to the country will have earned him.

We are going to bring peace to the country. Not the peace of rifles and bayonets, but the peace that comes from men's hearts and their good will.

In order to achieve all this, dear compatriots, rest assured that we will be able to count not only on our tremendous strength and our immense riches, but also on the assistance of many foreign countries, whose collaboration we will always accept if it is sincere and does not seek to force any policy of any type whatsoever on us.

Belgium herself has finally realized what direction history was moving in and no longer attempted to oppose our independence. She is ready to grant us both her aid and her friendship. A treaty to this effect has just been signed between our two equal and independent countries. We, for our part, although continuing our vigilance, will respect all commitments freely made.

Thus the new Congo, our beloved republic that my government is going to create, will be a rich, free, and prosperous country in both its domestic and foreign relations. But in order for us to reach this goal without delay, I ask all of you, Congolese legislators and citizens alike, to aid me with all the strength at your command.

I ask all of you to forget the trivial quarrels that are draining our strength and threaten to earn us the contempt of those in other countries.

I ask the parliamentary minority to aid my government by constructive opposition and to stay strictly within legal and democratic paths.

I ask all of you not to ask for inordinate raises in salary before I have had the time to work out an overall plan whereby I will be able to ensure the prosperity of the nation.

I ask all of you not to shrink from making any necessary sacrifice to ensure the success of our great undertaking.

Finally I ask you to unconditionally respect both the life and property of your fellow citizens and foreigners who have settled in our country. If the behavior of these foreigners leaves something to be desired, our justice will be swift in expelling them from the territory of the republic; if, on the other hand, they conduct themselves properly, they must be left in peace, for they too will be working for the prosperity of our country.

My dear compatriots, my black brothers, my brothers in the struggle, that is what I wanted to say to you in the name of the government on this magnificent day of our complete and sovereign independence.

Our strong, national, popular government will be the salvation of this country.

I invite all Congolese citizens, men, women, and children, to begin work to create a prosperous national economy that will be the crowning proof of our economic independence.

Honor to those who fought for national freedom.

Long live the independent and sovereign Congo.

Translated by Sarah J. Campbell and Matthew Jodziewicz.

Republic of Zambia

Formerly Northern Rhodesia, the Republic of
Zambia is located in central Africa bounded to the
north by Tanzania, to the east by Mazmbique, to
the south by Rhodesia, and to the west by Angola.
British colonization of Zambia begain in the mid
1800's. In 1889 a royal charter to the area was
granted. The charter was transferred to the British
Colonial Office in 1924. Northern and Southern
Rhodesia were united by the British in 1953
within the Federation of Rhodesia and Nyasaland.
Although the Federation was popular with the
Europeans, Africans feared the Federation as a
consolidation of European influence. Increased
gains in political power by the Africans resulted
in the December 31, 1963, disollution of the
Federation. On July 31, 1964, an agreement was
reached to grant Zambia independence. On October
24, 1964, Zambia became an independent republic
pursuant to the Zambian Independence Act of July
31, 1964.

An Act to make provision for, and in connection with, the establishment of Northern Rhodesia, under the name of Zambia, as an independent republic within the Commonwealth. [31st July 1964]

B E IT ENACTED by the Queen's most Excellent Majesty, by and with the advice and consent of the Lords Spiritual and Temporal, and Commons, in this present Parliament assembled, and by the authority of the same, as follows:—

1. On 24th October 1964 (in this Act referred to as "the appointed day") the territories which immediately before the appointed day are comprised in Northern Rhodesia shall cease to be a protectorate and shall together become an independent republic under the name of Zambia ; and on and after that day Her Majesty shall have no jurisdiction over those territories.

2.—(1) Subject to the following provisions of this Act, on and after the appointed day all law which, whether being a rule of law or a provision of an Act of Parliament or of any other enactment or instrument whatsoever, is in force on that day or has been passed or made before that day and comes into force thereafter, shall, unless and until provision to the contrary is made by Parliament or some other authority having power in that behalf, have the same operation in relation to Zambia, and persons and things belonging to or connected with Zambia, as it would have apart from this subsection if on the appointed day Northern Rhodesia had been renamed Zambia but there had been no change in its status.

(2) Part I of Schedule 1 to this Act (which relates to enactments applicable to Commonwealth countries having fully responsible status) and Part II of that Schedule (which relates to enactments excepted from the operation of the preceding subsection) shall have effect on and after the appointed day in relation to the enactments therein mentioned ; but that Schedule shall not extend to Zambia as part of its law.

(3) Subsection (1) of this section applies to the law of, or of any part of, the United Kingdom, the Channel Islands and the Isle of Man, and, in relation only to any enactment of the Parliament of the United Kingdom or any Order in Council made by virtue of any such enactment whereby any such enactment applies in relation to Northern Rhodesia, to law of any other country or territory to which that enactment or Order extends.

Zambia Independence Act 1964, c.65